THE EXECUTIVE AND THE ELEPHANT

A LEADER'S GUIDE FOR BUILDING INNER EXCELLENCE

•

Richard L. Daft

JOSSEY-BASS
A Wiley Imprint
www.josseybass.com

Published by Jossey-Bass
A Wiley Imprint
989 Market Street, San Francisco, CA 94103-1741—www.josseybass.com

Readers should be aware that Internet Web sites offered as citations and/or sources for further information may have changed or disappeared between the time this was written and when it is read.

Jossey-Bass books and products are available through most bookstores. To contact Jossey-Bass directly call our Customer Care Department within the U.S. at 800-956-7739, outside the U.S. at 317-572-3986, or fax 317-572-4002.

Jossey-Bass also publishes its books in a variety of electronic formats. Some content that appears in print may not be available in electronic books.

Library of Congress Cataloging-in-Publication Data

Daft, Richard L.
  The executive and the elephant : a leader' guide for building inner excellence /
Richard L. Daft.
    p. cm.
  Includes index.
  ISBN 978-0-470-37226-5 (hardback); 978-0-470-63661-9 (ebk);
978-0-470-63667-1(ebk); 978-0-470-63668-8(ebk);
  1. Leadership. I. Title.
  BF637.L4D34 2010
  658.4'092—dc22

33614056450348

                                                                    2010013839

Printed in the United States of America
FIRST EDITION
HB Printing   10 9 8 7 6 5 4 3 2 1

Contents

•

Preface

•

ALTHOUGH I DIDN'T KNOW IT at the time, this book on inner excellence began on my first trip to India. I felt a calling to learn about spirituality, and where better to start than India? Sitting on an ashram, reading and studying deep ideas, and trying to meditate were jolting changes in paradigm for me, as were the hot days and cold showers. At times my head almost hurt as I tried to integrate what I was learning in the East with concepts from the West; the spiritual and academic were not blending easily. Gurus from Eastern traditions did research into the mind by focusing on the mental dynamics within their inner world; Western social science focused on understanding other people in the outer world. Both lines of inquiry were sincerely searching for the truth, but in opposite directions. It took me a while, and multiple trips to India, to assimilate lessons derived from within into the lessons from the outer world with which I was more familiar.

As I absorbed a new way of thinking, a key discovery for me was the Eastern concept of using *Buddhi* or "intellect" as a mental mechanism to guide one's life, rather than living a life helplessly surrendered to one's senses, desires, and self-interest. As I began to comprehend this somewhat separate and higher way of thinking, I started seeing similar concepts in the West. The notion that people have two selves or two thinking processes now seemed to appear all around me, along with the nagging problem of how to regulate or manage one's emotions, impulses, and fears. Many people were asking questions about how to focus their restless mind and energy, how to avoid distractions, and how to manage themselves to lead or live more effectively. I saw a great deal of interest and inquiry from both psychology and neuroscience in self-regulation and in the extent to which people had so-called free will or were governed by unconscious desires and thought processes. In psychology, the higher part is characterized by conscious or metacognitive thought processes that are distinct from the nonconscious or simple cognitive processes. In neuroscience, the higher part is called the executive function in the brain's prefrontal cortex, and the lower part includes the rest of the nervous system.

In some sense, the two parts of the mind are not very complicated. One part is quick and impulsive, and at times its restless urges are too strong to control. This part wants immediate gratification; it has a short attention span and a childlike stubbornness in defending its own positions. The other part is slower and wiser, humble, determined; it doesn't overreact to things, and keeps the larger purpose in mind. I had my own issues finding more of the slow and steady within me to replace the reactive and restless. I researched and experimented with many techniques from East and West that would develop the part of my mind that could manage my own behavior.

This book is about the *how*, not the *what*, of improving your leadership. Changing one's personal habits or leadership style is not easy. Where do you go for help? There are hundreds of books on leadership that tell people what they should do as leaders. These books offer excellent advice, such as the five leadership principles, seven habits, ten timeless principles, fifteen secrets, and twenty-one irrefutable laws, all of which have value for readers. In contrast, my purpose in this book is not to give you another list of what makes a good leader but to provide the how of changing and improving yourself into the leader you want to be and can be. This book offers specific exercises and practices that show you how to start managing yourself to become more effective as a person and a leader.

When I started using these ideas to teach MBA students and managers how to strengthen their intellect, they reported back some progress in changing themselves. One problem was that people had a hard time identifying with their own conscious and unconscious minds. Things took off after I adopted simple names for the two parts. Participants in my classes and programs then really seemed to get it. The names that stuck were *inner executive* for the higher part (intellect) and *inner elephant* for the lower. Students started using the terms to describe themselves and their behavior. A few executives took the terms back to their workplaces as a point of reference to help people understand and transcend their less functional behavior. These notions had practical value, so the remaining challenge for me was to write up the ideas and practices in book form.

The final tally is that I am now living within a different paradigm and have experienced modest success teaching these ideas and practices to others. Pursuing inner excellence has certainly changed me. I hope some aspects of this paradigm of two parts within your mind will help you develop the higher part of you on your journey to becoming a better leader, spouse, parent, friend, colleague, or employee, along with greater focus on and satisfaction in whatever endeavors in which you engage. Your inner excellence is waiting for you to claim it. Why not get started now?

Acknowledgments

•

WRITING A BOOK SEEMS TO ME at the start like a solitary exercise accomplished through individual will. Soon it becomes clear that writing a book cannot proceed without the support and involvement of many people and organizations. On the academic side, I am deeply grateful for three books that helped me see the two selves clearly and understand how they worked. These books elevated my belief that the book I wanted to write was possible, and each of these books was so well conceived and crafted that I had an ideal to shoot for in my own writing:

> Jonathan Haidt, *The Happiness Hypothesis: Finding Modern Truth in Ancient Wisdom* (New York: Basic Books, 2006)
>
> Timothy D. Wilson, *Strangers to Ourselves: Discovering the Adaptive Unconscious* (Cambridge, MA: Belknap Press, 2002)
>
> Marilee C. Goldberg, *The Art of the Question: A Guide to Short-Term Question-Centered Therapy* (Hoboken, NJ: Wiley, 1997)

Many people and writings helping me understand Eastern spiritual insights into the mind and how to train the mind. The Santa Fe Buddhist satsang discussions provided wonderful guidance and instruction as I started my inquiry. The Diamond Heart books and programs helped expand my thinking to include Sufi wisdom mixed with Gestalt psychology. Later, I was profoundly influenced by the teachings and writings of Sathya Sai Baba, Ramana Maharshi, Joel S. Goldsmith, and *A Course in Miracles*. The writings of Eckhart Tolle were extremely helpful for showing how big spiritual concepts translate into everyday life. I want to specifically thank Sharda Madagula for guiding me through *A Course in Miracles* and introducing me to the publications of Joel S. Goldsmith, Mina Menon for hosting the Sai study circle at her home, and S. Mahadevan for his expert facilitation of the *Bhagavad Gita* discussion group. Participants in each of these discussion groups and programs made many contributions to my thinking, for which I will always be thankful.

For helping me refine personal improvement practices for leaders and professionals, I owe an extraordinarily large debt to the MBA and Executive MBA students who willingly participated in my coaching experiments here at Vanderbilt, and to the executives who attended my leadership programs and provided feedback from their experiences. I want to point out that MBA students are in their middle to late twenties, and Executive MBA students are typically in their thirties and forties. These students have substantial work experience and much experience as managers and leaders. They are practical minded rather than theoretical. Students in several classes tried experiments at my behest and provided feedback on what worked and did not work. I could not have written the book without their feedback on the exercises and practices. I am deeply grateful for their honesty about very personal issues. I have disguised their identities by using fictitious names and by sometimes altering the context of their experiences to protect their privacy.

I am also grateful to the Bridgestone/Firestone global development classes of worldwide senior managers, TVA's Leadership and Management for Accelerated Performance, Aegis Technologies, Oak Ridge National Laboratory, and a federal government agency for allowing me to test these ideas on their managers. Also, Michael Ray of Stanford University sent me exercises that he developed for his MBA classes. I appreciate Michael's generosity for letting me adapt several of the exercises for my classes.

Here at Vanderbilt, I especially thank Dean Jim Bradford, Owen Graduate School of Management, for his continuing support for this project, and for suggesting a quotation used in Chapter One. I also thank associate deans Bill Christie and Don Iacobucci for not overloading me with administrative projects, and associate dean Tami Fassinger for her enthusiastic support of my roles in executive teaching and as EMBA group doctor. I feel special appreciation for my assistant, Barbara Haselton, for her excellent and prompt support, especially her continuous filing and refiling that helped me find things and gave me time to write. I am also grateful to Pat Lane, my editorial associate, for her work researching some pieces of this book and for her outsized contributions to other books, freeing me for this project. Members of my academic group also were interested and supportive. Ranga Ramanujam suggested readings and provided helpful insights. Tim Vogus used a coaching model to teach his MBA classes, so our discussions provided valuable insights for me. I also owe an intellectual debt to other colleagues in my group at Vanderbilt: Bruce Barry, Ray Friedman, Neta Moy, Rich Oliver, David

Owens, and Bart Victor. I am also grateful for the superb service from our library, with special thanks to Laura Norris and Rahn Huber, who responded instantly to my many requests.

The people at Jossey-Bass also contributed significantly. Kathe Sweeney, acquisitions editor, signed this book and showed faith and patience for a project that was hard for me to describe. Kathe also brought together an excellent team. Alan Schrader was frank and very helpful for structuring the book's content into a logical sequence and for identifying elements that could be omitted. Anonymous reviewers also provided excellent feedback along with a number of suggestions that I adopted. My thanks also to Rob Brandt, Joanne Clapp Fullagar, and Michele Jones.

With my family I experienced the full duality of solitude and support. I spent endless hours isolated in my office, trying to keep my inner elephant on point, while also missing human contact. My wife, Dorothy Marcic, understood the message I was trying to communicate and was unwavering in her encouragement. Dorothy, along with my daughters Roxanne, Solange, and Elizabeth, were enthusiastic about the book and provided materials and insights about practices used in the Bahá'í faith. My daughters Danielle and Amy expressed encouragement for the book, and occasionally served as guinea pigs for a self-management technique or suggested a new exercise or practice they had discovered and found helpful.

To my wife, Dorothy Marcic,
For insisting that this book must be written and that
I was the only person who could write it, and for her
unrelenting encouragement to do so

PART ONE

•

The Two Selves

•

1.

The Problem of
Managing Yourself

*I am dragged along by a strange new force. Desire and reason
are pulling in different directions. I see the right way
and approve it, but follow the wrong.*
—Medea

*He that would govern others should first be the master
of himself.*
—Philip Massinger

BOB WAS HEAD OF A CORPORATE manufacturing division located in
East Tennessee. Because his division was relatively small, Bob made all
the hiring decisions himself. After receiving feedback from corporate
and reading books about the importance of delegation, Bob realized
his deficiency and made a pact with himself to engage others in key
decisions. Calling in the sales director, Bob asked him to meet with
several candidates for the customer service rep position and make the
hire. Three weeks later, that director brought his top choice to Bob's
office, along with an offer letter for Bob to approve. Dumbstruck, Bob
mumbled that he wanted to meet the final three candidates himself. He
was unable to go along with the director's choice, as he felt no rapport

with the woman or her thin resume. After meeting the other candidates, Bob hired the man at the bottom of the director's list. No matter how badly he wanted to delegate the decision, Bob could not let go. No matter how much Bob wanted the director to hire his own person, something compelled Bob to make the decision himself. "My mind has a mind of its own," he said. The decision was a disaster both for the now resentful director and for the new customer service rep. It was no surprise when both quit within six months.

Bob was experiencing an internal struggle with himself that he had neither explicitly acknowledged nor ever discussed before. Bob did see that he had failed to lead himself to do what he had promised himself to do. He somehow chose the unwanted controlling behavior over his intended delegation behavior.

• • •

Martha was a young sales manager for an advertising agency. She was fairly new at the advertising firm and was promoted to sales manager after her boss abruptly resigned. Martha inherited a difficult employee who was a strong producer but whose competitiveness caused resentment among other team members. The difficult employee's behavior seemed to get worse after inexperienced Martha took over. She said her intention to correct the employee was like "getting in my car to go east and the car insisted on going west, and I couldn't do anything about it." Martha did the right thing by getting her facts together and scheduling a meeting. "As I broached the subject of the prima donna's behavior, his reaction was defensive, and I backed down." That was her car turning toward California. "My sense of empathy or my desire to please others overrode my ability to be assertive and provide strong direction for him." She was clearly disappointed in herself. "I missed my chance. I later tried giving him 'motherly' advice, but he did not change." Martha's vivid image of her car turning in the opposite direction against her wishes illustrates the gap between her intention and action. A part of Martha knew what to do, but the other part would not comply.

• • •

An obvious question is, why are these leaders not behaving as they intended? They had the right idea each time, but somehow sidetracked themselves into undesired behavior. It is a puzzle why leaders choose unwise behavior when they are often aware of a smarter choice. That puzzle is the focus of this book.

The Conflict Between Knowing and Doing

Kings, heads of government, and corporate executives have control over thousands of people and endless resources, but often do not have mastery over themselves. From a distance, larger-than-life leaders may look firmly in control of their businesses and their personal behavior. What about up close? Personal mastery is a difficult thing. For example, can you think of any politicians in recent years whose personal behavior was revealed as opposite to their espoused values? Or consider *Fortune* magazine's article a few years ago about why CEOs fail.[1] The records of thirty-eight ineffective CEOs revealed that all were good at cognitive stuff—vision, strategy, ideas, and the like. Things broke down during execution. The CEOs' behavior did not follow through on their thoughts and words. Action did not follow intention. Things as simple as sitting too long on decisions, not confronting underperforming subordinates, or not delivering on commitments ended up harming the company. The CEOs had plausible excuses, but it seemed clear that their actual behavior did not reflect their stated intentions. They seemed to know what to do but were not doing it.

Have you ever had a clear intention and then failed to follow through? Jeff Pfeffer and Bob Sutton wrote a book called *The Knowing-Doing Gap,* in which they described the many ways in which corporate talk substituted for corporate action.[2] The same gap exists for individuals. I think that all managers and professional employees know what they *should* be doing, *how* to do it, and *why* they should do it. We know or can figure out the correct thing to do. Yet often we do not act accordingly. Our intentions and behaviors often refuse to align. In my consulting and executive teaching, I have come across dozens and dozens of internal conflicts between knowing and doing. One part of a manager wants to do one thing; another part wants to do something else.

I put off writing my monthly report until the last day every time, said the publisher of a food magazine. This procrastination drove him crazy because he could not understand or control it. He finished most other tasks on time, and the last-minute pressure on the report was extremely unpleasant. Each month he tried to start the column earlier, but failed to do so.

I often tell my direct reports I will do something and then I don't follow through. This bank manager did not know why she made casual promises she did not keep. The bad habit extracted a price in annoyed and frustrated direct reports, and they let her know about it. She was genuine in her intention each time she made a promise, but something often got in the way of follow-through.

I am reluctant to recognize and celebrate people's accomplishments. Why make a fuss over people doing what they are supposed to do? Celebrating accomplishments was a blind spot for this plant manager. He did not "get it" about the value of public praise and recognition. From others he had gradually learned that he "should" provide verbal recognition, but was slow doing so.

Listening is my biggest fault. Shortly after someone comes into my office, I tune out and start to think about e-mails. People who visited with this utility manager complained when he worked on e-mails while they talked. He tried to pay attention, but he typically lost the struggle after five minutes or so—a habit he believed made him a less effective manager. Why did he not listen to people when he believed that was the right thing to do?

I am mentally critical of others. I point out their flaws and failures. I am just trying to help people, but they do not appreciate it. Most managers do not realize that their thoughts toward others are disproportionately negative, so give this engineer some credit for seeing his own criticalness. He understood and admitted to his negative bias, but he did not know how to change it. He said he wanted to soften his critical approach, but never did.

Something will tick me off and I react. Often it is something small and then I have a mess. I know it would be better to hear the other side of the story before reacting, but I don't do it. This manager was a weekend Executive MBA (EMBA) student who reacted sharply and negatively to an e-mail I sent to fifty students in the class reminding them about a deadline. He took it personally and sent me an angry e-mail. When I called him, he apologized when we discussed the reason behind his e-mail. As we talked, he told me a story of recently calling a direct report into his office and accusing her after hearing a customer complaint. He was later chagrined to learn that the complaint was not valid. He said he understood there were two sides to every story and that the impact of his reactions on direct reports could be devastating. He wanted to change, but continued to overreact.

What is going on with these managers? Have they no self-discipline or willpower to be better leaders? Are they mentally weak or lazy? Do they lack resolve? I appreciate their stated desire to do right, but their behavior looks stupid because they admit to doing the wrong thing when they know the better choice. They are caught in something within themselves that they do not understand or know how to manage.

The big challenge in leadership is not in figuring out what to do but in actually doing the thing you know will produce great results. The challenge is learning to lead *yourself* to do what needs doing when it needs doing. Personal mastery aligns your behavior with your intention, and it is far, far harder to achieve than it looks.

The Universal Failure of Willpower

The behavior of these managers does not seem so unusual when you consider the failure of willpower in everyday life. I gave my MBA class an assignment to change something about themselves over a period of three weeks, and several students opted for healthier eating habits. One in particular decided to give up sodas. Ten days into the project, he was invited to a friend's house for pizza. The smell and taste of the pizza made him crave a soda "more than I have ever craved something in my life. There was something in my mind that directly linked the pizza with the soda, and the link was so strong I could not resist it." One part of him lost out to the other part. Personal resolve and willpower lost out to desire. This student was not alone. Most of the MBA students failed in their quest to improve themselves during the three weeks, and the remainder faded shortly after the assignment ended.

I have my own failures. One evening over dinner, I told my wife I was going to use the free evening to grade papers. Getting those papers finished would feel good and be a win-win for me and my students. With grading finished, I would have the next morning free to prepare for class, and I would be able to return the graded papers in class. As I left the dinner table, something pulled me toward the sofa in the living room to rest for a few minutes. Without my realizing it, my right hand reached for the remote and turned on the TV. "But I want to grade papers," a part of me protested. *Dancing with the Stars* was on, so I decided to watch it and then for sure I would grade papers. After thirty minutes, something pulled me out to the kitchen for a snack despite my not being hungry. I did not want that ice cream, but I ate it anyway. When the program finished, I noticed that *American Idol* was on next. The part of me that wanted to watch it was stronger than the part of me that wanted to grade papers. Grading papers would be much more satisfying than watching TV, but I lost the argument. Finally, late at night, I started grading papers, and then I got up early in the morning to finish them. Despite losing sleep, I was unable to finish the papers before I had to prepare for class. The students did not get their papers back in class. My mind had a mind of its own. My "stupid" behavior won out over my good intentions. My inner excellence was not at the level I would have liked.

Perhaps there is comfort in finding esteemed company in the failures of intention. Here is what the Apostle Paul said about himself:

> I do not understand my own actions. For I do not do what I want, but I do the very thing I hate. For I know that nothing good dwells within me, that is, in my flesh. I can will what is right, but I cannot do it. For I do not do the good I want, but the evil I do not want is what I do.[3]

"Everyone has the same amount of self-discipline, almost none," says Jim Loehr, a sports psychologist who runs a corporate athlete program that is popular with Wall Street executives and others.[4] People mistakenly think they can change their lives if they just try harder and summon enough willpower. It seldom happens. Just ask Opera Winfrey. She got her weight down to 160 pounds four years ago. Now she is back up to 200 pounds. "I didn't just fall off the wagon, I let the wagon fall on me," she wrote in O magazine.[5] Something like two-thirds of weight lost by dieting is regained within a year, 90-plus percent within two years, and over 99 percent in five years.[6] What is the delusion that makes people persist in buying weight-loss books and believing this time they will lose weight? Of course, their hopes are no more foolish than the 90 percent of owners of health club memberships and exercise machines who do *not* exercise. Their good intentions led to a purchase but not to new behavior.

Personal resolve apparently is not enough to change a bad habit, even with impending death to focus the mind and motivate action. Several studies of patients who underwent coronary bypass surgery and were given doctor's orders to change their diet and lifestyle to extend their life found that only about one in ten people adopted healthier day-to-day habits, such as proper diet and exercise.[7] Cardiovascular surgeons give diet and exercise advice expecting that patients will *not* follow it. The patients clearly understand the life-extending value of changing their behavior, and still do not follow through.

These examples show, first, that our mind can be unreliable when it comes to regulating our behavior. When we really want to use our willpower, it is likely to desert us. There seems to be a universal gap between what people think they will do and what they are actually doing. Managers, for example, often know the correct behavior to get results, but find it hard to change their behavior pattern. Second, they show that it takes two parties to have a conflict, and, metaphorically speaking, "both are within me." An internal division causes people's frustrations—the part that wants to do the new or better thing and the part that refuses or has something else in mind. This divided self is the key to understanding how to lead yourself to gain mastery over your behavior.

This book will explore the knowing-doing breakdowns that plague and mislead leaders and professional employees, and then describe practices that will strengthen one's higher intentions to assert control over personal behavior. These practices can reduce the gap between the divided self to create a more united and reliable self that chooses the wise behavior. To get started, let's look more closely at the divided self.

The Divided Self: Executive and Elephant

Think again about the list of inner conflicts expressed by managers and others so far in this chapter. The internal struggles revealed a divided self, with one self supposedly guiding and giving instruction to the other, which refused to cooperate. One self seemed stronger than the other, and too often the "wrong" self seemed in charge. A human being seems composed of two selves—one that is habit bound, impulsive, and emotion driven, and the other more thoughtful, circumspect, and rational.

A story from ancient mythology in India illuminates the point. Five stallions are pulling a chariot. The stallions are the five senses, each of which seeks gratification for itself. The driver is the mind. The mind is responsible for keeping the stallions under control and on the correct road; otherwise their strength will overpower the driver and wreck the chariot. When emotions and desires are strong enough to take control in a human being, a wreck is likely to occur. Benjamin Franklin said, "If passion drives, let reason hold the reins."

The idea of two selves has a long tradition in Western culture; they are represented in the battle between reason and emotion, superego and id, angel and devil, the light side and the dark side, good and evil, and the spirit and the flesh. In some religious groups, "The devil made me do it" is a way of describing the self that acts selfishly and without restraint as something different from the "real me." In psychology, these two parts have been called the learner self and the judger self,[8] the conscious mind and the adaptive unconsciousness,[9] the higher brain and the lower brain,[10] and the cool (cognitive) and hot (emotional) systems.[11] A recovery center for substance abuse labels the intense craving for alcohol or drugs the "beast" within. Each client, to recover, must learn to deal with that powerful beast.[12]

What this adds up to is that everyone has two parts, or two selves, so to speak, that sometimes are in conflict. The bigger part is unconscious and forceful, and manages most of our behavior. The other, smaller part is conscious and makes deliberate choices, and seems to play a subsidiary role, being used only on occasion when needed. Our unconscious processes pretty much run our lives, as revealed in our habit patterns of thinking and behaving. And they do a good job most of the time. We happily enjoy work and life when our behavior is aligned with the needs of the moment. We don't realize that our unconscious mind is busy running our life on automatic pilot—we feel as though we are in control of our daily behavior—until we try to change something about ourselves. A major problem occurs when the two parts are in conflict, such as when the conscious part wants to listen to the person talking and the unconscious part wants to check e-mails. Or when the conscious part wants to read a book, and an unconscious force wants to watch TV. When there is a direct conflict between the two parts, we discover that the unconscious part seems as strong as an elephant. If you have ever tried, you know that changing a deeply embedded habit seems nearly impossible. You also sense an elephant's strength when you cannot resist a desire or craving despite your conscious wish to do so. You are not in control of yourself after all. Changing something as simple as eating, drinking, TV viewing, or exercise habits can be enormously difficult, requiring a major effort, maybe even an outside intervention of some sort, and the desired change may fail anyway. But there is hope. It does not have to be this way if you adopt and follow some of the practices in this book.

The metaphors I use in this book for our two selves or parts are the *executive* and the *elephant,* which I will often refer to as the inner executive and the inner elephant. The inner executive is our higher consciousness, our own CEO so to speak. Visualize an executive riding on a large elephant, attempting to control it, with legs dangling on either side of the elephant's neck. The inner elephant symbolizes the strength of unconscious systems and habits.[13] The inner executive plays the role of providing higher-order choice processes that can guide the inner elephant. The intentional mind is small in proportion to the unconscious mind, much as an executive is small in proportion to the elephant on which it is riding. The executive has limited influence over the elephant's mental and behavioral processes. The strength of an elephant can cause a problem for any person. If the elephant wants to turn left or right in search of food, it will do so, regardless of the person's conscious wish to be on a diet. As long as our inner executive is in alignment with our inner elephant, which is most of the time for most people, we feel in control and everything is fine. However, when we want to go in a direction different from our inner elephant, struggle and failure often ensue.

An executive may appear weaker than an elephant, but the executive has some advantages. The executive sees a bigger picture from the top of the elephant, much like a traffic reporter in a helicopter who can see a traffic tie-up miles ahead. The inner elephant can see only the cars directly in front of it. The inner executive is also smarter, wiser; it can plan ahead and is the source of free choice. When faced with a challenging planning process, such as making travel arrangements for multiple family members from disparate locations to share a common vacation, the inner executive can work through and solve the puzzle. The inner executive can see the different parts of the bigger picture, and organize a unifying solution.

When a leader is unable to follow an intention with action, the reason is that the inner elephant is acting on its own by refusing to accept direction. The inner elephant is asserting its habits and preferences over the inner executive's wishes. For example, at times my inner elephant can overpower my inner executive in both aversion and attraction. My inner elephant has long had an aversion to daily exercise. My inner executive knows that morning exercise makes me feel good all day and that strengthening my quad muscles supports the knee I injured in a skiing accident. My inner elephant habitually directs me away from morning exercise toward the computer to do e-mails or to the kitchen for breakfast, while subtly suggesting that I will exercise later. My inner elephant also has a strong, nearly irresistible attraction to snack foods at social gatherings. Seeing tables loaded with delicious snacks, my elephant will take me to the food soon after arriving. This is not my executive's idea of healthy eating, but it knows better than to get in the way of a hungry elephant.

Learning to Lead from Your Inner Executive

All of us have these two parts within—the wise and intentional inner executive and the unconscious inner elephant, which does a good job for us most of the time. The friction between inner executive and inner elephant occurs when they have different ideas about desired behavior. The inner elephant is concerned about its own needs and comforts, and is often stronger than the inner executive. The inner executive can see the bigger picture even if it has not learned how to guide and control the elephant.

For a leader, the ideal situation is for the inner elephant to work as servant, the inner executive to work as master. Of course everyone faces situations where the inner elephant's urges seem far stronger than the inner executive's good intentions. This is like the inmates having more influence than the warden. Managers who do not have a well-developed inner executive will not lead themselves consciously and intentionally, just as a company without a CEO and executive team will not have an intended strategy or the capability to coordinate disparate departments for strategy execution.

When in its proper role, the inner elephant thrives as a follower, not a leader. Ideally, leaders will understand their own elephant, and will be conscious of its habits and needs. When a person is "unconscious," however, he or she tends to live at the mercy of the inner elephant, following its needs and impulses without concern for others or a bigger picture. When "conscious," a leader can be intentional about doing the right thing. Mike Hyatt, CEO of Thomas Nelson Publishers, told my MBA class, "Managing me is a full-time job. I manage myself to have the right impact on the company." Mike understands himself, and intentionally directs his behavior to signal the right cues to the Thomas Nelson culture.

I recall a research manager who refused to "be evaluated by his inferiors." Killian had an aggressive, unbridled inner elephant accompanied by a weak inner executive. In committee meetings, he revealed his smarts. His arguments overwhelmed any competing idea. His subtle disparagement of ideas other than his own and his shunning people who disagreed with him allowed him to win battles, but eventually created a backlash. His inner elephant was blind to the bigger picture of uniting, integrating, and building a research organization to include everyone. His boss, the vice president, suggested a 360° feedback process wherein Killian would get feedback about how others perceived him. He refused, and threatened to resign before he would accept feedback from his "inferiors." Although a gifted researcher, Killian never did break free of his unfortunate leader habits. He could not get into an executive mind-set that could see a bigger picture and be concerned with needs beyond his own. His inner executive was not sufficiently developed to understand and restrain his inner elephant. He kept ramming ahead unconsciously with ideas that represented only his personal beliefs and self-interest, and was eventually removed from the management position.

In my experience, professionals like Killian who have an ambitious, single-minded inner elephant that overpowers their inner executive generally are remarkable individual achievers, but often make poor leaders. Killian was a driven and highly published researcher, but the blind devotion to his own viewpoints did not translate into leadership of other people. When a leader does not have a bigger picture (one that includes other people) from which to guide his or her inner elephant, then the leader is more likely to act unconsciously, impulsively, and blindly, driven by personal beliefs, prejudices, and desires. Professionals with a weak inner executive often act like impulsive children, blinded by temptations that fulfill their strong personal needs. When a manager's inner elephant is so dominant, there are no second thoughts, no inner conflict, and little empathy for other people or ideas. Someone who is all elephant probably needs strong guidance from an outside executive.

To become better leaders, we must learn to manage ourselves by developing our inner executive to direct and guide our inner elephant. The laments and ineffective behaviors described early in this chapter were examples of leaders not doing what they knew they should do. Each case was an example of conflict within the manager, between the inner executive and the inner elephant. The inner executives within the managers knew all the ideal leader behaviors, such as delegating more, listening attentively, and completing a monthly report on time. Yet even when knowing the correct action, they failed to act on the ideal. I appreciate that most leaders do the correct thing most of the time. But when an internal conflict arises between intention and action, the inner elephant's unconscious response has asserted itself to override the inner executive's wishes, causing the less desirable behavior.

Purpose of This Book

So there you have it. The premise of this book is that managers often know what they should do, and why and how to do it, yet too often they do not. Why? Their inner elephant's unconscious desires and habits are too strong; their inner elephant won't follow directions. Their inner executive is not sufficiently well-developed to take charge. They have not learned to lead themselves. As leaders learn to recognize the two parts within themselves, and the occasional conflict between the parts, they can strengthen their inner executive and learn how to train, calm down, and guide their inner elephant to follow their inner executive's wishes.

In a normal person, the inner executive grows stronger with exercise and practice, which allows the inner elephant's bad habits and self-defeating behaviors to weaken and fall away. As your inner executive gets stronger, you become more conscious of the two selves and points of inner conflict. Achieving this awareness is a big step. Your inner executive typically has a notion of the right behavior, and you can be puzzled and frustrated by your occasional inability to act correctly. With a little practice, you can learn to execute the right action on the occasions of internal conflict rather than let the elephant have its way.

This book is about understanding and clearly recognizing your own inner executive and inner elephant. It is about learning *how* to help your inner executive manage your inner elephant as needed to behave according to your best intentions. Your inner executive already knows a lot about effective leadership. The challenge for you is to learn to guide your inner elephant toward that behavior despite its sometime obstinacy or neediness for the wrong thing. The solution is to learn to follow your inner executive's higher intentions and what it knows to be true. When leaders learn how to increase their self-discipline and self-mastery to manage themselves, they finally can become the leader they want to be, which is a feeling of inner excellence.

The trick is to lead yourself *first* so you can be a first-rate leader of other people. Leading yourself means seeing, understanding, mastering, and leading your unconscious but powerful inner elephant. You can appreciate that bringing your two selves into alignment and learning to be the master of your own behavior would have a terrific leadership payoff in satisfaction, inner peace, impact, and productivity.

Throughout the book, I present a variety of personal practices to help you gain mastery over your inner elephant—lessons in how to lead yourself. Many people I have taught and coached have found these practices valuable for achieving a higher level of self-discipline, more self-awareness and self-control, greater ability to follow their own higher intentions, less procrastination, weaker impulses, and a more positive viewpoint, including reduced anxiety and fewer negative thoughts toward themselves or others. These practices are derived from a variety of sources, including Western psychology and Eastern spirituality. I have been pleased at how quickly people can adopt these practices and see some change in their thinking and behavior.

I have used nearly all of the practices myself, and over the years, they have led me to experience increased feelings of contentment and peace. The falling away of simple urges, such as food cravings; the enhanced "flow" and immersion in my work brought about by the melting of resistance to doing important projects; the ability to reach out to someone in the moment to resolve a conflict—these feel wonderful and peaceful, like a load off my mind. The absence of inner struggle—one part of me wanting to do one thing, the other part the opposite—is a feeling of freedom. My hope is that you will try practices that appeal to you and experience similar feelings of peace and self-control.

Chapter Two will develop the concepts of the inner executive and inner elephant in more detail, and Chapters Three and Four will closely examine the inner elephant from different perspectives, with special emphasis on the many inner-elephant illusions, guises, mistakes, and problems that can lead well-intentioned leaders astray. Chapters Five through Sixteen describe ideas, personal practices, and exercises that show you how to engage and strengthen your inner executive to take charge of your inner elephant, shifting the balance between your two selves in favor of your inner executive and thus avoiding the problems identified in the early chapters. These practices are presented in an approximate sequence of difficulty; earlier chapters cover simpler ideas that can solve specific problems, and later chapters cover practices that strengthen the inner executive more generally. If you can find even one or two of the many suggested practices that appeal to you, and begin using them regularly, you can start making progress right away. As you learn to master yourself, you can become a master leader of other people.

2

Recognize Your
Two Selves

*The mind which yields to the wandering senses carries away his
wisdom as the gale carries away a ship on waters.*
—*Bhagavad Gita* 2:67

You are what you think.
—Lord Buddha

I WAS A COPRODUCER of a musical theater production of *RESPECT:
A Musical Journey of Women,* for which my wife was playwright. The
show had played in several cities. In this production, the group sales
person quit to work for another employer. It was imperative to quickly
find an experienced salesperson to contact area social groups, because
groups purchase their tickets several months in advance of attendance.
Launching a musical theater production, like launching a start-up, is
chaotic. The managing producer said he understood the importance of
group sales and repeatedly promised to find a new salesperson right
away, but his mind kept focusing on urgent short-term production and
marketing problems, e-mails, and the like. The important long-term
action was delayed. As the need for more ticket sales to groups became
urgent, he finally focused on finding a replacement, but it was too late.

Group ticket sales were dismal. The managing producer's intention had been clear, but he did not act on it despite wanting to do so. His mind kept focusing on other seemingly urgent details.

As described in Chapter One, the human mind operates as if there were two distinct mental processes or selves. The inner elephant is more or less automatic, reactive, strong, and unconscious; the inner executive operates at a "higher" level of awareness based on a bigger, more objective picture of what needs to happen. The managing producer for *RESPECT*, for example, seemed to have a weak intention (inner executive) toward dealing with an important long-term issue, preferring instead to react to immediate events (inner elephant).

Levels of Consciousness

All of us experience the inner struggle between two seemingly different parts of ourselves that want to do different things. The personal examples of inner-elephant and inner-executive behavior are supported by diverse and systematic evidence from neurology, psychology, and Eastern philosophy.

Neurology

Modern science reveals a similar duality involving the physical structure of the brain. The human brain is an enormously complex system that performs many functions. Neuroscience reports that the frontal lobes, particularly the prefrontal cortex, act as the CEO for the brain. The frontal lobes coordinate such brain functions as perception, memory, language, attention, attractions, and emotions. The function of the frontal lobes is to provide humans with self-awareness, purposefulness, intentionality, imagination, and foresight. This executive function endows us with human qualities. The brain's CEO decides direction, sets goals, makes plans to attain goals, and regulates behavior that is consistent with achieving its goals.[1]

Brain injury or neurological diseases of the frontal lobes impair the CEO function. Alzheimer's patients cannot make decisions in an ambiguous situation, such as selecting and coordinating clothes for the day. The loss of frontal lobe function may cause people to become stimulus-bound or field-dependent, which means they react immediately to any external stimulus or distraction the way a baby or small child would. Without the frontal lobe function, a person cannot stay on course to achieve goals. Without the inner CEO, there is no mechanism to control distracting urges or impulses. There is no sustained intention.

The field of education has embraced "executive function" as a way to understand differences in children that carry over into adulthood. The executive function is associated with the self-discipline necessary for goal-directed behavior. From an educational perspective, elements of executive function observed in children include planning and setting priorities, seeing a big picture and how elements fit together, and making alternative plans quickly when unusual events arise; getting organized, taking initiative to get started on a project, and persevering with a task through to completion; and restraining inappropriate emotions and behaviors. The executive function gets stronger as children grow toward adulthood.

When children experience "executive dysfunction," they may be impulsive, easily distracted, unable to plan ahead, and unable to tolerate frustration. For example, a student may have trouble determining the steps for a research project, determining needed resources, or setting realistic milestones. Other signs include difficulty waiting one's turn, difficulty switching gears, or acting out of frustration. For adults, the simple indicators of executive dysfunction might include the inability to plan meals several days in advance, spending income impulsively rather than adding to a savings account for future college expenses, difficulty managing a budget and deadlines for a small business, and inability to keep multiple projects going. Adults, like children, vary widely in executive function development and their ability to regulate themselves.

The CEO function within the brain of a human being is analogous to the executive function in a large corporation, army, or government organization. Every organization has to have an executive function that is distinct from the work of production operations, HR, or marketing. The executive function provides an overall vision and strategic direction and implements action plans to achieve the business's desired outcomes. The executive function monitors environmental changes, asks the right questions, makes sense of things, and builds agreement for proper direction, organization, and coordination. Just like a corporation, each person needs an inner CEO to guide his or her personal behavior.

Psychology

Mainstream psychology supports the notion of two selves as reflected in two distinct mental processes: (1) the conscious or intentional mental processes and the (2) nonconscious, automatic or externally triggered mental processes.[2] Psychology has abundant evidence that the vast majority of thoughts, perceptions, desires, emotions, judgments, and behaviors are the result of unconscious and automatic processes. An automatic process occurs without any conscious intention in response to an event or situation. One example is the feeling of stage fright that pops up automatically when a person has to give a speech. Another is the annoyance that many people experience when others behave "improperly." The feeling of annoyance arises by itself. In my case, frustration and critical thoughts start to enter my mind automatically when someone is twenty minutes late for lunch, or when a Web page takes more than fifteen seconds to open. My conscious mind did not create or choose those thoughts or feelings. The thoughts arise automatically from my unconscious in response to the event, as does the desire to read the newspaper in the morning, the felt need to prepare for class as the class time draws closer, and the sense of well-being I feel after being immersed in a project to completion or if I do something nice for someone. Most of my thoughts, feelings, and behaviors arise automatically in response to outside events. My conscious mind did not cause my inner reactions, but it was aware of them. The conscious mind, like a flashlight or spotlight in a large auditorium, is able to focus on and see one thing while the rest of the auditorium is dark. The dark auditorium is the unconscious mind.

The unconscious and automatic mental processes play a huge role in how we live. These processes are so pervasive and automatic that one writer called them our bio-computer.[3] The mental processes that operate language, memory, perception, and physical systems function largely outside of awareness like the hard drive of a bio-computer, much as the workings of one million employees at Walmart occur outside the view of its CEO.[4] The unconscious mind detects threats, judges people, makes inferences, and formulates stereotypes, all outside our conscious intention. When you speak on the telephone, your words flow automatically, as does your recognition of familiar people and places. You don't have to tell one foot to step in front of the other while walking or tell your fingers to push keys on the keyboard. To write this paragraph, I close my eyes and focus on the topic. Words appear automatically in my mind and I then write them down. When I teach, words automatically jump into my mouth. Without automatic language, I would have to find other employment.

The conscious and unconscious parts of the mind are designed to work together. The conscious mind is supposed to be the decider, the executive in charge, the boss that asserts itself when needed. The unconscious mind is like a search engine continually scanning the Internet and occasionally sending a message of interest to the conscious mind. The search engine's work is out of sight. The conscious mind is like the pilot of a modern jetliner, who provides little input while the plane flies on autopilot; the pilot is perhaps drinking coffee while reading gauges and checking messages sent from the airplane's automatic systems. The airplane's systems make adjustments instantly and effectively in response to environmental changes until it is time to land, when the pilot takes control. The primary role of the conscious mind is to act like a CEO by gathering data and providing systematic planning and adjustments. Its job is interpretation, planning, and objective evaluation. The unconscious mind handles the high-volume routine stuff. The unconscious mind has a lifetime of experience stored within and is ideally suited to the routine and automatic. Competitive ice skaters, like many other athletes, practice so much that during a performance they can shut off the conscious mind. Their unconscious and automatic systems will guide their bodies through the skating program.

Eastern Philosophy

Historical Eastern thinking offers a comparable view of a person's mental processes that reinforces the ideas from Western science. Hindu literature describes human consciousness as operating at multiple levels.[5] A human being tends to identify initially with lower levels of consciousness. The higher levels of consciousness are acquired gradually with maturity, effort, and personal growth.[6] Four levels of consciousness as described in Hindu literature are as follows.

LEVEL 1. This is the level of the physical body and five senses that interact with the environment. This level of consciousness is present in all organisms. People at this level behave on the basis of physical need and operate at the animal level of consciousness.

LEVEL 2. The mind (*manas* in Sanskrit literature) receives stimuli from the senses and translates the stimuli into actions, words, thoughts, and feelings. This level of consciousness tends to be directed by the needs of the ego as well as the physical body. The mind experiences emotions, and seeks pleasant sensations while avoiding the unpleasant. This level of consciousness is referred to as the "unintelligent will" because of its unthinking pursuit of self-gratification, and it makes shortsighted judgments based on pain and pleasure. People at this level are often inflexible because they are guarding and protecting their own beliefs, mental positions, and habit patterns. People at this level are considered unconscious because they are unaware of how their automatic thought patterns determine their behavior.

LEVEL 3.   The intellect (*Buddhi* in Sanskrit literature) is the higher mental faculty in human beings. It is the instrument of abstract knowledge, discernment, and thoughtful decisions. It organizes and interprets information from the senses to furnish intellectual discrimination and reason. It is an "intelligent will." It can think things through before acting and weigh consequences. It can seek the truth behind objects and events rather than react to face value, integrate diverse stimuli rather than react to a single stimulus, and pursue a larger purpose. The intellect enables people to enjoy deep intuitive understanding, choose action based on wisdom, be flexible in their responses, and be concerned for people and causes beyond self-interest and personal pleasure. People at this level are considered conscious because they can observe and manage their own thought and behavior patterns.

LEVEL 4.   The soul or spirit is the very core of being, the animating life force that is sometimes called the real Self (*Atman* in Hindu), which is the human connection to divinity (God or Brahman). This is the most subtle level of consciousness and can be known by only a very few people, who would be considered self-realized or enlightened. This is the highest level of human consciousness.

• • •

As illustrated in Exhibit 2.1, the inner elephant and inner executive correspond roughly to levels of consciousness or mental functioning described in Eastern philosophy, neurology, and psychology. The parallel between Western science and Eastern thinking is striking to me because these two fields grew out of different cultures and investigative practices. Western science is based on the study of the world outside ourselves. Psychologists study the behavior of people in the psych laboratory. Neuroscientists study other people's brains and nervous systems. Eastern sages, in contrast, study the workings of their own mind through introspection. They investigate by watching their own internal mental dynamics through meditation and contemplation. The convergence of Eastern and Western perspectives on basic levels of human consciousness provides triangulation on the concept of two selves.

The importance of the levels in Exhibit 2.1 is summarized in Einstein's statement, "The problems that exist in the world today cannot be solved by the level of thinking that created them." This means that a higher level of consciousness is bigger than the one below it. The higher mind has the potential to control the body, ego, and lower impulses, but it must be developed and used. Ideally, the different levels are aligned, which is

Exhibit 2.1. Levels of Human Consciousness

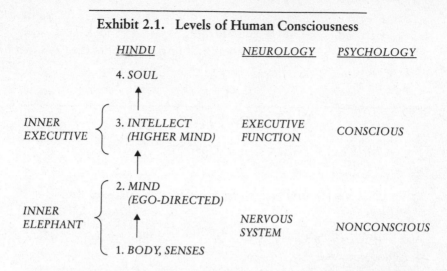

often the case. When they disagree, however, the lower consciousness may appear stronger than the wishes of the higher consciousness, and hence people make bad choices, do not do as they intended, act impulsively, fail to follow through, and so on. People start out at lower levels as children and, one hopes, engage more of the intellect or executive function as they mature. As people evolve to a higher level of consciousness, they experience a sense of greater free will in the form of self-regulation and personal control. The inner elephant's personal desires, impulses, fears, likes, and dislikes have less influence over choices and actions when people engage the higher level to solve the problems created by lower-level desires and actions.

Two Voices Within

Let's try an experiment so that you can experience the two parts of yourself—the unconscious and automatic, yet powerful, inner elephant versus the more intentional, versatile, and less used inner executive. This experience will help you see that your inner elephant is mostly in charge of thinking your thoughts and making your decisions. I use this experiment all the time with managers and students to help them understand the difference between the two parts of themselves.

Before continuing further with the book, follow the instructions in this paragraph. Sit comfortably and close your eyes. Focus your attention on your breath as it enters and leaves your nostrils. Watch your breath for approximately three minutes. If a thought comes along and distracts your attention, refocus on the breath as soon as you realize your attention has drifted. Bring your attention back to your breath anytime you realize that you are not focused on your breath. You might look at a clock before starting so you know the amount of time devoted to the exercise. Start now.

• TRY THIS •

Focus on Your Breath

1. Sit comfortably and close your eyes.
2. Focus on your normal breathing as air enters and leaves your nostrils.
3. Continue focusing on your breath for three minutes.
4. What happened?

What happened during the three minutes? Did your mind jump away from the focus on your breathing? Almost certainly it did, and probably many times. I apologize for mixing metaphors, but in India those seemingly random thoughts are called *monkey mind*. A typical attention span without an intruding thought is a very few seconds. Only a well-trained mind can hold a focus on the breath for even thirty seconds with no intrusive thoughts. Those thoughts jump into your mind automatically. In other words, these thoughts came into your mind *without any intention on your part*. Let me repeat that: the thoughts jumped into your mind automatically with absolutely no effort on your part. Indeed, you were not able to stop them. Your intention was to stay focused on watching your breath, but your unconscious and automatic mind (inner elephant) brought up distracting thoughts anyway. The thoughts did not obey your intention. The random thoughts reflected things of concern to your inner elephant, which did not care about your desire to concentrate on your breath. Those random thoughts are the tip of the iceberg of intrusive and insistent thoughts, desires, fears, dislikes, and so on that take over your mind and ignore your best intentions.

The exercise can help you experience directly and thereby clarify the distinction between your inner executive and your inner elephant. Your inner executive is the part that was intentionally trying to focus on your breath. The automatic, or involuntary, thoughts arose from your nonconscious inner elephant. And when your awareness was carried away by automatic thoughts, you were completely in the inner elephant's level of consciousness. When you "woke up," saw the thought, and returned your focus to the breath, you were back in the inner executive's level of consciousness. The inner executive has a capacity for higher-level intention, although it often loses out to the forceful impulsive thinking from the inner elephant. The unconscious mind can generate compelling thoughts automatically, whenever it wants, and does so.

These two levels of consciousness have been characterized as two voices in our heads, and we can learn to choose the one we listen to. The inner executive is subtle compared to the inner elephant. You might think of the inner executive as a whisper for which you have to listen carefully, and the other, by comparison, an insistent and noisy boom box.[7] You may have to turn down the volume on the boom box to hear the inner executive's voice or quiet urging.

Imagine that you have two big dogs to feed that are intensely hungry. Despite its hunger, one dog is docile and quiet. The other dog is barking loudly, becoming vicious, and straining at its chain to attack. Which dog will you feed first? The strong urges, reactions, and opinions of the inner elephant typically fill the mind and demand your attention. No wonder you get caught up in the inner elephant's intrusive thoughts and ignore the better judgment of the quieter inner executive. Indeed, this explains why the managing producer for the RESPECT production was responding to the ever-present start-up details rather than hiring a person to handle group sales. The automatic thoughts flooding his mind were about those details, which pushed aside the less urgent thoughts of finding and hiring a salesperson.

A little practice is required to observe both voices. People believe they are thinking their own thoughts, when in fact thoughts jump into awareness automatically, based on some internal or external stimulus, just as they jumped into your mind as you tried to focus on your breath. Thoughts based on your inner elephant's desires and dislikes are constantly flowing into your awareness without any effort or prodding on your part. You may sometimes insert an intentional thought, but all the thoughts will pretty much run together until you learn to tell them apart. Intentional thinking is hard work, takes practice and concentration, and is infrequent. Using intention is like learning to speak a foreign language to replace the one you now speak automatically. Just as you can intentionally learn a new language, you can increase the strength of your inner executive to take control of your thoughts. As an illustration, let's try another experiment.

Sit comfortably with your eyes closed and once again watch your breath for three minutes, and this time add another element. Say silently to yourself "in" on the first in-breath and say "out" again during the first out-breath, "in" during the second in-breath and "out" during the second out-breath. You can say "in" and "out" slowly to match the length of each breath. The point is to concentrate on the word in your head as well as on your breath. Continue counting and watching your breathing for about three minutes. Any time your mind jumps away, bring it back when you "wake up," and start over repeating "in" and "out." Start now.

• TRY THIS •

Focus on Your Breath II

1. Sit comfortably and close your eyes.
2. Focus on your normal breathing as air enters and leaves your nostrils.
3. Say in your mind "in" during inhale and "out" during exhale.
4. Continue focusing on your breath and repeating the words for three minutes.
5. What happened this time?

What happened this time? Did your mind jump away less frequently? Chances are that your elephant mind was quieter. The reason is that you added strength to your inner executive by saying a word, which is an *intentional thought* to replace your inner elephant's involuntary thoughts. Your inner elephant had less free space to generate random thoughts.

There are two voices—the familiar automatic voice from the inner elephant and the intentional voice from the inner executive. Stop for a moment and get clear about what your intentional thoughts feel or sound like. Close your eyes and count to ten slowly, seeing and hearing each thought clearly in your mind. That is what an intentional thought sounds like. Thoughts are pretty subtle, so if you are not clear about "seeing" or "hearing" the intentional thought as distinct from the automatic thought, don't worry. Try counting to ten again and sense how each count differs from the automatic thoughts that will jump in to carry you away. Once you have had a little practice, intentional thoughts will sound or look quite distinct from automatic thoughts that come into your mind on their own.

This experiment is a microcosm of the everyday relationship between your inner executive and your inner elephant. The inner elephant is surprisingly pervasive and strong. Most of the thoughts that guide our lives arise into our mind's awareness instantly, unconsciously, without effort, uninvited, and without intention or control on our part—just as pop-up ads appear on your computer screen when you surf the Net. For example, psychologist Martin Seligman reported how the pessimistic thoughts of depressed people (for example, "I'm not good at anything," "My clothes look like rags," "I screwed up again," "I can't get things together") flooded their minds involuntarily after a negative event.[8] These thoughts were not intentional; the participants wanted nothing more than to be free of those thoughts. Automatic thoughts play a huge role in our thinking.

Why Your Mind Is Filled with Automatic Thoughts

Why is the inner elephant's voice so dominant in your mind? Your lifetime's accumulated experiences are stored in your nervous system as part of your conditioned self, which is the inner elephant. You have a huge store of conditioned responses from previous feelings of pain and pleasure. Responses are based on millions upon millions of experiences recorded in the nervous system from the moment of birth. We learn to sense, anticipate, and move toward pleasure and away from pain. Every situation you face as an adult elicits a reaction in the form of automatic thoughts. A typical mind is occupied by automatic thoughts for perhaps 95 to 98 percent of its waking moments.[9] The unconscious mind is vastly larger than the unconscious mind, as illustrated in Exhibit 2.2.

The enduring quality of our conditioning experiences is illustrated by the way elephants are trained in India. Baby elephants are tied to a stake in the ground. The baby will try to pull away and free itself, but the

Exhibit 2.2. The Relative Size and Experience of the Inner Elephant and Inner Executive

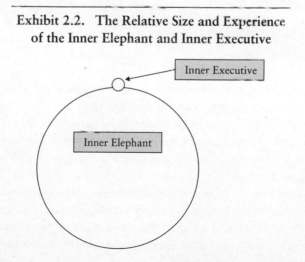

rope and stake are too strong. The elephant learns that the stake will not yield. When the elephant is grown, it can be tied with the same rope and stake. The five-ton elephant could easily break free, but its mind has been conditioned to believe in its captivity, and it will not even attempt to escape. The elephant's behavior is limited by the conditioned habits and boundaries of the past. The same conditioning occurs in a human being when a person learns to refrain from speaking out because of a volatile father. Another person might learn to be the life of the party in response to a depressed mother, and yet another wants to "go it alone" and avoid teamwork because of isolation as a child.

The difference for humans is that we have an inner executive. This intellect or intelligent will can be developed to guide our conditioned inner elephant into new and better behaviors. For example, when my inner elephant was upset with a mobile phone clerk for refusing to replace my broken phone, giving me an excuse as thin as gruel, I wanted to blurt out my frustration, and was about to do so. The thoughts and feelings of anger and frustration filled my mind. My inner executive, meanwhile, could "see" my urgent feelings and realized that they were temporary and would soon pass, that the exchange policy was not the clerk's fault, and that anger in this moment was inappropriate and dysfunctional. The inner executive had an overview and the potential to guide my behavior. If my mind had been completely taken over by energized anger thoughts from the inner elephant, I would have shouted at the clerk.

As the inner executive gets stronger, it can gradually replace unwanted automatic thoughts that arise. Psychology suggests that people can replace their inner elephant's dominant conditioned response with an alternative response, which is analogous to an adult elephant breaking away from the rope and stake. Anyone can assert intentional thoughts and actions, but initially it takes a lot of mental energy to transcend or replace the instinctual and conditioned responses that arise automatically.[10] With development, however, the inner executive can provide self-regulation to alter your automatic responses and reduce the depletion of mental resources.

As you become familiar with the voices of your inner elephant and executive, you will notice that they each have a unique feel. In general terms, the inner executive is anchored more in being than in doing, more in quiet than in noise, more in calm than in anxiety. The inner executive sees a picture bigger than the inner elephant's immediate desires or urgent thoughts. The inner executive's higher consciousness is the source of a balanced perspective, making decisions that are rational for all concerned as opposed to just pushing one's own view or seeking one's own interests.

Understanding the differences between the two parts will help you recognize them and gain ascendency over your inner elephant's unwanted thoughts or behaviors. I will explore leadership problems with the inner elephant in the next two chapters. Right now, let's highlight two key differences between the inner elephant and inner executive.

Unfocused Elephant Mind Versus Focused Executive Presence

I often work with managers who check their BlackBerries frequently. The worst case was a senior manager at a Tennessee state government organization. He could not sit still. He conveyed nervous energy, and his mind was jumping everywhere rather than staying focused on the conversation with me. Not more than a minute or two would pass before he would check something on his computer or PDA, even as I talked. After several self-initiated interruptions, he apologized. He closed the laptop and put the PDA out of reach. He then sat on his hands. He explained that he had recently learned that his direct reports' feelings were hurt when he constantly checked messages while they talked to him. They felt unheard and rejected. His overactive inner elephant was not focused on people because of its impulse to jump away and take his attention with it. When he became conscious of what he was doing, his inner executive devised the solution of closing the laptop and sitting on his hands to help him stay focused and present.

Many executives have to deal with their busy minds. When asked how he could improve as a leader, Steve Ballmer, CEO of Microsoft, said, "My brain races too much." He said that even when he has listened to everything somebody said, he sometimes wouldn't hear if his mind was racing. Ballmer said that to get the best out of people, they have to feel that they've been really heard. "So I've got to learn to slow down and improve in that dimension, both to make me better and to make the people around me better."[11]

The inner elephant's jumping mind is impulsive and does not want to be here or now. Each automatic thought takes the mind away to the past or future or to another location. The inner elephant is always hungry for stimulation. It always wants to "do" something. It is impatient. It gets uncomfortable if the pace is too slow, which is what you may feel when you have to wait for the elderly gentleman to write a check in the express line or when someone speaking takes too long to make a point. The inner elephant wants to bolt away and get to the next meeting or back to e-mail. It wants to push toward some other place rather than enjoy the present moment.

• TRY THIS •

Observe Your Inner Elephant

Put down this book and sit quietly for ten minutes. Do you feel thoughts or impulses that want to take you away from your stillness? That is your inner elephant. Can you sit still and let the impulses pass? If so, your inner executive is temporarily in charge by not acting on your inner elephant's impulses.

But the thoughts and impulses keep coming. One study reported that the minds of some college students were not on what they were doing as much as 80 to 90 percent of the time.[12] I gave an assignment to my MBA students to make a pencil mark each time they "woke up" after their mind drifted during a lecture class (not mine). The highest number was seventy-five, and twenty to thirty marks were common. The students were appalled at their own lack of concentration and presence.

Your elephant mind is like a shark that has to keep moving to stay alive. A story told by Eckhard Tolle illustrates how the inner elephant will create internal conversations to maintain its stimulation. While on a bus, Tolle observed an apparently homeless woman aggressively talking to herself aloud, as if angry at some unseen person, talking to that person in an animated way. You have probably seen someone like that and felt sorry for his or her disconnection from reality. When Tolle got to his office, the insight struck him that his mind worked exactly the same way. His mind also carried on animated conversations with unseen others, arguing his own point of view. He was the same as the "insane" woman in how their minds worked. The only difference was that the woman spoke her thoughts aloud while Tolle's mouth stayed silent.[13] As you learn to see your compulsive thinking, you too will see your mind's animated internal conversations with unseen others.

In contrast to the inner elephant, with its need for constant stimulation and action, the inner executive is more focused and present in the moment. It is attuned to the current situation, alert to the nuances of people and circumstances right here and right now, and able to respond accordingly. The executive mind can monitor one's own thoughts and feelings and ignore a distraction such as a new e-mail, to stay on point. One administrator I know stays focused by scheduling regular times each day for e-mail, and focusing on other work the rest of the day. That takes self-discipline from a strong inner executive. Executive presence is not about being a thousand-watt bulb giving off heat in the room. It is more like having a spotlight shining on you just being yourself. It is drawing attention from others without being excessively extroverted or trying to overwhelm people. Presence begins with an inner state of calm and being completely in the moment. It is being grounded in your own body rather than doing ten things at once or feeling fragmented, rushed, or hyperkinetic. Awareness in the moment gives you flexibility to handle the unexpected. Presence also means drawing people to you by connecting with them on an authentic level. It means being aware of your own thinking, feelings, values, or purpose in the moment and expressing them appropriately to deliver a congruent message.[14] The inner executive *is* presence.

Charles Holliday, chairman of DuPont, shared with me a story about a visit to Capitol Hill. He was walking with a senator when he was introduced to a young senator passing by. The second senator took about ten minutes to talk privately with Holliday. He asked a lot of questions about how DuPont was doing and about Holliday's family. The young senator did not talk about himself, promote himself or his pet issues, or make a pitch for money, which seemed unusual. He focused completely on Holliday to learn as much as he could. Then he thanked Holliday and went on his way. That senator was Barack Obama. Some observers say that Obama worked hard over his life to cultivate his presence, consciously developing his self-discipline,[15] or what I would call using his inner executive to establish dominance over the restless inner elephant.

Calm presence is great for business executives too. John Chambers, chief of Cisco, learned early in life from his physician parents that when an accident happens is the time you've got to be the calmest. Chambers said, "And yet that is when most people are not. . . . So I've learned when something with tremendous stress happens, I get very calm, very analytical."[16] One of my EMBA students, Ted, told me the story of visiting a cell phone manufacturer and speaking with the CEO. The CEO demonstrated complete presence. The CEO's mind was completely focused on Ted, with no sense of busyness or rushing. In turn, Ted's attention was drawn to the CEO. The CEO was not thinking about other things or shifting to distractions, as if he had all the time in the world. His well-focused mind could concentrate completely on Ted. Jeff Immelt, CEO of GE, is said to be utterly at ease despite any chaos around him or when facing difficult issues, such as from Wall Street. His mind is present to listen, stay on point, build consensus, and be an ambassador. Executive presence is being comfortable in your own skin, right here and now.

One study reported that the minds of champion athletes experienced one-half the number of thoughts as normal athletes.[17] This means that the champion's mind is less distracted; it has calm assurance and focus. For example, a champion baseball hitter's mind will think only of the pitch rather than be distracted by crowd noise or a hitting slump. Athletic flow or the "zone" is only in the present moment, not when the mind is distracted. Mental presence and focus are achieved by learning to concentrate the mind rather than let it flit to infinite distractions. The stronger the inner executive in relation to the inner elephant, the more a person's mind will be quiet, present, and focused.

Small Box Versus Large Mind

One day in class I asked an MBA student to shine a flashlight on the ceiling of the darkened classroom. If the surface area of the walls, ceiling, and floor represented the reality of the Owen School, that spot of light was a metaphor for one person's knowledge and perspective. A leader who is stuck in small, inner-elephant thinking tends to see only his or her own spot of light—his or her own thoughts, ideas, beliefs, strategies, and solutions. What can be smaller than one mind? When I asked all the students to shine flashlights in all directions in the classroom, much of the "reality" of the classroom wall and ceiling surface area was exposed, representing many minds.

The more you are attached to your own thinking, the smaller and tighter your box, and the more your mind is like an elephant tied to a stake in the ground. A leader operating from the inner executive, not overly attached to his own thinking, can take in the perspectives of others and the whole company. The inner executive is concerned with a reality bigger than its own thoughts and desires. The leader doesn't waste her energy fighting for her own view. The inner executive welcomes thoughts and competencies from many minds.

The inner elephant gets lost in its own thoughts and desires and cannot see beyond its own mental box of thought patterns, needs, likes, and dislikes. These automatic thoughts, mostly about personal likes and dislikes, are flowing constantly. Social psychologist Jonathan Haidt, in *The Happiness Hypothesis,* observes that a "like-o-meter" is constantly running in the heads of humans. We generate subtle like-dislike judgments toward everything we experience, even when we are not conscious of doing so.[18] The inner elephant makes decisions based on personal attraction and aversion. This is fine for food and drink, but can get in the way of balanced social judgment. In the book *How Doctors Think,* Jerome Groopman told how a doctor's mere liking or disliking of a patient could influence the selection of diagnostic tests and other aspects of treatment.[19] If a doctor likes a patient, she might be inclined to skip a test that would cause discomfort. If she dislikes a patient, she might blame the patient's behavior for his illness, and assign less treatment. The inner elephant's judgments based on like and dislike color even a presumably objective physician's medical decisions. A Chinese Zen master addressed this idea when he wrote,

> The Perfect Way is only difficult for those who pick and choose;
> Do not like, do not dislike; all will then be clear.[20]

A manager's mind cannot see clearly when his thinking is colored with automatic feelings of personal like and dislike. A great deal of research shows how a manager's feelings also can have serious impact on subordinates. A leader's unconscious dislike will create in-group and out-group feelings among subordinates. Unconscious favoritism creates disparities and anxieties among employees. A manager seldom realizes that his own small and personal preferences are the cause of the discontent or perhaps the failure of some direct reports. Intentionally treating direct reports with equal concern has been shown to increase team performance.[21]

The nature of the inner executive is to be objective and balanced, which gives it a picture bigger. To be objective means to perceive things with neutrality and detachment, free from social or personal influences. The inner executive plays a role similar to a neutral judge, referee, scientist, or journalist not obsessed with her own preferences or opinions. The facts will be examined with calm detachment to find the truth. A balanced view is a bigger view and is essential to make nonpartisan decisions. A leader has to make judgments, excruciatingly difficult judgments, but ideally without the bias of deep personal likes and dislikes. Judgments are business, not personal. Yes, you have to fire people when they do not perform. The inner executive does not take things personally and will fire someone because the evidence warrants it.

Ram Charan told the story about a new CEO who overheard a division manager describe on the phone how he was going to keep vital information away from headquarters (and the CEO), which could threaten the new regime.[22] The CEO kept his cool, did not react, and took time to investigate the big picture before making a judgment. He talked to several people and learned that cultural norms were the problem, not that particular individual. He then confronted the offending division manager, not to fire or berate him, but to listen to his reasoning and then set expectations for a new culture and system of information sharing and collaboration. The CEO's inner executive was not judgmental and worked at the big-picture level to solve a problem for the company.

I visited a general in a military acquisitions organization that used a duel-authority matrix structure. I was curious about how he encouraged people, regardless of rank, to meet face-to-face to hash out their frequent disputes. When I asked him what quality most accounted for the success of his matrix organization, he responded instantly: "A corporate mindset." He meant that people who were stuck in their own small point of view or who endlessly defended their own department were unable to resolve differences effectively. David Novak, head of Yum Brands, said much the same thing when asked what advice he would give young people: "I tell people that once you get a job you should act like you run the place. Not in terms of ego, but in terms of how you think about the business. . . . Think about your piece of the business and the total business. This way you will always represent a broader perspective."[23]

A great example of big-picture and balanced inner-executive thinking was Abraham Lincoln's second inaugural address, in which he saw the perspective of both sides in the Civil War and thoughtfully chose to continue the war to free the slaves.

> With malice toward none; with charity for all; with firmness in the right, as God gives us to see the right, let us strive on to finish the work we are in; to bind up the nation's wounds; to care for him who shall have borne the battle, and for his widow, and his orphan—to do all which may achieve and cherish a just and lasting peace among ourselves, and with all nations.

When you are wearing tinted glasses, the whole world looks colored. Only by becoming conscious of the glasses themselves can you recognize how they affect your perception. Your inner elephant is the tinted glasses. The higher consciousness of your inner executive can recognize the tint, which starts liberating you from the box of small and habitual thinking. With the development of your inner executive, your perspective will expand, you will be less enamored with yourself and more open to new ideas, and you will enjoy a bigger worldview. Leaders who operate from their inner executive have acquired new, tint-free glasses for themselves.

PART TWO

Ways You May Mislead or Delude Yourself

3

·

Three Tendencies
That Distort
Your Reality

*There are more things in Heaven and Earth than are dreamt
of in your philosophy.*
—Shakespeare

We don't see things as they are, we see them as we are.
—Anaïs Nin

JOHN WORLEY WENT TO COLLEGE and divinity school and is a Vietnam
veteran and ordained minister. He received a PhD in psychology by
correspondence from the Carolina University of Theology and worked as
a Christian psychotherapist. Worley developed a sixty-item questionnaire,
Worley's Identity Discovery Profile (WIDP), to help people understand
their personality and temperament. He built a successful business selling
the questionnaire to churches, businesses, individuals, and counselors.
He believed that he understood his own temperament and tendencies,
based in part from his scores on the WIDP.

Worley received an e-mail asking for his assistance transferring money
from the estate of a late Congolese president to the United States from

South Africa, for which he would be richly rewarded. "I can help and am interested," Worley e-mailed back. After receiving satisfactory responses to questions and issues he raised, Worley was optimistic about helping a woman in distress while becoming rich. Anticipating his fortune, he spent several thousand dollars consulting a tax attorney, and asked his daughters to list all their debts, which he would pay. Worley sent more than $40,000 of his own money to the Nigerian scammers for expenses and bribes. He deposited several hundred thousand dollars in checks from them into his bank account and transferred the money to foreign bank accounts. The checks were forged. The scammers disappeared, leaving Worley with both the financial and criminal liability. He received a two-year prison sentence and owes $600,000 in restitution.[1]

How did such a good person go terribly wrong? It seems obvious that Worley was naïve and gullible. Despite a life built on introspection and self-awareness, he did not see or understand the strength of his desire to be a hero and become rich, which blinded his rationality. Worley did not understand his inner elephant at all, and he is not alone. Nearly everyone makes poor judgments about themselves. Worley would arguably be considered a sensitive, human-relations type of person. Surely a hardheaded business executive would not be susceptible to personal misjudgment.

A key theme in popular books, including *Good to Great, Execution,* and *Winning,* is the need for managers to *face reality.* Great executives see things as they are, not as they want them to be. Businesspeople think of themselves as realists, gathering facts and reaching conclusions grounded in solid data. Are the conclusions as solid as managers like to believe? On the basis of their extensive corporate experiences, Larry Bossidy and Ram Charan note the following in *Confronting Reality: Doing What Matters to Get Things Right*:

> The best strategies, the most rigorous research, the clearest of operating plans—all are undermined because the key people behind them have missed the reality of the situation for one reason or another.
>
> The most common causes of such failures are filtered information, selective hearing, wishful thinking, fear, emotional overinvestment, and unrealistic expectations.[2]

The previous chapters described the frequent failure of willpower, and argued that the inner elephant can be hard to control, unfocused, small minded, and entrenched in recurring habit and thought patterns. The inner elephant's actions are often very different from our mental theories and intentions. It is especially difficult to see oneself objectively. So this chapter is going to address tendencies of the typical inner elephant, namely the three that cause its *inability to see reality*. Seeing the world accurately is not easy, even for fact-based businesspeople. The problem is between our ears. Our perceptions are based more on our needs and biases than on external events or data. Other people see supposed facts differently than we do, and they see us differently from how we see ourselves. For example, feedback from a personality questionnaire may provide insight, but people's ratings of their own personality do not correlate strongly with other people's ratings of them. Jane's perception of herself as agreeable and conscientious will be only modestly correlated with her friends' perceptions of her. Indeed, her friends' perceptions would show more agreement among themselves than they do with Jane's perception.[3]

Most distortions are in our favor. When I had a disagreement with an academic paper coauthor about the ordering of our names (based on our respective contributions to the research), it was because our minds "overclaimed" credit. This is common. Our minds exaggerated our own contributions, so both of us were wrong. Perhaps our overclaiming is no surprise, considering that 94 percent of college professors think they do above-average work. Husbands and wives engage in the same mental exaggeration when they overestimate their contribution to housework. The estimates of MBA students' percentage contributions to a team assignment have totaled 139 percent. Concerning athletic prowess, 60 percent of high school students saw themselves above average, 6 percent below. Judging their ability to get along with others, 60 percent saw themselves to be in the top 10 percent, and 25 percent considered themselves in the top 1 percent. Most people see themselves as having above-average intelligence. Ninety percent of drivers consider themselves to be safer than average.[4] The departure from reality is revealed in nearly everyone's rating himself or herself above average on something.

Why do we distort reality so much? A big part of the reason is that the elephant mind does not perceive reality—it *makes up* reality. Perception is a mental construction, not an objective representation of the external world. An objective stimulus in the world creates a subjective reaction in your mind. Seeing a bag of potato chips might trigger a like-dislike internal reaction of salivation or disgust. The inner elephant's mental interpretation is based on the reaction of hunger or disgust, which is the basis for the decision whether to partake. The external object is neutral. Your mind provides the positive or negative tint through which it perceives objects. This happens so quickly that the tint is hard to recognize. Your previous experiences determine your reaction to everything, whether the object is scotch whiskey, potato chips, your boss, your spouse, a political candidate, or the new Prius driving by. If you have no experience with salty snacks, you probably will not even notice a bag of potato chips. If you have experience, you may feel a craving or repulsion that will shape your interpretation.

We see the world inside our heads, not the external world, and we assume our internal picture is dead-on. The mind is so fast and seemingly clear that we accept the internal picture uncritically and may be surprised when someone disagrees with us. The real problem with our interpretation is not the false picture but rather our *belief* in the false picture. You and I each think we see the world as it really is. The same world is there for others to see, so, of course, they will agree with us. If not, they must have been given inaccurate information or have misguided intentions that need to be corrected. In some larger sense, we appreciate that different viewpoints have value, but in the moment, it is hard to understand how other people can be so blind or ignorant to the truth of how the world is. Intelligent and right-thinking people see the world as we do.[5]

Each of us is trapped in our elephant-self's thinking, which is based on the limited experiences we use to interpret the world and know ourselves. That leaves much room for error. The thoughts and pictures in our head look real and true; hence they are difficult to transcend.

Our internal picture seems true enough to get us through the day, but the reasoning behind it may not be solid. This is a bit like the Hindu concept of *maya*, which says that the external world is an illusion. Watching the world is like watching a dream, but we think it is real. The buildings and people are literally there, so the illusion is in our mind's representation of them. Consider the Buddhist story of the farmer paddling his boat upstream. He sees a larger vessel headed downstream directly toward him. He tries to get his boat out of the way, and he shouts to no avail. The boat crashes into his boat with a splintering thump. Enraged, the farmer shouts at the boat's driver, "You idiot! Are you crazy? Why did you hit my boat?" Then he realized no one was in the boat. It had broken free from the dock and floated downstream on its own.

The point is that there is never anyone in the other boat. All vessels are empty until we supply our interpretation. If you learn to slow things down and see your own thoughts and interpretations, the illusion can come into focus. Once you see it, a critical thought about someone, a desire, a craving, or a feeling of frustration that habitually appears in your mind can dissolve before your mind's eye, the same way a dream dissolves when you awaken.

There are various ways in which the inner elephant instantly and automatically distorts and influences our decisions and behaviors. No doubt our mind is a complicated mass of images and desires. Our inner elephant has quirks and tendencies for the inner executive to manage. Three of the predictable tendencies of a typical inner elephant—judging others and the self, creating illusions, and defending the self—are especially important for sustaining false images and avoiding reality, both of which may cause misperceptions and misjudgments.

Your Internal Judge

A reasonable question is, Can you be an effective leader when your mind is constantly finding fault with others? While driving your car, have you ever experienced critical thoughts toward another driver? Perhaps the driver in front of you is going slowly when you want to go fast, or the driver is talking on a cell phone and fails to respond to the green traffic signal. Does your mind fill with negative thoughts toward the other driver? I bet it does. Meet the internal judge, the first of your inner elephant's predictable tendencies. The judge may criticize in both an outward or inward direction.

The inner elephant's outward thoughts toward people tend to be excessively and irrepressibly negative. Recall the like-o-meter described in Chapter Two. If you are a human being, your thoughts are constantly judging others and probably are not balanced between good and bad. The inner elephant is more finely tuned to see things it does not like than it is to see things it does like. It reacts to "bad" things more predictably, strongly, and quickly than to good things. The evolutionary explanation is that the mind had to be more vigilant toward threats in order for primitive people to survive. Spotting a threatening predator is more essential to survival than spotting berries for lunch. A negative bias is good for the species.[6] Thanks to evolution, when my wife does something that annoys me, my mind reacts instantly with a critical thought, which I have long since learned not to verbalize. When she does something nice, the act often goes over my head unnoticed, so my mind remains uncluttered with thoughts of thankfulness and appreciation.

Many of the managers I teach are not aware of how critical their minds are because they have never thought about it. I suspect many people have never known anything other than critical thoughts. John Izzo, author of *Awakening Corporate Soul* and *Values Shift,* tells the story of a research project at the University of British Columbia.[7] Students were given permission to observe family dynamics, and while so doing made a mark for each positive ("Good job, thank you") and negative ("Get yourself together; clean up your mess") statement. The ratio of positive to negative comments was 1:13. This was shocking, but might be expected in families with young children. A similar study of statements between people in business revealed a positive-to-negative ratio of 1:8. The mental preference for the negative was also found in a study of college student gossip, which showed a relative frequency of positive to negative of 1:9.[8] These scores of real interactions are far from the recommended "ideal" ratio for healthy marriages or work relationships of four or even five positive statements to each negative statement.[9]

According to research at the Center for Creative Leadership, 75 percent of managers with promising careers derailed because the managers displayed qualities such as an abrasive or insensitive style, arrogance, being difficult to work with, constant disagreements with senior management, and being poor at team building or involving staff.[10] The negative bias toward others is not a good motivational tool and will not enhance a leader's career. Unable to recognize or correct their inner elephant's bad habits, the managers were moved aside.

Examples of the internal judge as discovered by my MBA students include the following:

> "The thing that usually sets me off about others is a lack of reason, logic, or planning. Nor will I let myself be illogical. I am highly critical of others' sloppy thinking."

> "I kept a log and wrote down 127 critical thoughts toward others over three days. Most of the time I criticized their looks, style, and posture."

> "I pay too much attention to people's physical appearance and how they act. I am alert to anything I don't like, especially hair, loudness, makeup, fitness, etc."

> "When I was accepted for a residency program, I checked out on Facebook the co-residents I will be working with. I was flooded with critical thoughts as I looked at their pages, evaluating their looks, schools, and social life."

> "I kept a log of negative thoughts for one day. I am a school administrator. I counted 18 negative thoughts toward students and 241 toward adults during seven hours. I guess I don't care much for parents and other adults."

The 241 was a record for my students. The negative judgments toward others are based on personal like-dislike and do not represent a balanced view or see the innate humanness of another person. This can be a problem for a manager at work when negative feelings toward someone flood her mind. Your judge sees things from a selfish point of view and has little empathy or consideration toward others. It is hard to be optimistic and motivate people when your mind is critical of them. If a direct report makes a mistake that really annoys you, your judge may react emotionally with an overly negative view of that person as a poor team player; as having a bad attitude, lack of motivation, or lack of engagement or commitment; or as a troublemaker causing conflict. These conclusions may be exaggerations brought on by the inner elephant's annoyance and need to blame someone. The judge's impulsive thoughts are not good data on which to act. The inner executive's job is to see and detach from the harshly negative judgments so as to see the situation in a balanced way. Action taken from the balanced perspective is more likely to be correct. As mentioned in Chapter Two, a manager has to make hard judgment calls, but without the need to be negatively and harshly judgmental.

Another reasonable question: Can you be an effective leader when your mind is constantly finding fault with *you*? The judge will often turn its criticism inward, which is sometimes called the inner critic, the superego, or the voice of judgment.[11] This is the automatic voice of blame and criticism inside your head that points out how inadequate you are. It constantly evaluates your behavior. It whispers, "You handled that badly," "I am too old [young, inexperienced, poorly educated] for that job," "I can't stand this anymore," "Don't ask her on a date—you'll be rejected," "People will think badly of me if I speak up," "Why can't I be more serious [thinner, more handsome, happier]?" And so on.

The unfortunate impact of the inner self-judgments is that they inhibit your leadership behavior. The judge raises doubt, reduces self-confidence, and increases fear that others are thinking badly about you, thereby blocking your underlying creativity and initiative. The internal judge keeps you from acting on the possibilities in life by keeping you timid, safe, inhibited, fearful, and unloving. The internal judge is like a bad headache, which, if removed, will yield a big increase in leadership creativity and capacity.

The internal judge was designed to play a useful role in your life. Having a voice to tell you to eat your vegetables, drive the speed limit, and not drink too much alcohol helps keep you on track. Setting a high standard that motivates you to greater effort and higher achievement is a good thing. We can live with a moderate judge. Too often, however, your judge is upholding an ego ideal or unrealistic standard set during your childhood that for the most part you have outgrown. You made early decisions about ideal standards for yourself based on feedback from parents, friends, and society. The greater the distance between your self-concept and your ego ideal, the louder and harsher the voice of the internal judge. If you do not compare well to your high ideal, even if it is unrealistic, you will take a beating from your judge. Moreover, your judge is likely to be louder and more punishing during times of stress, when you feel depressed, when you are alone in a gathering of strangers, after making a mistake, or when someone is upset with you.

Your internal judge is not adding to your leadership capability. When I introduce this concept to a group of managers, many discover that the internal judge had held them back, mostly because they were not aware of that voice. They took the voice for granted, believed it was telling the truth, and were not conscious of its inhibiting effect. I have found a few fortunate managers who have a subdued critic that does not play much of a role in their lives. For the rest of us, a key learning is to recognize the voice and see that it *does not tell you the truth*. This is a big step toward increasing the inner executive's awareness, which will enable you to ignore or perhaps extinguish the critic at some point. Following are some written comments provided to me by MBA students and managers discovering their judge's criticisms of themselves. See if you recognize yourself in any of these statements.

"I realized that judging other people and especially myself are a huge part of my life."

"When peers give me good feedback, I believe it is not true. My inner critic says, 'they don't know the "real" me.' I am afraid people will find out that I really have no idea what I'm doing."

"My critic kept telling me that it's sappy to make people happy and that I appease people too easily."

"My inner critic obsesses about body image and work performance. Everything I do I am comparing, judging, wishing, regretting. I hold myself to perfection and strive to meet that goal. I judge others badly if they don't hold to the same level of perfection. Now I see all that was stupid and irrelevant."

"I noticed that my inner critic assumes that I know what others think of me. Self-critical thoughts emerged through the personification of some other person's thoughts about me. I cannot possibly know for certain what anyone thinks of me."

"I was amazed at the number of times I criticize myself in one day. Many times, I blame myself and feel guilty for procrastination and falling short of my plan."

"I think my elephant absorbed societal judgments. My inner Judge hits me with a long list—too fat, lazy, not smart, bad leader, slow worker, bad writer, and so on."

"I am not sure who I would be without these critical thoughts toward myself; however, I would like to reduce the role they play in my life. They tear me up inside at times, and cast doubt on several things I attempt to do. I regret that I am so conditioned to them that they influence my behavior."

The overly harsh judgments and criticisms toward yourself and others are a problem because they distort reality. That may be hard for you to see if you have believed that voice your entire life. You are conditioned, so it takes time to disentangle from the judge so that your inner executive can see things objectively. The judge voices a one-sided view that is always negative. These thoughts arise in your mind based on your fears and childhood experiences. You believe the thoughts because they are all you know. You identify with the critical thoughts, and think you created them. Not true. You are caught in the grip of the inner elephant's entrenched and automatic thought pattern. Remember, your critical thoughts are a biased interpretation of events. The judge never speaks the balanced truth. By learning to "see" the critical thoughts as automatic pop-ups in your mind and by using your inner executive to interpret them objectively, you will no longer believe them and can start to gain power over them.

Your Internal Magician

Italian journalist Ricardo Orizio interviewed seven exiled dictators, including "Baby Doc" Duvalier of Haiti and Uganda's Idi Amin. He chose dictators who had fallen from power to learn if they had gained perspective on their actions. Newspapers and history books would describe these dictators as ruthless, immoral, crazy, and power hungry. Yet they saw themselves as *victims*, unfairly treated by those who brought them to power and betrayed by constituencies they were trying to help. They saw the damage inflicted (ordering the deaths of three hundred thousand people, or plundering a nation into endless misery) as essential steps to save their country. Self-justification was the hallmark of all the interviewees. Their minds believed their own reasonable and rational explanations for their abominable actions. The last thought that would occur to these wretched individuals would be to apologize for the atrocities they and their comrades committed.[12]

How do we explain these mental gymnastics? Another predictable tendency of the inner elephant is the magician, which makes up experiences and interpretations from thin air. The magician part of your mind confabulates, which means that it automatically fills in mental gaps with fabrications that you believe to be true. At one extreme are the people who have a memory disorder and tell, and believe, stories about their abduction by creatures from outer space or of visiting their parent yesterday despite the parent's death ten years ago. Some "recovered memories" about early childhood experiences or abuse may also contain confabulations. On a simpler level, if a student is given a story to read and then asked to retell it from memory, there will be errors of commission as well as omission. Students will add details that make sense to them, and they will believe the story additions to be true from memory. Our need for things to be consistent and rational influences our memory recall.

Anybody can confabulate, even people with good memories and healthy personalities. The simple explanations for stock market changes (for example, "The price of oil went up $.50 today, so the market went down") provided on the evening news look like confabulations to meet the need for rationality. The inner elephant hungers for simple, rational explanations, and will fabricate—and believe its own fabrications—when necessary. In one experiment, people were shown cards with pictures of faces, and asked to choose the most attractive. With sleight of hand the pictures were switched before the subject was asked for a detailed explanation for the selection. Looking at the wrong picture, subjects provided elaborate explanations about the eyes, hair color, and personality of the substituted face. The internal magician routinely provides rational explanations it believes to be true when people do not know why they made a particular choice.[13]

Another example occurs with hypnosis, when subjects will give rational explanations for behavior caused by posthypnotic suggestions. A subject was told that when the clock chimed, he was to walk up to Mr. White, place a lampshade on his head, then kneel down and say "Cuckoo" three times. Mr. White was a gloomy, nonhumorous individual. When the clock chimed, the subject precisely carried out the suggestion.

He was asked, "What in the world are you doing?" The subject replied, "Well, I'll tell you. It sounds queer but it's just a little experiment in psychology. I've been reading on the psychology of humor and I thought I'd see how you folks reacted to a joke that was in very bad taste. Please pardon me, Mr. White, no offense intended whatsoever."[14]

It did not occur to the subject that he did not know why he acted so unpredictably. And the hypnotized man believed his own fictitious explanation. The mind's internal magician will readily fabricate explanations that justify our decisions and behavior.

This has relevance for managers because they will be inclined to fill in seemingly "true" details to justify a course of action or an intuitive decision made without careful investigation of facts. The recent book by Scott McClellan, *What Happened,* claimed that President Bush made big decisions largely on instinct and without digging into the underlying facts.

If that is the case, then it would not be a surprise if the internal magicians of the president, the vice president, and other advisers who believed in a decision made up logic to defend it, and they would genuinely believe their logic.

Harvard psychologist Daniel Gilbert, author of *Stumbling on Happiness,* says that the brain is so good at the filling-in trick that we are not aware it is happening. We tend to accept the brain's products uncritically and expect them to be true.[15] For example, Sir Clive Thompson was the highly successful CEO of Rentokil in Europe in the 1980s and 1990s. Profits increased 20 percent every year for a decade from acquisitions of small companies with excellent margins. To maintain growth, Thompson decided to change strategy and acquire large companies. One acquisition increased Rentokil's size by 30 percent, which was followed by another that more than doubled the company's size. These large deals proved unsuccessful, with share value falling in half and then falling in half again. What was Thompson thinking? Groups of his managers had voiced skepticism and argued that prior success with acquisitions would not apply to large companies. A subsequent analysis suggested that part of the problem was Thompson's flawed pattern recognition: to him the large acquisitions seemed similar to small ones, but they also were very different. Thompson's mind filled in the difference gaps, rendering him incapable of hearing the contrary evidence his managers were offering. The unconscious filling in misled him badly. The company was unable to recover, and Thompson was asked to resign.[16]

Probably the most persistent and widespread appearance of the magician is in people's assumption and belief that they intentionally think their own thoughts. The first chapter described how the inner elephant is something of a bio-computer that operates automatically most of the time. Thoughts, desires, anxiety, emotions, fears, and cravings appear in our minds on their own without effort on our part. Yet we often act as if every one of these was created by us. We are attached to our mental positions and will often fight for and defend a thought as if it were engraved in stone and delivered from on high. We will attempt to win any argument that challenges the opinion appearing in our mind, especially in the realms of religion, politics, values, or hiring decisions. Yet with practice and awareness, we can learn to distinguish between thoughts that show up automatically and those we create intentionally. We can learn to discriminate between the automatic thoughts we want to hold on to and those we want to ignore. This discrimination involves the higher-level awareness of the inner executive, which can be strengthened with exercises and practices described later in this book.

Your Internal Attorney

The attorney is another predictable tendency of your inner elephant. Your attorney is in charge of the psychological immune system, which protects you from the pain of rejection, failure, loss, and other misfortunes. You probably recall from a psychology course that people have psychological defenses, such as repression, reaction formation, scapegoating, denial, and projection. A well-developed internal attorney will do just about anything to distort reality to protect you from truths that may hurt. The attorney will jump in to defend you against others and will even convince you that a mistake is not your fault. The attorney is on permanent retainer and will act in the blink of an eye. It acts like a psychological immune system that defends the mind against unhappiness in the same way that the physical immune system defends the body against illness. Unfortunately, when the attorney is effective, it makes us immune to reality.[17]

Natalie is an administrative assistant in an office furniture outlet. Her boss took off on a two-week vacation and did not tell her about it. Natalie had ongoing projects to coordinate with him and no way to reach him, causing much difficulty for her. When he returned, she brought up the subject to figure out a better procedure in the future. He responded, "I don't have to tell you when or where I go on vacation. You are not my keeper." The boss's inner attorney defended against any suggestion of wrongdoing, and he sounded like a child reacting to a parent.

Ethan is director of parts inventory for a snowmobile dealership, and the computer records were found to be inaccurate. Ethan designed the inventory control system. He said that his mind concluded that his people were making mistakes or that perhaps shop personnel were completing forms incorrectly. He couldn't believe that his system or his own leadership was the cause of the problem. I once heard a professor blame the school and the students for his low teaching evaluations. "If the school would recruit students capable of understanding what I teach, my evaluations would be just fine."

What is the common theme underlying these examples of internal attorneys? Chris Argyris has spent much of his career studying defense mechanisms among organization managers. He concluded that defense mechanisms are always *anti-learning*. When the internal attorney goes on the defensive, it blocks investigation into the manager's reasoning process. The attorney is focused only on protecting a conclusion, not on finding the truth. It will typically state its conclusions, claim they are valid, and then not allow inquiry into the conclusions. "Don't argue with me. Do it my way. I know what I am talking about." These defensive statements are self-serving and overprotective. The harm to the individual and the organization arises from the elimination of accurate feedback, inquiry, and hence productive growth and change.

The defenses of senior managers can quickly become defensive routines for their organization. Defensive routines are thoughts and actions that protect old ways of doing business and dealing with a management team's reality.[18] In other words, defensive routines occur when everyone drinks the Kool-Aid about the organization's way of doing business, and hence managers refuse to examine their views.

In one company, senior executives designed a resource allocation committee to fund improvement projects from several divisions. The division heads made excellent presentations that reflected much time and effort and creativity. The senior executives at the company developed a project list in order of funding priority and opened the list for discussion.

The president felt that the ordeal was painful for managers because the rejections hurt. The dollars available were insufficient to cover all requests, and the senior executives did not enjoy explaining their reasoning. To prevent this emotional pain the next year, the procedure was changed to ask managers to send in written proposals, and the committee made its decisions in secret.

The lack of discussion reduced the pain, at least for the senior executives, but sharply reduced learning for division participants. Because division managers could not learn the reasoning behind the decisions, especially with regard to the unfunded projects, they concocted schemes to fund their projects surreptitiously, such as by hiring part-time employees who were not part of the standard budget.[19]

Another problem with the internal attorney is that it prevents employees from assuming personal responsibility for problems and mistakes. It will blame others. The owner of a boutique consulting firm told me that the one quality he could not tolerate in a consultant was the inability to admit mistakes. A strong internal attorney would prevent a consultant, and hence the consulting firm, from accepting mistakes and thereby adapting to clients' needs. The second time he saw a consultant blame someone else for a personal mistake, the consultant was in trouble. A strong internal attorney acknowledges only successes while blaming others for perceived failures. Managers with limited internal attorneys are typically more flexible and valuable because of the learning they facilitate by taking personal responsibility.

The internal attorney's defenses are automatic. People do not defend themselves with thoughtful intention. They typically are not aware of what they are doing. The internal attorney instinctively defends a viewpoint to hold on to beliefs or self-image. A typical defense tries to minimize negative feelings and not rock the boat by bringing up personal issues. The misguided belief that impersonal rationality is the way to resolve issues is the driving force for avoiding personal feedback and relationship issues.

Vanderbilt's EMBA program assigns students into a permanent study group for two years. I serve as "group doctor" to facilitate discussion of group issues. It is hard for many of these managers to bring up complaints about each other, even when the group members want to hear it. No one wants to be seen as rocking the boat. Group members typically ignore issues until someone is too upset to keep quiet. Surprisingly to the groups, a discussion of interpersonal dynamics, when held, clears the air and enables everyone to learn and improve. Misery is transformed into satisfaction simply by talking through perceived work inequities that bothered some group members. The internal attorney's protectiveness blocks this kind of discussion.

• • •

The three predictable mental tendencies of every inner elephant are the judge, the magician, and the attorney. The judge is overly critical of the self and others, the magician makes up stories to explain our behavior in rational terms, and the attorney defends our mistakes as if they were not mistakes at all. All these mental tendencies are designed to maintain a sense of psychological well-being, but in fact they prevent us from facing reality. All of us are living within our own view of ourselves and the world, and usually we are not even aware of our particular worldview because it is so well protected. Everyone has well-worn ruts of thinking and behaving that are held in place with self-justification. Robert Wright, author of The Moral Animal, said this of what I am calling the inner elephant: "[it] is, in large part, a machine for winning arguments, a machine for convincing others that its owner is in the right—and thus a machine for convincing its owner of the same thing."[20]

Perhaps equally important, we are always doing what is right in our own mind. We are doing the best we can within our own system of perceptions and interpretations that reflect the limited framework of our mind. Every thought, interpretation, and action is just the right thing in that moment to each of us, even if it horrifies others. Every thought that appears is a conditioned response that served a valuable purpose at one time in our life, even if it is dysfunctional now. We will only act on what is in our mind until we learn to see its limitations. We can learn to peek outside our own worldview and thought patterns by developing the higher consciousness of our inner executive. Once we see how automatic our behavior is, and how self-reinforcing our own thinking is, it becomes easier not to take ourselves too seriously. We can be much more accepting and tolerant of ourselves and others once we see the basis of our perceptions and misperceptions. Using our inner executive with its balanced view of things can go a long way toward facing a new and more accurate reality.

4

Every Leader's Six Mental Mistakes

*Blessed are those who can laugh at themselves, for they shall
never cease to be amused.*
—Anonymous

*All explorers are seeking something they have lost. It is seldom
that they find it, and more seldom that the attainment brings
them greater happiness than the quest.*
—Arthur C. Clarke

WHEN I FIRST CAME TO VANDERBILT, I struck up a friendship with a
professor named Allison. Allison was out of town when a question came
up that needed a decision about a family gathering she was going to
attend. Allison's assistant could not reach her, and had seen us together,
so she asked me about it. I saw the right answer immediately. The
solution was obvious, so I told the assistant to go ahead on my say-so.
When Allison returned and learned what I had done, she was livid. My
decision was a huge mistake for her and her family and caused them
much grief. The good thing about Allison was that she did not suppress
her sentiments. She spoke directly into my face as she checked off the
long list of faults that made me an impossible person with whom to be a

friend. As her momentum built, she got to the final item that made me utterly insufferable. "And the absolute worst thing about you is that you trust your own perceptions. And let me tell you Dick Daft, YOU DON'T KNOW SHIT!"

After much contemplation, I saw that Allison was right. My mind had instantly concluded that it knew the right answer and reacted instantly with that "right" answer, but it had not evaluated concrete data about the family gathering or waited to gather other perspectives, including hers. My mind had made many assumptions about the facts of her situation, about my ability to understand her situation, and about whether I had a right to assert my opinion. Allison was correct. Trusting my instant interpretation as if it were absolute truth was the cause of her grief. My mind had believed its own perception and had reached a conclusion that had no more substance than air.

The images in our heads are bright and clear, and seem so true. Yet our inner elephant's distorted thinking can readily lead us astray. This chapter is going to explore some perceptual habits of the inner elephant that get in the way of seeing the world accurately: its tendency to react too quickly, think too inflexibly, want too much control, feel emotional avoidance or attraction, exaggerate the future, and seek satisfaction in the wrong places.

Reacting Too Quickly

I was visiting the founder and CEO of a medium-size company. I asked him why his office was on a separate floor from the hubbub of management and operations. He explained that when problems came up, he was unable to resist his reaction to tell people what to do, so he had moved his office away from day-to-day problems. His reactions that worked when the company was small were now seen as intrusive micromanagement. He had to remove himself from the action because he couldn't stop his compulsion to fix things his way.

Managers live in a reactive world. Having been a manager, I appreciate that an entire day is one e-mail after another, one phone call after another, one problem after another—all requiring quick action. Quick responses are often needed, and work well when you can pause a moment to see the bigger picture and provide a wise response. Otherwise, you may find yourself only reacting automatically rather than acting from your intentions. Dany Levy, founder of DailyCandy.com, said, "I have gotten better about not checking my e-mail as incessantly. . . . Everything I was doing was just a reaction to something."[1] John Donohoe, president and CEO of eBay, described the same trap: if he spent all day checking his

BlackBerry, he became reactive rather than proactive: "Being reactive is a lot easier than being proactive, and e-mail and the BlackBerry are natural tools to facilitate that."[2]

Sometimes a too-quick reaction has an emotional charge. Richard Anderson, CEO of Delta Airlines, said that in senior jobs there is a tendency to push really hard and that change can never be fast enough. Early in his career he would react with a temper, which he now sees as squelching debate and sending a terrible signal about how the managers reporting to him should act. His CEO at the time took him aside and gave him a serious instruction about his temper, which changed his approach. His advice for leaders now is to hold back the instant reaction: "You have to be patient enough and make sure that you always remain calm."[3]

A less damaging reaction I often see is the interrupting of someone who is speaking. The manager's interruptions are not hostile, but sometimes convey irritation and lack of patience toward the speaker. Other times the interruption just seems a strong impulse to make one's own point *right now* rather than wait. The interruption signals a lack of calm presence to hear someone out.

Have you ever overreacted to something or interrupted someone when your point seemed urgent? Instant reactions often feel urgent, which makes the impulse hard to control. If you feel that urgency, when you were a child your inner elephant probably wanted to "eat the marshmallow." In a study at Stanford, preschool children were offered a marshmallow to eat. If the children could refrain from eating it until the researcher returned from an errand (fifteen minutes, which children were not told), she would give them a second marshmallow. So the preschoolers could choose between one marshmallow now or two marshmallows later. Researchers followed the children over the next twenty years, and a striking difference appeared between those who ate the first marshmallow and those who waited. The children who resisted their impulse showed greater life resilience, handled stress better, more persistently pursued goals in the face of difficulty, were more confident and dependable, and took more initiative than those who ate the marshmallow immediately. At that early age, some of the children already were managing their inner elephant, and it paid off with greater maturity and success as an adult. Follow-up research supports the finding that self-control at an early age is an excellent predictor of long- and short-term success, sometimes more reliably than IQ tests.[4]

Too-fast reactions come up easily at work. Being patient is hard. In one case, Lance, the marketing director, saw Nate, his direct report, leave the office of the chief marketing officer (Lance's boss). Nate looked both ways, then walked the opposite direction down the hall. Lance noticed that Nate was carrying a file for their biggest client. Lance was furious and followed Nate to his office, where Nate looked flushed as he faced his boss and said, "What's up, Lance?"

"What do you think you're trying to pull? Why didn't you come to see me about the Philips account? Who do you think you report to? If you want to discuss our accounts, come to me. If you ever go around me again to see Mark, you will be out of this organization! Now, tell me what's going on."

Lance was embarrassed and apologetic when he heard Nate's explanation. Nate had inadvertently dinged the CMO's car in the parking lot and went to see him before refiling the Philips material that he was working on at home. He was flustered about telling the CMO, who wasn't too upset. Fortunately, the insurance companies would handle it.[5]

Have you ever reacted too quickly? What is the second-fastest thing in the universe? It is your mind jumping to the wrong conclusion based on skimpy data. It happens all the time. In this case, the marketing director's inner elephant jumped to the instant conclusion that he was being left out. Rather than assume the best and gather data to be on solid ground, he spoke to Nate from his premature conclusion, which came across as an attack.

There is nothing unusual about the mind's tendency to jump to instant conclusions. Our inner elephants have radar-like vigilance to threats in the environment, and instantly judge, conclude, and react based on small scraps of data. Neuroscience research supports the view that many decisions are instantaneous and not conscious. Serious intention is required to slow things down. By scanning the brains of people as they make decisions, researchers have shown that the choice-making regions of the brain are activated before people are aware they have made a choice. The rationale for the decision is constructed after the fact.[6] If the marketing director had engaged his inner executive, he would have ignored his initial reaction, stepped back to acquire more information, and assumed positive intent from Nate. Slowing down your reaction will typically produce a better response. Robert Iger, CEO of Disney, corroborates this idea in noting that an important leadership lesson he learned was to "manage reaction time better. What I mean by that is not overreacting to things that are said to me, because sometimes it's easy to do."[7]

The inferences in our heads seem so true in the moment. The most extreme example I heard was of the senior vice president who became suspicious when people around him started acting funny after the CEO was to retire in order to have heart surgery. Thinking he was in line for the job, the VP noticed that people were avoiding him and not answering his calls. He concluded that a rival would get the job, and wrote a letter of resignation to present at the next day's emergency board meeting. When he arrived at the boardroom, he discovered that it was a surprise party for both his upcoming birthday and his promotion to CEO, which explained the secrecy. Luckily for him, he still had that letter in his pocket.[8]

In another case of instant wrong reaction, a young manager was making an important presentation. His boss was in the audience and looked at his watch a couple of times about midway through. The presenter saw that the presentation was not going well, so he rushed through the remaining points, cutting the presentation short. Afterward he apologized to his boss. The boss responded that he loved the presentation, and had even checked his watch to see about rearranging his schedule to stay longer at the meeting.

All these incidents show how reacting too quickly, which the inner elephant does so naturally, often leads to a dead *wrong* conclusion except in the mind of the beholder. In addition, the beholder believes the instant conclusion so intensely that the inner elephant may defend the wrong-headed conclusion against contrary evidence.

Inflexible Thinking

Once the inner elephant jumps to a conclusion about something, it typically does not like to change its mind. Your inner magician and attorney will fill in any needed details and defend against competing views. Why? To maintain your sense of well-being, prevent or reduce psychological pain, and let you feel good about yourself. Once your inner elephant settles on a viewpoint or belief, it resists letting go. For example, one study recruited adult males who were committed Republicans or Democrats. The subjects listened to several statements about the presidential candidate they supported and the one they opposed. Then they heard a statement that each candidate had just reversed his position. Both the Democrats and the Republicans judged the opposing candidate harshly for the reversal and let their own candidate off the hook. The same data about opposing candidates were interpreted to fit within the subjects' existing views.[9] Once a person's underlying beliefs are locked in, they are very difficult to change with data, which are interpreted to fit with the person's viewpoint.

One reason views are hard to change is that the mind's conclusions are anchored in emotions. The brain activity in the political study was caught on MRI film, and showed that subjects' choices were strongly influenced by unconscious emotional reactions. These brain images confirmed that people react to data or events with an instinctive gut response. The gut response is an immediate like-dislike or yes-no, and then cognitive justification follows to support what the gut liked in the first place. (This is how I buy a car. My gut decides quickly, then my wife hears the subsequent logical arguments that justify spending the money.) Changing that gut feeling for or against something is not easy. It takes a well-developed inner executive to know when to ignore the gut. The gut feeling may be right, or it may be wrong. No matter, because the conclusions are as hard to change as telling you to stop liking your favorite beverage or snack food and to start liking ones you detest. These preferences hold up over time and cause you to pick out bits of new data that confirm your beliefs.

Have you tried to discuss politics, religion, or other emotion-laden topics with people who have strong beliefs? Did you change their mind? My guess is that you can provide fact after fact with no impact. I saw a TV news documentary about a natural history museum developed by believers in creationism. There were dinosaur exhibits just like those in any other natural history museum, but the guide explained to visitors that the dinosaur events all happened during the last six thousand years. The inner elephant has what psychologists call a confirmation bias—that is, it pays attention to data that confirm its beliefs and ignores evidence that undermines them. People tend to interpret things to fit their beliefs rather than use unbiased thinking.[10]

Executives are not exempt from inflexible thinking. The press characterized Richard Fuld, ex-CEO of Lehman Brothers, as the poster boy for staying attached to his own belief that all decisions were made correctly prior to Lehman's bankruptcy. The district attorney in the 2006 rape case against Duke University lacrosse players stuck to his guns until after he lost the case, despite skimpy evidence against the students. He was eventually disbarred after the fiasco. Marshall Goldsmith, author and well-known senior executive coach, told a story about his clients' lack of flexibility. He posed this story to them: You want to go to dinner at restaurant X, and your significant other wants to go to restaurant Y. You have a heated argument. You go to restaurant Y. The food and service are terrible. Do you critique the food and point out that your partner was wrong, or do you shut up and make the best of it? Seventy-five percent of Marshall's clients would say something like, "See, I was right. I told you this place stinks," putting into words their inflexibility.[11] It is very hard to let go of your own gut feelings and mental preferences. It is all you know. The mind-set, habits, and skills that made you successful tell you to stick to your guns. However, things change, and if the mind does not accept the current reality, it can create problems for everyone.

Wanting Control

The inner elephant has a real desire for control, probably as a way to feel safe. For example, have you noticed that you are more vigilant when you ride in the passenger's seat rather than in the driver's seat? When you are not in control, the car seems to go faster, the car in front looks closer, and you are likely to push on an imaginary brake. When driving, you may feel nervous or frustrated about drivers you see chatting on cell phones, but feel perfectly comfortable talking on a cell phone yourself. As a homeowner, you may be skeptical about the use of pesticides by neighbors, farmers, or corporations, but feel okay with the pesticides you use.[12] Your inner elephant is more comfortable when you are in control. Research into waiting times in phone booths and parking lots offers other examples. People take longer to wrap up a phone call or to leave a parking spot when they know someone is waiting, as if they slow down and refuse to be rushed as a way to stay in control.[13]

Chris Argyris's research into manager defense mechanisms found that the organizational hierarchy often generates a struggle for control. In a so-called decentralized company, headquarters told division heads, "You are in charge." Division managers liked this idea and adopted the attitude, "If you trust me, you will leave me alone." Then the trouble started. Headquarters wanted to be involved beyond normal accountability reports. Division managers typically resented the intrusion. Argyris argued that even if the HQ and division managers switched places, and thus had great empathy for their counterparts, the control dynamic would be the same. The struggle over control perpetuates in organizations and seldom gets resolved.[14]

Giving away control is something many managers have to learn because it often seems more efficient to them to maintain control. If your inner elephant micromanages other people, your satisfaction will be at their expense. Your inner executive can honor people's need for control so that they feel safe, happy, and motivated to achieve high performance.

Probably the most famous control study discussed in business schools is the experiment using loud random noises to disrupt subjects' work. Some groups were given a button to push if they felt it was absolutely necessary to terminate the noise. Other groups had no button. None of the people with the button actually used it, but the feeling of control made the noise less disturbing. Subjects who had no control button to reduce the random noise were more annoyed and gave up on difficult tasks more easily. Giving people a control button had a positive impact on performance.[15]

Ellen Langer's research in a nursing home demonstrated other benefits of feeling in control. On one floor, residents were given control over many aspects of their daily life—choosing plants, watering them, and selecting movie night, for example. The administrator gave a talk to residents emphasizing their responsibility for themselves. On another floor of the nursing home, the administrator's talk stressed the staff's responsibility to care for residents as patients. The nurses selected and watered the plants, selected movie night, and so on. The result was that the responsibility-induced patients became more active and reported feeling happier and more alert than the residents who were encouraged to feel that the staff would take care of them. The more astonishing outcome was that only 15 percent of the responsibility-induced group died during the subsequent eighteen months compared to 30 percent in the cared-for group.[16] When the nurses intentionally relinquished control, residents thrived.

Findings like these may explain why, when people do not have control, their minds may engage in something called the *illusion of control*, in which they believe they have more control than is actually the case.[17] They ignore reality to believe they are in control even when outcomes are random or unconnected to their behaviors. I have watched colleagues who understand statistics bet on craps or the roulette wheel or dog races. I could see the illusion of control in the way they blew on the dice, threw hard or soft, and searched for the correct roulette number. The law of large numbers says that the underlying odds always prevail over time, and of course the house will win, yet gamblers believe they can make a difference. Anyone is susceptible to superstitions, which are attempts to gain control over the uncontrollable, which again is an illusion. An authoritarian manager's illusion of control can be seen in the attempt to have complete control over others, when in fact people will defy and undercut that control behind his back.

The point is pretty clear that everyone's inner elephant wants to have control and is happier when in control. The lesson for leaders is to engage their inner executive to give control to others. Alan Mullaly, CEO of Ford, told the story of his first job as an engineering supervisor. He had to approve the work of other engineers. After the fourteenth draft to meet Mullaly's standard, one engineer quit. When Mullaly asked why, the engineer said Mullaly might make a good supervisor someday, but right now, "this is just too much for me to be supervised this tightly."[18] That experience taught Mullaly that his job as supervisor was to engage a bigger picture of mission and purpose (inner executive) and let people be in control of their own work.

Emotional Avoidance and Attraction

I like the story from India about a young man hiking in the hills with a walking stick. At dusk, he saw a poisonous snake on the trail and shouted an alarm. He beat the snake to death and then headed for home. The next morning he returned with a friend to see the dead snake, and found he had beaten not a snake but a rope. His mind had imagined the very thing he was afraid of and had not seen what was really there on the ground. Likewise, the mind has the potential to see a gold chain in the place of a rope. The illusion depends on the inner elephant's emotional connection to what it sees.

You and I are guided through life and work by the thoughts, ideas, desires, impulses, dislikes, gut feelings, and so on that appear in our minds. The vast majority of these thoughts and images show up automatically in our heads without any conscious intention on our part. This is the way we are designed, and it works fine, most of the time. The problem occurs when you want to perform a task and your inner elephant does not, or your inner elephant desires to do an activity that your inner executive does not. Many problems our inner elephant faces in a leadership role can be boiled down to these two issues. We know we should perform a task, yet our inner elephant balks or refuses as if seeing a snake, and we end up in a state of avoidance or procrastination. Or we choose not to do something, and our inner elephant surges ahead anyway out of attraction and habit, potentially causing a problem for ourselves or others. An extreme case of avoidance would be a phobia (for example, of heights or spiders) that freezes us in terror. An extreme case of attraction would be an addiction (alcohol, work) that we cannot resist. Phobias and addictions are beyond the scope of this book, but some ideas for handling these extremes also work for gaining mastery over your inner elephant's annoying attraction and avoidance habits.

Avoidance

Let's consider your wish to do something when your inner elephant balks and will not go forward. Let us say you have a report due at the end of the week, and you are avoiding it. You would love to complete it, but cannot get yourself started. This is procrastination, which afflicts nearly everyone at some point. I see it occasionally with managers as well as with students and professors. For example, a manager fails to follow up as agreed or delays providing information as promised. One manager wanted to spend more time walking around talking to people and visiting customers, but always delayed doing so in favor of working on operational matters. Another manager did not want to take time to consult with others about decisions, despite knowing she should do so and even after promising her people she would do so. Yet another manager promised to submit two employees' work for company awards and delayed until the deadline passed.

To procrastinate means to "delay an intended course of action despite expecting to be worse off for the delay."[19] You do not want to delay, but do it anyway, because your inner elephant resists more strongly than your intention. You can try to force yourself to do the activity, and sometimes that works, especially if close to a strict deadline. But it is stressful to work at the last minute. Procrastination is the opposite of flow, which is the effortless absorption in a task with full mental involvement, energy, and focus.

Procrastination is real pain. It is an invisible barrier in your mind that prevents you from moving into a task. The reason is that there is something about the avoided task or situation that your inner elephant perceives as a subtle threat. You probably don't feel actual fear, as in the case of a phobia, but the fear emotion is underneath, and you are aware that you are avoiding something. Resistance to a task means that the task symbolizes something from your past that triggers modest anxiety, and hence your inner elephant wants to avoid it. Modest anxiety typically happens quickly and automatically below the surface of your awareness.

Attraction

Attraction or desire is a strong feeling of longing for an object, sensation, or outcome. You may feel desire for a cup of coffee in the morning or several Diet Cokes during the day, to do certain favored tasks when you are working, or to click on the e-mails that interest you most. In the world at large, desire can cause problems by enslaving people to their wants for money, food, status, comfort, love, and so on. The desire of investors for predictable high returns and to be part of an "in-group" helped Bernie Madoff succeed with his Ponzi scheme. Desire is the basis for most financial scams. The attorney who was coexecutor of Brooke Astor's estate is under indictment for his desire to steal money from the estate. He admitted that he had to keep a closer eye on the "bad things inside" him that he could not control.[20]

The attractions that appear in our minds are powerful, as illustrated in Homer's description of Odysseus's escape from the sea nymphs whose singing was so alluring that sailors would jump overboard to pursue them. Odysseus asked his men to bind him to the mast, forbidding them to release him until after they had passed the sirens' island. Then he ordered his men to plug their ears with wax. When he heard the singing, he struggled to release himself, begging to be untied. His men were deaf to his entreaties and stayed the course, saving Odysseus and the ship.[21]

Strong attractions, such as the need for perfection, can cause problems for managers. A few of my MBA students are perfectionists who can't restrain their desire to redo a group project to make it look the way they want, even after I explain that this behavior is fatal for leaders who have to accomplish work through others. Managers may also feel the need to act on their unthinking desire always to be right rather than let other people shine, to perpetually find fault with other people's ideas, to win every disagreement, to blame others when something goes wrong despite being culpable, or to speak harshly when upset. I have also observed a few managers who follow their desire to promote themselves rather than concentrate on their immediate work, unable to trust that their good work will be recognized. Others follow their personal desire to habitually horn in on the credit for the successful work of other people.

Several exercises in the chapters that follow will help you manage your troublesome avoidance and attraction behaviors. Learning to use your inner executive to accelerate forward when your inner elephant wants to delay and to put the brakes on some of your inner elephant's desires is a good idea, especially when doing so will increase your performance and morale and that of your employees.

Exaggerating the Future

A small team of academics and teachers was involved in developing a new curriculum for high schools in Israel. After about one year, team members estimated that they would need eighteen to thirty months to finish their work. Data from other similar projects suggested a period of seven to ten years for completion, not even counting the projects that were never completed. Team members admitted that they had no special talent, and their resources were below average. Yet the team forged ahead with optimism that most of the work would be finished in about two years and the curriculum implemented successfully soon thereafter. The curriculum was finally completed eight years later. Disappointingly, the curriculum was rarely used.[22] The team would have been better off canceling the project eight years earlier. Unfortunately, the team members were unable to view their future realistically.

Why did the team misjudge the future so badly? The exaggerated prediction of future events is related to the issue of emotional attraction and avoidance we just looked at. When the inner elephant is attracted to a future outcome, it overoptimistically anticipates good results and underestimates potential difficulties, so it fails to see the problems ahead. Overpromising and underperforming happen to everyone. Hofstadter's Law states (and mathematically proves) that every task takes longer to complete than estimated, even when one has added time to take the law into account. For example, daily to-do lists and project plans are notoriously optimistic and are seldom completed as expected. Plans are often based on the inner elephant's best-case scenarios, leading to frustration down the line.[23]

The same thing happens in the opposite direction. When the inner elephant dislikes or wants to avoid an outcome, it will pessimistically see more difficulties and problems than will actually occur. Your elephant mind can make a mountain out of a future you dislike. Surely you have dreaded a task and then after getting started found it wasn't so dreadful after all. The inner elephant exaggerates the size or complexity of negative events, similar to the feelings that often lead to avoidance. This happened to me with tax preparation one year when the issues were complicated. I told myself I could not bear the pain of twelve hours of work on something I dreaded. I finally got to it at the last minute, and my preparation took only about four hours, and was kind of fun once I got into it. My inner elephant had exaggerated the amount of time by eight hours. Grandma was right: "Nothing is ever as bad as it seems at the start." Nor is it as easy as we expect for those things we desire. The inner elephant tends toward positive and negative exaggerations about the future depending on its emotional orientation toward an object or event.

The bias toward optimism is an important leadership quality that engages followers in the vision. Who wants to follow a pessimist who sees only the difficulties ahead? But doses of objectivity are needed to help anticipate the future realistically. For executives and managers responsible for large change projects, the rosy, optimistic picture often poses a problem. The production delays on the giant Airbus A380 and the Boeing 787 Dreamliner may illustrate the tendency to overestimate the ease of completing a huge, complex, multinational project. The optimism that drives these projects forward makes it hard to anticipate problems accurately. Mergers such as Time Warner and AOL, or more recently between Bank of America and Merrill Lynch, are typically driven by the same optimism. Love is blind, which explains why about two-thirds of acquisitions and mergers destroy value compared to the optimistic expectations that drove the deals.

Another example is the run-up to the Iraq war a few years ago. When Larry Lindsey boldly estimated the absolute cost limit as $100+ billion to Congress, White House operatives claimed that his figure was way too high, because they supported the war. So far the Iraq war's cost is climbing toward $1 trillion.[24] The cost (so far) was underestimated by a factor of ten. In terms of manpower needed to fight the war, General Shinseki, Army chief of staff, told a congressional committee in 2003 that several hundred thousand soldiers and up to ten years could be needed to achieve security and stability in Iraq. This realistic estimate was soundly rejected by Donald Rumsfeld and Paul Wolfowitz, optimistic supporters of the minimalist approach to war, as "wildly off the mark." Optimism won, and Shinseki's retirement was encouraged. Three years later, General Abizaid, chief of U.S. central command, said, "General Shinseki was right."[25] Blind optimism prevented leaders from seeing the harsh reality of the upcoming war.

Chasing the Wrong Gratifications

The most frequently stated underlying motivation for an inner elephant's behavior is to achieve some degree of happiness and sense of well-being. Psychologists since Freud have said that everyone wants to be happy. To the question of what people show by their behavior to be the purpose of their lives, Freud responded, "They strive after happiness; they want to become happy and to remain so."[26] This is reasonable enough, but the inner elephant can act like a child chasing after the wrong gratifications. Finding happiness is a challenge because the inner elephant often seeks things that do not provide lasting satisfaction.

Consider the elementary school children who played in an area not far from the window of the bedroom in which a retired man worked and napped. After a few days of noise, he asked the kids to play elsewhere, but they refused. The next day he said to them, "If you kids come back and play here tomorrow, I'll give each of you one dollar." They came back the next day and played even more enthusiastically. He paid them each a dollar and said, "If you will come back tomorrow, I'll give you each fifty cents." That was still a good deal, so the kids showed up on time and played their usual loud games. When they came to collect, he paid the fifty cents, and then offered them one penny if they would come again the next day. These kids were insulted at being paid only one penny. One said, "Forget it." They never came back again.

Why the change of heart? When the kids started, they were intrinsically motivated to play in the spot near the man's window. They played there for the fun of it. As soon as they received pay for playing there, they started to see themselves as doing it for the money. The money caused them to lose sight of the original fun. The old man understood that given a choice, the inner elephant within each child would choose the external reward and thereby lose sight of the intrinsic fun. Once their minds believed that they were playing for a reward, when the reward disappeared, so did they.

The inner elephant loves the temporary good feeling that goes with external rewards, whether in the form of a trip, plaque, promotion, or more money. The question is, Does the elephant's love for external rewards produce happiness and satisfaction? Edward Deci carried out some of the first experiments on intrinsic versus extrinsic motivation. He gave subjects four challenging block-building puzzles to complete. One set of subjects was not offered any reward; the other set was offered cash to complete the puzzles. Later the groups spent time in a "free choice" room where various activities were available, including block-building puzzles. The group that did not receive any money showed considerably more interest in the puzzles than the paid group. Deci concluded that the financial reward was the key reason for the paid group's lack of interest. Those subjects saw completing the puzzle as a way to get a reward rather than as a source of personal interest or fun. Deci replicated the experiment with headline writing for students working on the college newspaper. Those who received pay to write headlines later showed less intrinsic interest in doing so. Their minds seemed to conclude that doing a task for money meant they did not like it very much.[27]

There are many studies that have attempted to answer this age-old question about which is more satisfying, means or ends, the chase or the victory, the journey or the destination, intrinsic or extrinsic outcomes. Time and again, results indicate that greater personal satisfaction comes from the means, the chase, the journey, and the intrinsic. There seems little doubt that performing a task for intrinsic satisfaction feels better than working only to receive an external reward. Finding happiness is easy—just do what you enjoy. You can have happiness right now. Indeed, pursuing an extrinsic reward undermines a person's intrinsic satisfaction, creativity, and risk taking.[28] Absorption in work is a great pleasure and will last. An external reward is short lived, so happiness is temporary. When the boss or organization emphasizes external rewards, as the old man knew, intrinsic pleasure is diminished. Unfortunately, the inner elephant is gullible and easily seduced into chasing after shiny objects to the exclusion of pure enjoyment.

Greg Brenneman, chairman of CCMP Capital, said, "I've talked to a lot of people on Wall Street where their entire fulfillment came from the answer to, 'Is my bonus bigger this year than last year?'"[29] He went on to say that leaders can help people step back and ask the question, "Where do I get fulfillment in my life?" There is great satisfaction in making progress toward a meaningful goal, but when the goal is solely to receive an extrinsic reward, the day-to-day intrinsic pleasure is reduced.

When money becomes the sole focus of work, the inner elephant has overpowered the higher wisdom of the inner executive in the false pursuit of happiness.

The inner elephant only knows to move toward pleasure and away from pain. The trap caused by chasing objects of desire is illustrated in the Indian story about capturing monkeys. Monkeys are curious and have little control over their desires. They can be caught by placing a banana, nuts, or a piece of fruit inside a clay pot with a small neck. When the monkey reaches into the pot and grasps the fruit, it can no longer retract its hand. The monkey believes something inside the pot has a hold of it. The monkey is unwilling to let go of the fruit. It is the monkey's own desire for the fruit that traps it and allows it to be captured.[30] The same may be true of those executives on Wall Street.

Early in my career when I was supporting a young family, I accepted a consulting project primarily for the money. The work became painful because I felt no intrinsic pleasure. At that time, I did not understand that the extrinsic reward would displace intrinsic satisfaction. I found it difficult to complete that project just for the money. On another occasion, I accepted an advance against royalties to write a book. I felt some commitment to the book, but once I had money in advance, that became the main reason to complete the book. Again, I did not understand why my heart was no longer in the book project, and I struggled. Rather than continue to suffer, I finally returned the advance. Never again did I accept an advance to write a book.

Extrinsic rewards such as money do reduce fear and allow one to compare oneself favorably to others, but this is all about the ego—the province of the inner elephant. Research compiled by Alfie Kohn shows that time and again, a person's inner elephant will choose the extrinsic reward and then be unfulfilled.[31] Physical and ego pleasures such as food, drink, status, money, and winning an argument are especially short lived. How many desserts can you eat before the next bite becomes unbearable?

The inner elephant desperately seeks but cannot find lasting happiness. As children we learn to be rewarded for being good. Unconsciously we believe that "loving me means you will meet my needs." We want the world to continue meeting our needs to make us happy. We haven't learned as adults to question our desires and their satisfaction.[32] The thrill—of a bigger house, a BMW, jewelry, a wide-screen TV in every room, or the big promotion—always wears off. A manager who works eighty hours a week instead of sixty, expecting the additional prestige and purchases to bring lasting happiness, is on the "hedonic treadmill."[33] You can keep running faster and faster without making progress toward greater life satisfaction. The inner elephant can chase money into infinity, acquire luxury goods beyond imagination, and never experience the joy of performing a task just for pleasure. That is why the adage "Love what you do and the money will follow" is good advice for finding satisfaction. You will find the satisfaction and happiness that everyone else is seeking.

PART THREE

•

How to Start Leading Yourself

•

5.

Engage Your Intention

The universe is change; our life is what our thoughts make it.
—Marcus Aurelius Antoninus

When there is no vision, people perish.
—Ralph Waldo Emerson

MUHAMMAD ALI HAS BEEN CALLED the master of intention.[1] He developed mental skills that improved his physical skills in the ring. His oft-repeated phrases "I am the greatest" and "I float like a butterfly, sting like a bee" shaped his mind as much as they angered opponents. These statements were declarations of intention, as were the poems he recited publicly before a match. A few lines from the poem in which he predicted the outcome of his rematch with Frasier showed his mental intent:

> Ali swings to the left
> Ali swings to the right
> Look at the kid
> Carry the fight.
> Frasier keeps backing
> But there's not enough room
> It's a matter of time
> Then Ali lowers the boom.[2]

Writing and repeating poems and phrases crystallized intentions for Ali; when repeated often, they shaped his belief system and guided him toward victory. Ali also used visualization to rehearse an entire fight in his head. In his mind, he could feel the fatigue in his legs, the deflection of a punch to his body, the counterpunch to the face of his opponent, the roar of the crowd. For the Joe Frazier fight in the Philippines, Ali created a voodoo doll. Talk about visualizing an intention! He carried the doll with him, and he would take swipes at it in front of the TV cameras. All of Ali's pranks, which some observers saw as childish play, "sent an intention to his body to win and his body responded by following orders."[3] Ali revealed his power of mental intention when he said, "To be a great champion, you must believe you are the best. If you are not, pretend you are."[4]

How do we take control of our body and mind—the inner elephant—as Ali did? We live in a world filled with unrelenting opportunities for distraction, in which our inner elephant shows obvious attention deficits when it jumps from important work to unimportant distractions, cannot stay focused for long periods, and sees the world through a lens that often seems to obscure reality. As described in previous chapters, the inner elephant may seek interpretations, cook facts, jump to the wrong conclusions, quickly defend its errors, be impatient, act rashly, avoid unpleasant work that needs doing now, and pursue outcomes that don't satisfy, often while accepting its behavior uncritically and without question. There has to be a better way to manage your inner elephant.

Like Muhammad Ali, you can take advantage of your inner executive to create intentions that influence your elephant to overcome ineffective habit and behavior patterns. Your inner executive contains your intelligent will, which can define the direction the elephant should go. However, simply pushing your inner elephant in the desired direction is often not enough, especially when it is avoidant or resistant. The trick is to engage your inner elephant in the intention, to shape expectations so that the elephant "gets it" and wants to move forward. You can learn to bring your intention to life in your mind so that your inner elephant can absorb and embrace it. Then it will perform as directed with little effort on your part.

This chapter describes how to use your inner executive to guide and coach your inner elephant by bringing your intelligent will to life in your mind. This chapter will explore how to use intentional visual images and verbal statements to manage your inner elephant through periods of resistance or procrastination. Some techniques are easy and almost natural, as they should be. Some you have probably tried, perhaps without realizing it.

Avoidance behaviors like procrastination are annoying and frustrating, as described in Chapter Four. You feel as though there is a barrier that prevents you from moving forward just when you most need to. As described in Chapter Four, the cause is modest anxiety that triggers an avoidance reflex. It often happens quickly and automatically below the surface of your awareness. All you may know is that you have a pattern of avoiding certain things when avoidance is not rational. You and I are guided through life and work by the thoughts, ideas, desires, impulses, dislikes, avoidances, gut feelings, and so on that normally appear in our minds automatically, with no conscious intention. The solution is to learn to use your conscious intention or will when you want to perform some task that your inner elephant wants to avoid.

Visualize Your Intention

When I was a kid living in Stromsburg, Nebraska, I occasionally visited a friend on a farm. I learned about hand pumps that provided underground water for livestock. During chores, sometimes the pump did not produce water, so it was primed by pouring water down into it. The water seemed to improve the suction, and after a few pumps, water would flow forth. Little did I think at that time that the inner elephant behaves the same way—pour water in to get water out. Pour into your inner elephant what you want to get out, and it is likely to happen. Here's how.

I visited a friend who was director of leadership development at USAA in San Antonio, so I sat in a class he was teaching. He gave participants and me a handout with the following instructions: "Please rate the sentences I will read on how easily you can pronounce them. Repeat the sentences to yourself." He read twenty creative sentences similar to the following:

> The slithering snake slithered down a steep sliding board.
>
> The plump chef liked to jump rope.
>
> The medieval minstrel strolled along the babbling brook.[5]

Much to my consternation, after rating the twenty sentences, he then asked questions to test our memory. "Who liked to jump rope?" "Who strolled along the babbling brook?" and so on. I was embarrassed. I could remember only four or five answers, and I got those because of generous grading. To make matters worse, several people in the room remembered fifteen to nineteen answers correctly. How could they remember so many? My friend teased me and other low scorers for being poor leadership material.

The instructor, and now ex-friend, finally revealed that the reason for the widely different scores was differing instructions. The participants who had great memories had been told, "Please rate the sentences I will read on how well you can form a vivid mental picture or image of the action of the sentence." Twenty complicated sentences are far too many to remember, especially when you were not asked to remember them. The people who visualized the action of the sentence remembered *three times as many* sentences as those who were told to repeat the sentence in their mind. This amazed me, and I have used the exercise with many executive groups since. The result is always the same. People in the visualization group miss only a few answers and remember two to three times as many as the verbal repetition group.

Clearly, the inner elephant "gets" and remembers a visual image. Visual images are a powerful way to communicate to your elephant. I read a study in which students who visualized exactly when and where they would write a paper completed 75 percent of the papers on time; without the visualization, only a third of the students submitted the paper on time. When people take the time to visualize exactly what they are going to do, they are much more likely to do it.[6] Another study showed marked improvement for basketball players who practiced free throws for thirty minutes and spent thirty minutes visualizing themselves shooting perfect free throws, compared to players who practiced for sixty minutes without imagery. In a study of Olympic skiers, a group receiving imagery training were improving so much faster than the nonimagery control group that the study was suspended so that all participants could take advantage of visual imagery.[7] This is almost too easy—your inner elephant will respond obediently to visual instruction from your inner executive.

Some of the students and managers I work with use visualization as mental rehearsal for upcoming tasks about which they feel some anxiety or resistance. For example, I received an e-mail from Robert, a thirty-six-year-old account manager who delayed his application to the EMBA program for two years because of anxiety about test taking. His first big challenge was the statistics course.

> Dick, I want to make it a point to thank you for the visualization
> techniques in your class. I was terrified of the statistics test and talked
> to the instructor. He suggested taking a couple of practice exams.
> I used visualization to mentally rehearse taking the practice exams
> with zero stress, clear focus, and increased confidence. It worked.
> I visualized even more for the real exam, and I did fine. If I felt
> stress, I closed my eyes, took deep breaths, and envisioned how easily
> I completed the practice problems. I aced the course. Thank you.

Visualization works for salespeople too. One salesman told me how visualization was helping him cope with his introverted personality in the extroverted profession of selling banking products:

> Developing new customers is hard for me; my natural tendency is to shy away from calling on new customers. To combat my resistance, every morning for five minutes I started visualizing myself picking up my office phone and calling my list of prospects to set up appointments. My inner elephant's fears tried to take control, but I persisted. I became calmer and made calls easily, yielding five additional appointments this week.

Another salesperson visualized the whole sales process in detail:

> I sat down in my chair in the hotel, closed my eyes, and visualized the appointment from the opening greeting and personal chitchat through to the end. I could see myself and the client handing materials back and forth, and myself discussing my company's differentiation. I visually fielded tough questions and provided solid answers. I even visualized my smile and greeting. I am pleased to report that it worked wonderfully. My new president joined me on the call. I was calm, confident, and able to make my case about why my company was the only logical choice. The client agreed. My new president was impressed. Visualization was an opportunity for me to practice without consequence.

Visualization has a direct impact on your mind and body by calming an automatic "flight response." A manager told me about a project that he needed to complete but just could not get to work on. Every time he told himself to start on the project, he would find something else to do instead. He decided to sit for five minutes and visualize doing that task. After the five minutes were up, he reported, "I felt motivated and focused. I wanted to accomplish the task and actually got it finished fairly quickly." In another case an MBA student club officer was overwhelmed with so many e-mails that he dreaded reading them, a daunting task in that moment. "It was my birthday and I wanted to do something else. Instead, I sat for three minutes and visualized myself quickly and efficiently answering all unread messages. Then I went to my computer and answered all e-mails in record time. I also found that visualizing for other daily tasks kept me focused all day." Another MBA student who was perpetually late to meetings started visualizing, the night before, his arrival on time at all the day's appointments. Over two weeks, he was late for only one class and one group meeting. Your inner elephant is likely to respond to new visual intentions in the same way.

To stimulate serious procrastination within MBA students, I give them exercises that they want to avoid. One assignment is to introduce themselves to a "scary person" who intimidates them and to get to know that person; a more challenging assignment is to ask a person for his or her seat in a public place, without explanation, when other seats are available. The first assignment triggers inner anxiety; the second assignment breaks a social norm. Hence, both cause serious procrastination. Visualizing the task in advance reduces anxiety and rehearses the calm step-by-step actions to be performed. One student reported, "I tried asking for a person's seat three times without visualization, and I could not do it. So I visualized for ten minutes, and my fears dissipated and I could see myself making the request. I asked with a calm voice. The person looked at me like I was crazy, but she gave me her seat. I was elated." Another student used visualization to get herself to step through ongoing resistance to cleaning her house.

> I visualized myself getting out of bed at 7:30 A.M., and I was up and about in five minutes. Wow, this works! I then did visualization exercises for doing my operations paper, cleaning the kitchen, taking out the trash, vacuuming, and doing laundry. These are all things that I have been avoiding. Visualizing seemed to channel my executive intention and ignored the elephant that was telling me to watch television instead. It was almost like jumpstarting the action. After visualizing, my elephant was not able to get in the way of my productivity.

Sports Visualization

The most striking examples of coaching one's inner elephant with visual images come from sports. The mind clearly teaches the body how to behave. Most college coaches and athletes practice some form of visual mental rehearsal. Focused intention, sometimes called mental practice, visualization, or motor imagery, is a part of the regimen for swimmers, skaters, skiers, golfers, track and field athletes, tennis players, and weightlifters. Here are two stories from *The Mental Game of Baseball,* by H. A. Dorfman and Karl Kuehl. A relief pitcher for the California Angels, who spent too much time on the disabled list during three previous seasons, earned four saves and held the opposition scoreless over twelve and two-thirds innings. He gave credit to a sports psychologist who taught him to visualize. Instead of pitching every day to stay sharp, now he did the pitching in his mind and saved the wear and tear on his body. Carl Yastrzemski, the Hall of Fame left fielder who played with the Boston Red Sox, said, "The night before a game, I visualize the pitcher and the pitches I'm going to see the next day. I hit the ball right on the button and know what it's going to feel like. I hit the pitches where I want to. I keep some bats at home. If I want a stronger picture, I pick one up and do some hitting in the living room."[8]

In 1986, Charles Garfield, a retired world-class weightlifter, had an experience with sports scientists from East Germany and the Soviet Union. He was not in competitive shape, but they taught him to relax and visualize, and to his surprise, he managed to bench press 300 pounds, just barely, which was 20 pounds above his normal 280 pounds. Then the scientists added 65 more pounds, an impossible 21 percent increase. The scientists guided Garfield into a deep state of relaxation and visualization; suddenly everything came together, and he felt a surge of strength in his body. His mind became convinced he could do it. The world around him seemed to fade. With total confidence, Garfield lifted the 365 pounds![9]

An even more striking example to me of visualization's power was research at the Cleveland Clinic Foundation that compared participants who worked out with weights at a gym to participants who worked out in their heads. Regular visits to the gym provided a 30 percent increase in muscle strength. Those who stayed home and did a mental rehearsal increased muscle power by almost half as much.[10] Can you believe that? An earlier study at Chester College reported a similar finding. People who worked out increased their physical strength by 30 percent, whereas those who imagined themselves working out achieved a 16 percent increase.[11]

Russian scientists assigned Olympic athletes to four groups that were given different training schedules. Group one did 100 percent physical training; group two did 75 percent physical training and 25 percent mental training; group three did 50 percent physical training and 50 percent mental training; and group four did 25 percent physical training and 75 percent mental training. Group four, which devoted 75 percent of their time to mental training, performed the best.[12]

How is this possible? The intentional thought or visual image is sufficient to create the same brain signals as the physical act. The intentional visual image is part of the inner executive, the intelligent will. The visual intention produces the neural instructions to carry out the act. The electrical activity in the brain is the same whether you are visualizing doing something or actually doing it. This is a powerful thing—your mind's visualization sends signals through the nervous system to the muscles and fibers of your body. EEGs reveal that electrical activity in the brain is the same whether people are doing something or just thinking about doing it. By visualizing an activity, you are sending your body a mental intention to do the activity, to speed up or calm down, or to perform in a specific way, and your body will listen.[13]

Visualization Guidelines

Visualization brings the future into focus exactly as you want it to happen. It is a great way to send a clear intention to your inner elephant. Visualization as I teach it might also be called mental rehearsal or motor imagery because it focuses on the specific behaviors that produce an outcome. It focuses primarily on the process, not the outcome. Most people have the ability to visualize action images in their mind. When teaching visualization to managers, I typically stay simple and practical by starting with something from their own memory. You might try it right now.

1. Visualize your bedroom or living room at home or your office. Close your eyes and take a couple of minutes to view in your mind the major features in the room. In your mind, move around and view each feature, one at a time.

After having the managers visualize one room, I typically discuss how it went, and then have them try visualizing a second room to get their minds warmed up. You can do the same right now.

2. Now visualize yourself completing a familiar task in a familiar setting, such as at work or home.

3. The next step is to identify something you have been avoiding, putting off, or feeling anxious about. Then visualize yourself in the location of that activity, and see yourself performing the required action without resistance, flowing through it effortlessly and enjoyably. Repeat the action a few times to imprint it clearly on your inner elephant.

• TRY THIS •

Visualize Your Intention

1. Sit comfortably, close your eyes, relax.
2. Visualize from memory the features of a familiar room.
3. Visualize yourself completing a familiar task in a familiar setting.
4. Select a task toward which you feel some resistance.
5. Visualize yourself completing the task easily and enjoyably.
6. Repeat the visualization several times.

Learning to visualize for practical application is that simple. The trick is to actually do it. The following are some general guidelines I normally suggest to heighten the inner executive's ability to prime the inner elephant:

○ You get the best result if you visualize the activity at the same speed you will actually perform it. If you rush through the visualization, it will have less impact. An athletic performance may last only a few seconds, but your task may take longer. So take time to repeatedly visualize the critical parts of the task. Mentally rehearse the moments of giving a sales presentation that are critical for you, or visualize your desired posture and gestures when giving a speech.

○ Try to "feel" yourself in the situation using multiple senses. Perhaps feel the temperature in the room, your hand on the podium, the emotion of personal enthusiasm, and even see the customer's reaction. Kinesthetic sensations are a key part of the mind-body link. The more specific, concrete, and detailed your mental rehearsal, the more your inner elephant will operate as visualized during the actual event.[14] The clearer, more specific, and more detailed the mental action, the greater the effect on your body.

○ If you have trouble creating visual images, I suggest that you start by imagining yourself holding a lemon, squeezing it, rolling it, cutting it in half, smelling it, tasting it. The lemon's pungent odor and taste will arise in your imagination. For additional practice, try visualizing a future event by mentally creating your perfect vacation spot, perhaps on a ski mountain or beach. See, feel, hear, and smell the details of the house, people, and activities. If you want to stretch yourself, try visualizing colors—red, yellow, purple, orange, blue, green. However, visualizing colors is not necessary for a typical mental rehearsal. This is a way to add to your visualization capacity.

Jim Fannin, a consultant and mental coach for professional athletes, said that about 84 percent of participants see a mental image through their own eyes (first-person view), as they do in ordinary life. Thirteen percent see the action from above or the side (third-person view), observing themselves as part of the entire scene. In Fannin's experience, either of these views is effective. About 3 percent of people have difficulty seeing anything in their mind's eye.[15] If you are one of the 3 percent, practice visualizing familiar scenes and colors in your mind. Practice changing and mixing colors. Look directly at an object in the room, then close your eyes and keep the image in your mind's eye. Repeat. Then create something in your mind that you do not physically see, such as the face of a friend. Be patient. Then visualize yourself performing a task in the future.

• • •

Many managers find themselves putting off writing, planning, giving feedback, or having a confrontational meeting. Again, a visual mental rehearsal allows you to flow into a planning or writing task or to rehearse the dynamics of a difficult conversation. Mental rehearsal reduces anxiety and procrastination.

The main thing to remember is to visualize a specific sequence of behaviors that prime your inner elephant with mental pictures of exactly what you want to do. This is the rehearsal prior to the actual event. Visualize at the correct speed, see specific details, and use multiple senses. If visualization is hard for you, there is another option—verbal priming, which we will explore after briefly considering how to use visual images to lead others.

Leadership Show and Tell

Visual images work for communicating to other people as well. That is one reason why the notion of leadership "vision" is so important. People want to see a picture of where they are going. They want to know the purpose, intention, or "why" of their work, and one picture really is worth a thousand words. Bernard, the chief operating officer for the U.S. division of a global risk management and insurance brokerage firm, told me how he used a picture to facilitate change when he took over. After visiting many brokerage offices, he found that definitions of success differed widely. It soon became clear to him that three criteria of financial performance were essential: profit (bottom line), the percentage increase in profit, and revenue growth (top line). A large office might emphasize profit, a growing office might emphasize revenue growth, and an efficient office might emphasize percentage profit increase. Most executives were good at achieving one score rather than all three. To get office executives focused on all three aspects of performance, he drew a picture of a simple triangle with one performance indicator (P, delta P, delta R) at each point. When executives came together, they were encouraged to debate the "three points of performance" triangle projected up on the screen and discuss ways to achieve high scores on each.

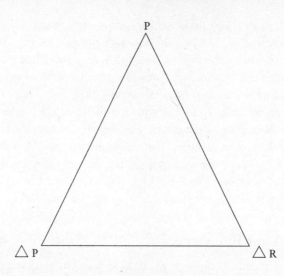

Bernard said that results dramatically improved in less than two years, with sharply increased growth rates and profit margins. He emphasized "Pictures, not PowerPoints" for communication. He told me that during previous corporate transformations, he learned that he could effectively communicate change by either repeating a point ten times verbally, sending it out five times via e-mail, or showing a picture twice. The simplest picture is many times more powerful than no picture at all for changing the behavior of other people's elephants.

Show *and* tell is a powerful way to communicate. Visual images dominate the impact of words. Some studies show that 80 percent of learning is visually based.[16] However, our inner elephant is busy and wants to just tell others what to do and then get on to something else. Taking a few minutes to "show" a picture can penetrate deeply into the awareness of another person and change his or her perception. As a young manager, Daniel Amos, chief executive of Aflac, said he learned never to have a sales meeting where he did not read a customer letter or have a customer present.[17] Having a customer in the room is the ultimate show and tell.

A few managers who have participated in my programs have told me of their communication successes, particularly when trying to change things. One executive in Asia flew his team of direct reports and their direct reports to visit customers' businesses and witness firsthand how they worked and what the customers wanted. He no longer had to lecture them, because they could see for themselves what customers needed and why. A plant manager, dealing with a recalcitrant union during a turnaround, shut the plant down for one day. He set up a "fair" in which competitors' products could be seen, touched, and examined firsthand by shop-floor employees. They could compare prices too. He also invited a few customers whom employees could talk to about their perception of the plant's output compared to that of competitors. Showing rather than telling brought the union membership on board for change. In another case, a manager made a brief audiotape of three corporate customers complaining about service deficits. The anger and frustration could be felt in the voices on the tape. The manager played the tape during a meeting with his staff. He said the shift in their perspective was instant. Hearing what customers were feeling shocked them out of their status quo mind-sets, whereas his previous "talking" at them had little impact.

Verbalize Your Intention

Elaina was a poised young woman, but sometimes in the heat of the moment she became upset, emotional, and irrational. Elaina was hard on herself in those moments, with such thoughts appearing in her mind as "This always happens to me," "I screwed up again," or "You're so stupid." This self-talk did not reestablish her poise. So she tried rehearsing some positive statements that her inner executive could interject in a moment of crisis, including "I am staying calm," "I am going with the flow," and "I am lightening up." As it happened, her car broke down just before a long drive across country. She was in a fight with the dealership that supposedly had fixed it, and used her new self-talk to stay calm and poised. In her e-mail to me, Elaina said, "During the ordeal with the dealership, I forced my executive to take control. Several times I stopped, closed my eyes, took deep breaths, and repeated the new phrases. I found this very effective! It helped me relax and think rationally using the executive function rather than the elephant's reactions. I will continue with this. Thank you."

Elaina used *autosuggestion* by inserting intentional positive statements about how she wanted to behave to replace the negative thoughts that automatically popped into her head. Autosuggestion tells our inner elephant how to behave. The notion of autosuggestion got its start with Emile Coué's book *Self Mastery Through Conscious Autosuggestion*, published in 1922. Coué was a hypnotist and psychologist in France who gave up his original practice because patients got better results with auto-suggestion. His focus was on physical ailments, and he reported many successes. Charles Baudouin published *Suggestion and Autosuggestion* in France at about the same time. He built on the work of Coué and reported similar positive results from autosuggestion for physical ailments. One of the first, best-selling self-help books in the United States, Napoleon Hill's

Think and Grow Rich, devoted an entire chapter to autosuggestion. The basic idea of autosuggestion is to seed your unconscious mind (inner elephant) with a repetitive self-instruction that today might be called positive self-talk or a pep talk. Daily repetition can continue until the thoughts become internalized and replace the automatic negative talk. It is something like a placebo effect. If our inner executive repeats an intentional thought, we are more likely to believe it and behave in a way that will make it happen. The specific instruction in Coué's book is as follows:

> Every morning before getting up and every evening as soon as you are in bed, shut your eyes, and repeat 20 times in succession, moving your lips (this is indispensable), and counting mechanically on a long string with 20 knots, the following phrase: "Day by day in every way, I am getting better and better." Do not think of anything in particular, as the words "in every way" apply to everything.
>
> Make this autosuggestion with confidence, with faith, with the certainty of obtaining what you want. The greater is the conviction, the greater and more rapid will be the results obtained.[18]

Experiments in the psychology laboratory show the clear impact of verbal mental priming on a person's behavior. Participants were asked to complete various word problems at the behest of a psychology professor, such as unscrambling sets of words into a sentence or filling in missing letters to complete the spelling of words. If the words pertained to rudeness, participants were more likely to interrupt the experimenter when finished. If the words pertained to politeness, the subjects were more likely to wait ten minutes until the experimenter was finished. If the words pertained to authority and power, some men were more likely to judge a woman confederate as attractive. In one experiment, words such as "hostile," "an insult," and "unkind" were flashed on a screen so quickly as to not be consciously recognized. Later, subjects interpreted other people's behavior as more negatively hostile and angry compared to subjects who were exposed to positive words.[19] Verbal priming can indeed shape the inner elephant's thinking and behavior, even when we do not know it is happening. Other studies have shown significantly greater performance for people who are exposed to words of achievement ("succeed," "master"), and greater cooperation when exposed to cooperative words ("fair," "share").[20] The great thing is that your inner executive can do the priming to take you in whatever direction you want to go.

Today there is a better understanding of just how much negative talk the inner elephant fills our minds with, which reinforces our hesitation, avoidance, fear, and procrastination. How can you push on your accelerator to go forward when your internal judge is throwing thoughts into your mind such as "idiot," "dummy," "I hate doing this," "stupid," "imbecile," "loser," "I will never make it," "I can't do it," "I stink," and "You're going to fail again." Your body will respond to the thoughts in your mind. If these negative thoughts are alive in your mind, how can you change them? The value of autosuggestion is to change the persistently negative and critical thoughts toward yourself, the task, or other people into positive, helpful, supportive thoughts that help you move forward. If most of your automatic thoughts are negative or critical, intentionally pushing back against this negative word flow with positive thoughts is a first-rate idea. What is there to lose? Daily mental instruction can substitute a positive thought, attitude, and mood for the automatic negative comments that flood your mind continuously.

Coué's original instruction was to repeat the statement out loud. This works in the initial stages of training your mind while you are at home in your bedroom, especially if your mind keeps jumping away. For regular use during the day, it is better to learn to repeat words silently in your mind. See what works for you. Coué was on track with his suggestion of practicing morning and evening, which are ideal times to prime your subconscious for the day ahead. Your inner elephant is more open to suggestion when it is relaxed. You can also prime your inner elephant any time during the day in a quiet moment or before an important meeting or event. Napoleon Hill recommended writing down an entire specific plan for achieving your goals and reading that aloud twice daily. That is extreme, but you get the idea.

I have received excellent feedback from people whom I have coached on autosuggestion. One manager and one MBA student in particular liked Coué's original statement, "Day by day in every way I am getting better and better." Parker was extremely left-brained, articulate, and well spoken, but he hung back in school and social settings. He started repeating Coué's statement about ten times both before school and before bed. When in his car, he said it out loud. Parker's hope was to "put myself out there more." Repeating the suggestion provided almost immediate traction. He offered comments in every class during the first week. During the second week, he mentioned to his job search adviser that he was working on extending himself more. Her reply shocked him: "Yeah, I can really see the difference." When he attended a school function with his wife, she commented, "Parker, you seem like a different person." For a second-round job interview, he was nervous because of a previous awkward encounter with the interviewer. While driving to the interview, he kept reminding himself that he was getting better and better as he visualized introducing himself and projecting confidence during the interview. It seemed to work because they chatted for an hour and a half.

During the third week of autosuggestion, Parker felt a desire to stop by people's offices and say hi, which he had never done before.

Also during the third week, Parker modified the instruction to help him with golf. During golf his temper would take over with a single error, which led to club slamming and loud, derogatory comments about himself that would ruin the entire golf experience. His modified instruction was, "Every stroke and on every hole, I am getting better and better." When he made a big mistake, he quickly started repeating the statement. His temper did *not* get the best of him. After screwing up a shot, he stayed calm and poised for the first time in years. Approaching the next hole, he repeated the statement several times to get completely into a positive mood. He birdied the hole.

I saw Parker a month after our initial coaching session, and he looked relaxed and in a better mood than I remembered. He was thrilled with his ability to manage himself into new behaviors by repeating the instruction. He said it was the first time in his life he had experienced personal improvement in a short time. I saw Parker again two months later. He said his outgoing behavior continued as if permanent, and he was no longer repeating the autosuggestion.

• TRY THIS •

Verbalize Your Intention

1. Select an autosuggestion phrase to help correct your behavior.
2. Repeat the phrase twenty times morning and evening when relaxed. Start with ten repetitions if that feels more comfortable.
3. Say the phrase aloud until your mind learns not to jump away.
4. Repeat the phrase slowly and focus on it completely.
5. Use beads, knots in a string, or your fingers to count.
6. Repeat the phrase during other opportune times, such as when driving or exercising.

Reed considered himself to be hyperanalytical and hypercritical, and I would agree, given his personality test scores and our interactions. He did not take people's feelings into account when assessing a situation. I had witnessed him react with a critical comment almost before a person could finish a sentence. During the first week, he tried to repeat Coué's instruction as much as possible, such as when doing routine activities like brushing his teeth, driving, and showering. Reed told me, "Really focusing on the words helped me avoid distractions. My concentration was better. My mind seemed to slow down." He found that having fewer negative thoughts and slowing down his brain didn't make him dumber. He felt more present and able to step back and view a situation from another person's perspective. He found himself empathizing with other people rather than being critical of them. It was a breakthrough for him to be considering more than just cold facts. During the third week, Reed became aware of his critical thoughts toward others. Each time a critical thought arose, he consciously replaced it with the instruction "I am getting better and better." During a business social function, he worked on praising others during conversations. Afterward he asked his wife for feedback. She had noticed his new behavior and said the comments were genuine and appropriate. Reid said it felt great to compliment and highlight another person's strengths at the business function.

Here are some other examples:

> A medical resident came up with her own phrase, "I am right here, right now," to keep her mind focused on the present when dealing with patients.

> I consulted with Casey, a military officer, and he developed the instruction "I am loving people more" as a way of achieving his goal of appreciating people. He said he noticed immediate improvement in the way he saw others; he was taking more time to listen to what people were saying and what they meant. His impulse to solve their problem was weaker. He repeated his instruction ten to twenty times per day.

> Alec had an "edge" when talking to others. His black-and-white thinking was very fast, and instant judgments flowed out of his mouth, which demotivated his direct reports. He adopted the phrase "I am slowing down my judgments," and told me a few days later that it was helping.

> Haley started a joint law and business degree immediately after completing her undergraduate work. She was in her last year and totally burned out with school. She tried the autosuggestion "I am becoming more engaged in school." She told me later that it was enough to get her through her final semester.

> Faye forthrightly said she knew that she was cold, task focused, and often a jerk. She was very directive, and tried to control every detail of the work of her salespeople. She had tried some things to change herself without much luck, but believed autosuggestion would work for her. We came up with "I am slowing down to love

others." I talked to her on the phone after a few weeks, and she said her heart was softening. She was starting to like people.

If you are interested in autosuggestion, here are the basics of how I teach it:

o *Stay in the present tense.* Your phrase should refer to what you are doing right now rather than to the past or future. It is not as effective to say "I will be present" or even "I am present" as it is to say "I am becoming more present." The best phrasing is the progressive form of present tense, which means using an "ing" on the verb. Examples are "I am going with the flow," "I am lightening up," and "I am becoming more outgoing." This form awakens the inner elephant to move from now toward the desired future state.

o *Speak gently, respectfully, and positively.* Do not give an order to yourself, such as "Be more outgoing!" Try to avoid negative phrasing, such as "I will not get angry" or "I will try to be less anxious," although sometimes a negative word is unavoidable. Positive phrasing, such as "I am becoming calmer" or even "I am letting go of this anger," tells the inner elephant in what direction to head. Remember, you are talking to a person, so give your inner elephant consideration and respect. It is more likely to respond positively if you do.

o *Say it like you mean it.* Say it slowly enough to feel and be fully aware of every word. Be fully engaged in and focused on the repetition. It should not be mechanical or unfeeling. Have some conviction in your mind and faith in the outcome as you repeat the words. It is the meaning of the words that counts. Immerse yourself in the phrase.

o *Visualize your intended actions while repeating the statement.* This adds impact for some people. After your mind gets comfortable with the repetition, you may find it easy also to picture your desired behavior. This doubles the cues to your inner elephant, providing both verbal and visual intentions.

o *Stay with it.* For a basic shift in your elephant's temperament, such as becoming more appreciative or slowing down your reactions, you should repeat the phrase as often as possible in addition to scheduled morning and evening repetitions. You will see the biggest improvement in the first few days, with a gradual slowdown thereafter. I devised a 3-3-3 rule if using autosuggestion every day. If the suggestion is working, you will probably notice some small change or traction within three days. After three weeks, some change in mental pattern will endure. After three months, a new behavior pattern will endure. The longer you stay with it, the more permanent the impact.

o *Use autosuggestion for short-term results.* You may want to use autosuggestion to motivate your inner elephant for a specific, short-term behavior, such as to start working on a project you have been avoiding, coach yourself to speak up in meetings, or make a public presentation. A great example is Alain Robert, a Frenchman with an obsession for climbing tall buildings (on the outside). He has climbed five of the ten tallest buildings in the world. If thoughts of concern, exhaustion, or fear creep into his mind, he immediately starts repeating (loosely translated), "I have confidence in myself, and I succeed in all that I undertake." This gets him over the top.[21] Your task may not be as daring, but as you prepare for a task that you have been avoiding, you might say things like "I am flowing into my work" or "I am feeling ready to immerse myself." In the case of a baseball pitcher, the self-talk might be "Good low strike here" or "I am focusing only on this pitch."

I have presented Coué's original autosuggestion—"Day by day, in every way, I am getting better and better"—to many people, but most prefer a phrase tailored to their specific issue. The following are some examples of other phrases people have tried:

I am handling this moment.

I am feeling enthusiasm about the upcoming meeting.

I am slowing down and engaging (for someone who rushed through his meetings).

I am feeling more peaceful.

I am becoming more intentional.

I am slowing down my response.

I am becoming less critical.

I am listening more carefully.

I am staying relaxed.

I am speaking up more easily.

I am becoming more expressive.

I am flowing into my work.

I am giving up control.

I am letting go of my need to control things.

I am giving up my perfectionism.

I am taking more time for people.

I am taking my inner judge less seriously.

I am feeling happier.

I am enjoying my work [or life] more.

I am becoming more positive in my thinking.

I hope you are getting the idea for how to use this powerful tool to lead yourself. The trick for you is to get clear about your intention. What little piece of behavior do you most want to change? This may take some thought and discussion. The choice of the correct autosuggestion depends on what you want to accomplish. Once you have chosen your phrase, repeat it ten to twenty times morning and evening while in a relaxed state, either aloud or in your mind. Also repeat it during the day if you have downtime or if any strong negative thoughts arise. I think you will be surprised with the results.

• • •

Visualization and autosuggestion are basic but powerful tools for leading yourself. The underlying requirements for each are to be clear about your intention and then to translate it into pictures or words. A visual picture shows the unconscious inner elephant exactly what to do. Visualization typically requires a separate quiet time to do the work with eyes closed. Repeating autosuggestions seems more natural to many people, and it can be carried on in the mind while doing other things, such as driving or listening. The mental rehearsal associated with either tool can help you eliminate avoidance behaviors, such as procrastination, or impulsive behaviors that are not in your best interest. Experiment with these tools and see what works for you.

6

Follow Through
on Your Intentions

*Because things are the way they are, things will not stay the way
they are.*
—Bertolt Brecht

*He who conquers others is strong; he who conquers himself
is mighty.*
—Lao-Tzu

DURING PETER'S COACHING SESSION, he wanted to talk about procrastinating on his to-do list. He was pretty well organized, but he would avoid or delay doing some items on his list. He understood why people procrastinate—they feel some unconscious anxiety associated with the focal task—but that insight did not help him. He wanted to complete the to-do list without any resistance. The items on his to-do list were big, such as "Study for corporate valuation exam," which did not provide much traction for his inner elephant. It would be as clear to say "Learn finance" or "Learn French."

My advice was for him to make a second to-do list of only the items toward which he felt resistance. On that list, first thing in the morning, he was to break down each item in great detail, listing every incremental step to complete that task. The trick was to make explicit every detail he could think of and to write it down on the morning list. Each item had to be readily doable. That way, he could enjoy checking off each item as he completed it. I asked him to let me know how this worked when I next saw him. Two weeks later, he told me it was working really well. There was something about writing down smaller tasks that made them easy to complete. The list provided concrete instruction to his inner elephant, and the small tasks seemed to reduce his fear of the bigger task.

As luck would have it, three days after meeting with Peter, Yvette stopped by with a similar issue. She had what I thought was an effective to-do list, which she said she used regularly, but still resisted some items on her list. I suggested that she try an experiment by breaking those items into refined detail, writing down the tiniest task possible, preferably first thing in the morning, and then seeing if she could complete them during the day. We brainstormed some subtasks before she left my office. I saw Yvette a few days later, and she said that writing down the more detailed list helped her. She still felt a little resistance, but could readily push through it by performing a single subtask.

Write Down Your Intentions

There is something powerful about writing down your most specific intentions. It takes several minutes to think through specific subtasks, but doing so is effective compared to relying on your memory or the thoughts and impulses jumping around in your head. Writing things down will give clear, unambiguous instructions to your inner elephant. There is also something liberating about writing things down. In one research program, hundreds of people wrote about an important emotional issue that affected their lives. Most found it hard to put these troubling incidents down on paper. However, the writing exercise produced significant benefits over the long term. Compared to people who did not write about emotional issues, participants reported better moods, students got better grades, employees missed fewer days of work, and there was improved immune system function as reflected in fewer doctor's visits.[1]

Why does writing down emotional experiences have such beneficial effects? One explanation is that obsessing about unresolved emotional issues causes stress that takes a mental and physical toll. Writing down the specifics of an event gets them out of one's head so that the experience can be viewed objectively. The written word is also more specific, coherent, organized, and clear, which makes the emotional event more understandable and meaningful. In the case of a to-do list, writing down tasks and subtasks crystallizes the mind's vague generalizations into concrete, doable tasks. Recall from Chapters Two through Four how the mind easily magnifies and exaggerates issues, becomes distracted, and embraces self-serving illusions. You can face reality by writing things down.

Writing things down requires more precision than carrying intentions in your head. The transformation from a vague thought to a clearly written sentence is important. The added precision and clarity provide structure for your inner elephant. In my own writing about nonemotional issues, the first draft is pure mud. I'm always shocked to see the mess that was in my head. When the mess is written down on paper, I can see it more objectively, and after several revisions the ideas become more clear and precise. Moreover, after writing something down, you get to see it as well as hear it in your mind. Abraham Lincoln used these tricks as president of the United States. When emotionally upset, he would write a letter to clarify his distress. Often the letter would be too harsh, so he would simply write "Not sent" on the back of the letter. But his mind would be clear. Also, Lincoln would frequently read aloud. When asked why, he said he remembered things better when he engaged two senses—both sight and sound.[2]

Writing things down can help in other ways. For example, Pittsburgh Steelers head coach Mike Tomlin has made copious notes since he was in high school about what he sees and does. He has stacks of notes in his basement from which he can find exactly what he did in a past football practice or how he handled a difficult player. The notes are now a road map of Tomlin's meteoric rise to his present position.[3] Taking notes is a great aid to memory. You may recall as a student how you only retained long-term the concepts and solutions that you managed to write notes on for later review. Most parts of the lecture for which you did not take notes disappeared from memory. Our mind is not a good place to store things, yet we often live in the illusion that our memories are effective, or perhaps we just don't have the initiative to write things down.

Getting back to Peter and Yvette, how can you use writing to increase your inner executive's control over your inner elephant? How you begin your day is powerful because it sets your conscious intentions for the day. Beginning the day with highly specific written instructions places your inner elephant in harness to achieve your goals.

Abundant research has demonstrated that setting goals will clarify and focus your mind. A vivid picture of the goal outcome can energize your inner elephant toward right action. For even greater influence over yourself, spend some time thinking through specifically *how* to achieve each goal. Even with clear goals, Peter and Yvette experienced a problem translating some goals into action. If your elephant detects the slightest flicker of something difficult or distasteful, it may resist and shy away, similar to a racehorse avoiding the starting gate. Unless you have two or three handlers to guide your elephant into the gate, you are unlikely to follow through as desired on a distasteful goal, perhaps doing other things instead.

The solution that worked for Peter and Yvette was to spend a few minutes in the morning to set what psychologists call explicit *implementation intentions*.[4] Implementation intentions can be thought of as defining the specific step-by-step activities that will lead to your goal or desired outcome. Your inner elephant is more likely to move ahead if it can see each tiny, concrete step. The steps create a structure for your inner elephant to start on its way toward your desired outcome. Explicit, detailed, concrete instructions are especially important when the inner elephant wants to veer away. So, when you feel resistance, spend time writing a list of steps to achieve each outcome on your to-do list, or at least the ones your inner elephant wants to avoid. You might include the specific time on which to work on each step, which will further harness your inner elephant.

• TRY THIS •

Write Down Implementation Intentions

1. Write normal to-do list for the day's activities.

2. Identify items for which you feel resistance.

3. Identify minuscule subtasks for resisted items.

4. Write down every minuscule subtask.

5. Complete each subtask and scratch it from your list.

A special value of defining each implementation step is that it helps people *get started*. And just getting started is ultimately the solution to a problem of procrastination or psychological resistance. Do whatever you can just to get started. Once started, you will become immersed in a task, at which time it is just like any other task and you can flow through it. The best use of implementation intention is to specify each small activity, mainly so you can get started. Recall from Chapter Four that the inner elephant exaggerates the negative. The elephant can turn a rope into a snake when it does not like what it sees. Writing down specific implementation steps brings you back to reality, reducing the mountain to a molehill that is easily ascended. The specific steps also provide the clarity to direct the inner elephant toward the task you want to accomplish.

Consider, for example, women who set the goal of performing a breast self-examination sometime during the next month. Of the women who wrote down exactly where and when they would perform the examination during the next month, 100 hundred percent did so. No matter how strong their original goal, only 53 percent of women who did not form an implementation intention did the self-exam. In another study, participants who were induced to specify when and where they would take a pill each day missed fewer pills than participants who had the same goal to take the pill but did not specify when or where. In another study, one group of students created written statements of the goal to write a short curriculum vita before 5:00 P.M. that day; the other group did not specify when or where they would complete the CV. Of the students who specified when and where they would write the CV, 80 percent did so. None of the participants in the comparison group did so. Clearly, written implementation intentions remove mental barriers to the initiation of action toward a goal. A general intention without specific implementation steps is an inner elephant illusion.

Another inner-elephant trap is distractions. You can strengthen your intelligent will and help your inner elephant avoid distractions with clearly specified intentions. If you have to work on a project, perhaps you can leave your e-mail unopened until noon. Or plan to avoid your compulsion to surf the Internet. Be sure to write these actions down in advance and to check them off when accomplished. If your intention is to eat healthy food, you can name in advance which foods to avoid, such as desserts or specific snacks, and specify instead that you will eat a piece of fruit, right down to the type of fruit and the time to eat it. This will tend to inhibit a habitual response of reaching for a dessert or other food you want to avoid.

An undergraduate student had an absolutely horrible time achieving his goal of writing a research paper on how climate change might affect bears in Montana. His inner elephant avoided that paper at all costs. He avoided his teachers and fellow students who might ask him about it. His disdain for the assignment increased as time passed. Ignoring the growing pressure, he embraced distractions, such as partying and hanging out with friends. The burden of avoiding that paper used all his energy. Finally, with help from a counselor, he was able to break down the huge goal into a series of implementation steps. The counselor helped him put each step onto a calendar with times assigned. With emotional support from his friends, the student was able to stick to his schedule and complete the paper.

The major step for most people is to take time to break down a huge task into a series of tiny subtasks and writing down the subtasks, each as an easily doable separate intention with a precise daily schedule. The investment of time and effort pays off big. This is similar to using project management on one's inner elephant. The paper-avoiding student learned to begin each day with the written intention to complete specific subtasks that day; when combined with emotional support from his friends, this method got him through the paper with a grade of B.

Each workday needs a game plan. Writing down specific details for daily plans is important, especially for tasks that inhibit you. Your inner elephant responds to highly specific structure and instruction. During a summer internship, one of my MBA students had to compile all the accounting information and provide e-mail directions for an overseas vendor firm's data entry. He found it a gut-wrenching task that he wanted to put off as long as possible. To manage his inner elephant, he put together a detailed process list for what needed to be done first, second, third, fourth, and so on. Then he visualized himself doing each task. After the visualization, and with the detailed list in hand, he found the project much easier to accomplish. After finishing task number one, he immediately felt some accomplishment when he checked it off. Each task completed was a victory. The overall task went much faster than it had previously and was far less painful. Another MBA student had been avoiding the passport renewal process for weeks. So she sat down and made a checklist of all the activities needed to get the passport, including having a picture taken, filling out a form, writing a check, going to the post office, and so on. Once she had written the detailed list, she found it easy to dive right in. A few hours later, her passport application was in the mail as she finished something she had been avoiding for weeks. She went out and celebrated.

Do implementation intentions work in cyberspace? Yes and no. One student told me that she started her day by planning a schedule of specific to-dos on an Outlook calendar and said it helped a lot. It made her more organized during the day, and rather than bouncing from event to event, she felt more intentional and in control. Another student told me just the opposite, however. For her, using the computer was less effective than writing things down. She said there was something powerful about using her hands to physically write down each task and subtask. Paper calendars and planners are more concrete and may provide more benefit from writing things down than do digital media. Other people have said they reverted to paper planners because it made them more productive, but could not tell my why—it just felt better. I think digital media are fine for keeping track of your day, but if you are procrastinating and need a push, then handwriting each specific subtask on paper may provide greater benefit.

Set Deadlines

Polly was in tears because she was about to be fired from her EMBA group, which would make it nearly impossible to graduate. The volume of work in the Vanderbilt EMBA program is too great for someone to do alone, especially the group deliverables, which required several minds. Polly is creative and spontaneous, and loves to complete projects with a burst of energy near the time due. She claimed that she does her best writing at the last minute, perhaps pulling an all-nighter. This behavior drove her team members crazy. They didn't have time to review, add to, or improve the paper when Polly finished it so late. Moreover, for projects led by other team members, Polly typically didn't turn in her contributions in time to be included before the final revision or presentation. Her team members were frustrated because she did not pull her share of the heavy workload, and they were ready to fire her. As EMBA group doctor, my job was to help the team resolve this issue.

One thing I understood is that nearly everyone occasionally puts things off, and nearly everyone responds to a deadline. Maybe that was the answer for this group. Why is the U.S. Post Office so crowded on April 15? Why do undergraduate students put off studying for finals until the day before the exam? Why do business executives work on an important presentation the weekend before the board meeting? There is something powerful about a deadline staring us in the face that causes our inner elephant to get moving. Elephants respond naturally to deadlines. The pressure of a deadline works on its own to get a person moving. Polly apparently needed a deadline too, otherwise why would she put everything off until the last minute?

Researchers claim that people put things off because of *time discounting,* which means that we rationally discount the value of future outcomes and give more weight to immediate outcomes.[5] In other words, immediately available rewards or punishments have a disproportionate effect on preferences compared to delayed consequences. I will admit that discounting impact of an approaching deadline does not feel like a "rational" choice to me. When a deadline is far away, I feel light and at ease. As the deadline gets closer, I feel mental pressure. It is hard to describe, but there is a psychological change as the deadline gets closer. As the drop-dead date approaches, my mind becomes more focused. The share of my thinking allocated to the project increases. My behavior is similar to that of a rat in a maze, which becomes more animated and energetic as it gets closer to the goal box and its reward.

The natural pressure from a deadline works with most people. I found myself using deadlines with PhD students and direct reports. PhD students are notorious foot-draggers and procrastinators when working on their dissertation. I found that a scheduled weekly meeting served as a deadline. Moreover, I let the students decide what they would accomplish before the next meeting. They could make their own choices about what to do and when they would finish it. I provided the same leeway to direct reports for their improvement projects when I was associate dean. They were free to make decisions about what would be accomplished and when we would meet, but the deadline worked its power on them. It was hard to show up with nothing accomplished. The impact on PhD students was even greater because without some accountability for a deadline, they could drift for weeks or months without tangible progress.

The impact of deadlines has been shown repeatedly in the laboratory. In one experiment, forty-three students were given a forty-minute in-basket exercise of handling various papers and memos that would typically pile up in the office during a four-day business trip. During the exercise, they were interrupted by a phone call requesting answers to a five-minute survey. Participants who were near the end of the in-basket assignment hung up the phone almost immediately. However, if participants were interrupted near the beginning of the exercise, when they had more time before the deadline, they took time to answer a few questions and a few even finished the survey.[6]

Polly's EMBA team and I worked with her to apply deadlines that would motivate her to finish her work sooner. Polly's solution was to set intermediate, self-imposed deadlines starting two weeks before a major project was due, which would help her complete her work and papers on time. She also asked her fellow group members to give her strict daily deadlines for the work they needed from her. The team created an "official" ceremony every two weeks to schedule work details and set specific deadlines. Polly's work began to be completed on time; her contributions to the group increased. She was not fired from her group, and she received her degree.

You can probably do the same thing to prod your inner elephant forward through work it may resist. One secret is self-imposed deadlines. In a course at the Massachusetts Institute of Technology, which consisted of ninety-nine professionals, one subgroup of students was given fixed, evenly spaced deadlines for the submission of three short papers; other students were allowed to set their own deadlines.[7] At the end of the course, students with self-imposed, evenly spaced deadlines showed higher grades than students whose self-imposed deadlines were last minute. Self-imposed deadlines were nearly as effective as externally imposed deadlines when they were evenly spaced. In a related study, students were paid to find grammatical and spelling errors in written documents. Once again, students who worked with evenly spaced, self-imposed deadlines did much better than participants who set their deadline for the last minute. In these two experiments, externally imposed deadlines showed greater ability to get a person's inner elephant moving than did self-imposed deadlines, but self-imposed deadlines were much better than waiting until the last minute. Polly took advantage of both kinds of deadlines by setting her own intermediate deadlines and by asking her teammates to impose deadlines on her.

• TRY THIS •

Set Deadlines

1. Identify a task for which you feel resistance.

2. Break the task into subtasks.

3. Set a time and date for completion of each subtask.

4. Involve others in setting deadline if possible.

5. Let deadline pressure guide your inner elephant.

Have you ever agreed to a commitment—to give a talk, take a trip—that was scheduled far into the future and about which you were lukewarm? Because the deadline was far off, it seemed as though there would be plenty of time to prepare for the commitment. No problem, so you accepted. Then commitment time arrives. You don't want to do it and strongly wish you had not committed, and you may even try to get out of it. The far-off deadline creates an illusion of no pressure. Setting a self-imposed near-term deadline creates pressure as an effective tool for managing yourself, because your inner elephant feels the pressure as the deadline approaches. When the deadline is many months away, your inner elephant will easily misjudge and overcommit. Your inner executive can make wiser and more realistic decisions about the distant future.

Design Tangible Mechanisms

I spent a small part of my academic career doing change management consulting, which often involved facilitating discussions among groups of middle- and upper-level managers, many of them with aggressive personalities. I would lay out the ground rules for the discussion—only one person can speak at a time, no interruptions, everyone gets equal time, and the like. Within a few minutes, the managers would revert to their old habits—fighting for speaking time like dogs fighting for a bone, interrupting whoever was speaking, and dominating the discussion. To maintain the ground rules, I would call time-outs to point out infractions and teach adherence to the rules. My time-outs took time, were not very effective, and hindered spontaneity.

My solution was to use a talking stick or talking ball to direct traffic. I introduced the small, soft ball with the simplest instruction possible: "This ball has the power. If you are holding the ball, you are empowered to speak until finished. If you don't have the ball, you are empowered to shut up and listen." The transformation was dramatic. I no longer had to call time-outs. Anyone could raise his or her hand to request the ball. Sometimes the group would pass the ball in sequence so everyone had the opportunity to speak fully, even without asking. Suddenly, people started listening. Interruptions dropped to zero. Within an hour or two, the ball helped managers break years of poor communication habits.

Why was the talking ball so effective? My original ground rules failed because they were abstract and conceptual; the ball was tangible and real. As discussed in earlier chapters, the mind is not reliable. The mind's concepts are vague and illusory; the mind generalizes, exaggerates, does not listen well, and interprets things according to its own need. Counterbalancing this vagueness, abstraction, and subjectivity requires something tangible and objective. Vagueness quickly surrenders to a concrete physical or mechanical object that creates structure and brings order. The tangible mechanism, such as a talking ball, acts as an anchor of sorts for the mind's meandering. For example, a study asked volunteers to guess how many African nations belonged to the United Nations. Half were given the number ten as a starting point (How much larger or smaller than ten?) and half were given sixty as a starting point (How much larger or smaller than sixty?).[8] The minds of the volunteers were heavily influenced by the objective, concrete starting point. Those who started with ten guessed an average of twenty-five African nations in the UN; those who started with sixty guessed an average of forty-five.

Tangible mechanisms will help save you from yourself. The external, concrete mechanism replaces the vagaries of your mind. Your inner elephant can relax and let the mechanism do the work. For example, a calendar on which you set your schedule for the day is a mechanism. So is a simple to-do list that guides you through the day. Writing things down is a tangible mechanism because you will have a document that provides structure and clarity. You might set an alarm to remind you to take your medicine. Some people set alarms on their computer or wristwatch to remember to exercise or go to dinner when absorbed in e-mail or Internet research. Another kind of mechanism is a computer program used by writers that shuts off access to e-mails and the Internet during prespecified writing periods. I often set objects where I will see them, if not trip over them, as a mechanism to remind me to take needed action, such as carrying a book home or mailing a letter. Some people use Post-it notes in conspicuous places as a tangible reminder to do something their mind will forget.

Jim Collins uses mechanisms to guide his behavior as an independent consultant, researcher, and writer. The first mechanism is a rule to spend 50 percent of his workday on creative pursuits like research and writing books, 30 percent on teaching-related activities. The remaining 20 percent of his time goes to all other things he has to do. Collins uses a stopwatch he keeps with him at all times to record times for each activity on a spreadsheet. Another mechanism is the "four-day rule" that stipulates no more than four days with a single client in a given year. When teaching a course, Collins handed out one red card to each student—a tangible mechanism they could hold up to claim the floor to speak at any time during the semester.[9] Steve Ballmer, CEO of Microsoft, uses a tangible system to manage his time. He sits down with his assistant and lays out time priorities for the coming year, including time with family, vacations, and periodic reflection times ranging from half a day to one week. The assistant lays out required time chunks on the calendar, and the time left over is available for other business demands.[10] Roger Iger, CEO of Disney, puts walking around on his tangible schedule; otherwise the gravitational pull of business events would prevent his meeting employees face-to-face.[11] Likewise, your inner executive can plan and design tangible mechanisms to provide guidance for your inner elephant.

Rules and procedures have power as a mechanism. They can be written down and posted as needed to help the inner elephant remember and make the correct decision. Terri Cullen devised a $500 rule for her marriage. If she wants to buy something that costs more than $500, she checks with her husband first. Her husband is a saver who never owned a credit card prior to their marriage. Terri saw herself as a spendthrift with a wallet full of credit cards and more than $20,000 in debt, mostly for student loans. The $500 rule was designed to get her spending habits under control. Using the rule to set financial boundaries and be honest about finances helped Terri steer clear of arguments that can tear couples apart. The rule keeps the lines of financial communication open. Terri and her husband went on to create a system of both separate and joint accounts that gives them a sense of control over what they earn yet forces them to jointly set savings goals and make big money decisions. The spending rule made Terri a more careful shopper, and their rule-based mechanisms took a lot of pain out of their marriage.[12]

Social Contract

At the beginning of our youngest daughter's first year in college, she and her roommates were urged to discuss a "roommate contract." The discussion was meaningful, but did not trigger the desired behavior as the semester progressed, nor limit the undesired behavior, as she had hoped. The roommates returned to the kitchen table and wrote down a new agreement about visitors, personal responsibilities, and the like. Suddenly, everything crystallized. The written agreement stuck. The roommates all "got it." The tangible mechanism of a written social contract was a nifty way to constrain impulsive or inconsiderate roommate behavior.

The social contract or compact is a commitment device that makes agreement about behavior specific and concrete. A social contract can be as simple as talking though a point of disagreement and agreeing to new behavior, but an important step is to write down the specific points of agreement and desired behaviors. If you have ever negotiated a contract, you know how points that were so clear in your mind suddenly are not so clear when writing them down. And when a point is written down, the agreement you thought you had with another person based on verbal discussion may not be agreeable at all. As previously discussed, writing things down is an excellent tangible mechanism because it brings clarity, precision, and objectivity by getting thoughts outside your head. The more specific and tangible a mechanism, the better it will guide inner elephants.

One of my most extreme experiences as group doctor for the EMBA program was with a group that was flying apart by the end of the second semester. It was the worst-performing group I had ever coached. One individual was participating very little, and other members were furious at him. Two of the other members had a personality conflict, and some of their behaviors were designed to annoy each other rather than support the group. These two members had "individualistic" temperaments and were slow to adapt to working in a group. EMBA students must be in a group to complete the program. Three group members asked permission to fire the free rider, which would ensure his failure in the program. The free rider woke up to the problems he caused, and said that medication had disoriented him during the semester and that he would stop taking it. I had previously tried various strategies to corral these wild elephants, including deadlines, verbal agreements, and the like, but nothing worked. All I could think to do was make a list of behaviors the group wanted to achieve and a list of things the group would no longer tolerate, and to write a social contract. The group members liked the idea, and spent a three-hour meeting hashing out the contract. It included zero tolerance for the free rider and limited tolerance (a second chance) for dysfunctional behaviors by other members. This contract had extensive and precise detail, just what elephants need. I would meet monthly with the group to review progress on the contract.

Discussing and writing that contract, combined with a signing ceremony that included an EMBA administrator and me, had a transforming effect. I was amazed. The written and signed contract had an immediate and compelling impact on member behavior. There were no deviations of which I was aware. The monthly review meetings for compliance had little to report. Writing down what "good" and "bad" group member behavior looked like, along with appropriate penalties for the bad behavior, made everything clear to all parties. A social contract can exert a strong influence in changing the habits and behavior of inner elephants. By the end of semester three, I considered this group one of the more efficient in the EMBA program.

If you like the idea of a contract to motivate your desired behavior, but don't have anyone to sign a contract with, you can make a contract with yourself. In psychology, this is an effective strategy for self-management.[13] Three Yale behavioral economists started a Web site called stickk.com, at which you can select a goal and sign a contract to achieve that goal. If you fail, it will cost you money. All you need do is go on the Web site, specify what you want to achieve within a time frame, put up some money as a stake, and designate a referee to confirm the truth of your reports. You can even designate friends and family as emotional partners or supporters to cheer you on. Making a contract with themselves is probably working for most of the twenty-three thousand users of the Web site.[14]

Checklist

The big idea in this chapter for managing your inner elephant is to *get things out of your head* and into an external, tangible mechanism of some sort. One great mechanism is a simple checklist. This is like a to-do list, only it is official and repeatable. Johns Hopkins University published the results of implementing a five-step checklist in intensive care units in Michigan. Doctors were reminded, for example, to wash their hands and don a sterile gown and gloves before putting an intravenous line into a patient. The result was astonishing. The infection rate went from 4 percent to zero, and the program saved more than fifteen hundred lives and nearly $200 million over eighteen months—all from a simple little five-point checklist.[15] A similar benefit was found in a large international study of how to avoid mistakes during surgery. Scrawling on the patient with permanent marker to show where the surgeon should cut, asking a person's name, and counting sponges after surgery reduced the mortality rate by almost half and complications by more than a third.[16] Why? A checklist helps with memory recall, especially for mundane things that are easily overlooked by a distracted nurse or physician. Intensive care units are especially distracting places because of drastic events. The mind is pretty fuzzy even under ideal conditions and can easily miss a minor detail in critical care chaos. Under pressure, even the best health care professionals fail to follow basic steps proven to stop infection and other major complications. Like everyone else, they may act from old habits or unconscious impulses. The checklist mechanism provides tangible, written guidance that won't be overlooked.

Interestingly, many of the physicians in the Michigan study resisted the checklist. Some were offended by the suggestion that they needed a checklist. With all their education, many doctors believed that the knowledge in their head was superior to a checklist.[17] Doctors have egos just as you and I do, and their inner elephants want to stay in control rather than turn over control to an external list or object. One point made in Chapter Four was that people find it gratifying to exercise control. Control is hard to give up. I tried a simple checklist to make sure my assistant and I didn't forget anything when I taught an executive program away from Vanderbilt. My fear was that I would forget a key video or exercise, which had happened a time or two. Even with the anticipated peace of mind as an obvious benefit of a checklist, I felt some resistance to writing things down. The new center of things was going to be the checklist, not me. My mind would be replaced by a checklist. My assistant could do the packing without me. It was almost an insult to my inner elephant. Well, I did complete the checklist. It feels good now because preparing for a trip is so effortless, and I haven't had a single crisis concerning missing material. But I felt the same resistance the Michigan physicians must have felt when asked to give up control to a simple and apparently mindless checklist. However, the simple tangible mechanism turned out to be far smarter and more reliable for health care than anyone expected.

Scorecard

Another mechanism that converts muddled thinking into tangible reality is a scorecard. A scorecard provides concrete feedback on any behavior about which you are willing to keep a count of some kind. The count is a way to see objective facts as a key step in managing your behavior. Recall the scorecard in Chapter Four of the educator who had 241 critical thoughts toward parents in a seven-hour period, or that in Chapter Two of the MBA student whose mind wandered seventy-five times during a class while he was trying to pay attention.

Don't focus on changing an undesired behavior; just count it. Keeping count on a scorecard will increase your awareness and provide unvarnished feedback. In psychology this is called *self-monitoring*. You can count almost anything, and your total will serve as a benchmark for comparing behavior change. Marcus was from South America and disliked American drivers.

> My anger comes from what I see as inconsiderate and unsafe actions on the road. Examples are driving too slowly, not moving when required on four-way stop signs, and swerving into my lane. My response is to get very angry, many times to yell, and sometimes to drive aggressively. I know this is not good for me and it can be unsafe.

Marcus counted the number of times he became angry while driving during a normal week (benchmark) and then kept a scorecard during three weeks of trying to change. During the benchmark week, he experienced seven driving incidents, of which five triggered his anger (71 percent) and two (29 percent) led to an aggressive change in his driving. During the first week of behavior change, his anger reaction dropped to 47 percent and his aggressive driving to 21 percent, a healthy improvement. By the third week, his anger reactions dropped to zero. Marcus's scorecard "provided motivation and hope that I could change, which I did."

MBA students have kept a scorecard for the percentage of assignments turned in on time, the amount of time wasted on watching TV or other unproductive activities, the number of fruits or vegetables eaten each day, the percentage of appointments attended on time, and the like. One student kept track of how many times she said "you know" or other trite phrases like "whatever" or "it is what it is" in conversations. The average number of phrases dropped from 3.7 to 1.2 per day, and the percentage of phrase-free conversations jumped from 29 percent to 82 percent over a three-week period.

Uri, a manager at a phone company, kept track of the number of times he interrupted direct reports in meetings. His benchmark score showed three interruptions per meeting during the first week. During the following week of attempted change, the urge to interrupt was consistent (thirty-two urges during eleven hours of meetings), but actual interruptions dropped by one-third (to twenty-two). Upon reflection, of the twenty-two interruptions, only five were valid points that Uri needed to make. By the third week, the desire to interrupt dropped to less than one per meeting as Uri became more of a facilitator and orderly participant. With patience, he learned that points he wanted to make would be made by someone else.

> This was very revealing as I realized I was not allowing my employees to use their full worth by playing out the conversation, and be fulfilled as decision makers. Initially it was difficult to hold back, but I felt a strong sense of satisfaction from being disciplined enough and from seeing my employees' sense of gratification making the decision.

A simple count on a sheet of paper creates a scorecard and objective feedback that can help you, like Uri and others, make important changes in your personal or leader behavior.

Emptying Your Head into a System

The idea behind a tangible mechanism is to reverse the phenomenon of "out of sight, out of mind." You may forget something that is left in your head. If you can see it outside yourself, you will remember and act on it. A tangible mechanism improves management of your inner elephant by substituting something objective and concrete for the vague and uncertain mind, a winning trade-off for most people. The more the mind's clutter can be emptied out into an external mechanism, the easier it is to control yourself.

That is why I like the mechanisms developed by David Allen in *Getting Things Done*, a system for controlling your inner elephant.[18] His advice works for me for staying organized. His step 1: *Empty your head.* In order to clear your mind, you have to write down on separate scraps of paper everything that is demanding part of your attention. All of those duties, tasks, projects, and commitments can be organized into buckets of similar themes. But first, write them all down on separate pieces of paper. His step 2: *Decide on the "next action" for every item.* This specifies the implementation intention described earlier—the detailed step-by-step process that will achieve your goal of completing that project. Step 3: *Organize the information.* It can be put on your calendar, PDA, or to-do list showing when and where the next actions will be completed. Use whichever mechanism works for you. Step 4: *Perform a weekly review.* Do this at the same time and place each week, perhaps Sunday evening. This review provides essential feedback on the extent of completion of various projects. This review is a good time also to empty your head of new activities or commitments with which to repeat the cycle of defining "next action" implementation intentions to be plugged into your system.

You can let the system do the work, just as the talking ball did the work of managing my facilitated conversations with executive groups. You just have to show up to feed in information each week and interpret the results. Rather than fight with your inner elephant, help it download its mental burden into a tangible mechanism system, and you will do well.

If you are lucky, perhaps you can purchase or become part of someone else's objective system. My wife, Dorothy, joined Weight Watchers to lose weight. She discovered and embraced a wonderful system that Weight Watchers provided. Counting "points" for foods translated her food consumption into a simple number that was easier to keep track of than calories. She could plug information into the computer each evening and get immediate feedback on how she was doing. Weekly meetings provided social support and feedback on weight loss or gain. After about two months, her inner elephant was becoming trained, and the unwanted weight came off and stayed off as the system took hold. The system provided a concrete structure and easy-to-follow instructions that made it easy to conform to the desired behavior. Dorothy explained her success as being part of a system that took day-to-day eating decisions out of her unreliable mind and into a set of structured, concrete, and specific mechanisms.

Remember This

Create Tangible Mechanisms

Design a concrete object or method—a tangible mechanism—to help you accomplish a desired task. Mechanisms include rules, calendars, or reminders that do not rely on memory. The following are effective mechanisms for guiding behavior:

- Talking ball for conversations
- To-do list to organize your day
- Software to eliminate distractions
- Contract to commit to behavior
- Checklist to eliminate errors
- Scorecard for feedback
- Personal system to direct and support new behavior

7.

Calm Down
to Speed Up

*For after all, the best thing one can do when it is raining is to let
it rain.*
—Henry Wadsworth Longfellow

Always take an emergency leisurely.
—Chinese proverb

NIKOLAY, AN EXCHANGE STUDENT from Eastern Europe, was struggling
three weeks into the fall semester. He was to be at Vanderbilt only one
semester and was having a hard time. He was in my MBA leadership
class and came to see me. Nikolay could not focus or concentrate, was
lonely, missed his family and badly missed his girlfriend, and was falling
hopelessly behind in his finance course. He could not seem to study in his
room or in the library. He felt a mental block toward finance and could
not force himself to do the assignments. As we talked, I sensed a person
who was utterly unfocused and mentally fragmented because his mind
and emotions were all over the place. The anxiety from procrastinating
in finance made him miserable. Because my course dealt with behavioral
issues, Nikolay asked if I had advice that could help him.

To help Nikolay get his foot on the accelerator in his mind and off the brake, I gave him a simple assignment: take any homework needing to be completed and go sit at one of the tables in the school hallways or lobby that was already occupied by one or two other students. "Make sure other students are at the table when you do homework. Just sit with those students and see what happens. Do all your homework while sitting close to other people. It does not matter whether you know them." Early the next week, Nikolay came in again after class, and he was a lighter person. His face was relaxed. He said he was better able to focus and concentrate. Although not totally caught up, he had completed major finance homework assignments. His misery index was much lower.

Get Connected

What transformed Nikolay? It was getting connected to others, even if by just sitting near them. I explained to him that having other people close by tends to calm and focus a fragmented inner elephant. He had been experiencing an *avoidance behavior,* which is an escape from unpleasant situations or feelings such as anxiety, nonrational fear, or emotional distress. Avoidance behavior is a symptom of underlying anxiety, of which Nikolay was not aware. My advice was to find someone to sit close to in order to finish the homework. Does this sound weird? When you see friends studying or working together, you might think they would be distracted, but in fact they are better able to stay calm and get work done. Some students have told me that if they are unable to concentrate at home, they go to the library where others are present, and they focus better.

I learned the technique of being with other people soon after moving to Nashville. I had a book deadline, felt enormous pressure, and could not write. Newly divorced, I could not focus on or push my way through the material. I did not understand what was wrong with me. Each time I sat down at my desk at home to write, the impulse to go out for a donut or pick up my dry cleaning took over. I did everything but write. I managed to struggle through a few simple things, but the more complex material defeated me. I described my difficulty to a colleague in psychology, and he said "No problem. Tell me when you want to start on the difficult material, and I will come and sit in your office." "No way," I said. "I like to work alone." "Just try it," he said, "and see what happens. I will sit in the corner opposite you and work on e-mail. I won't say a word or bother you at all." I was desperate, so I agreed to his suggestion.

Well, when he was in the room, I miraculously (to me) focused on the most difficult material and plowed through it without resistance. What a relief! He explained that having another person in the room grounded my scattered emotions and calmed my anxiety, thereby enabling me to focus and concentrate. This is similar to "supportive" therapy in psychology wherein a therapist accompanies a phobic client to calm the client's anxiety while the client approaches a fear-inducing object, such as an airplane flight. It was a powerful lesson. It was as if I had an emotional child (baby elephant) inside me feeling distress of which I was unaware. I was only aware of the avoidance behavior. Having another person present calmed down the distressed inner child so that I could move forward and concentrate to write the difficult passages. For the next several months, until I healed from the divorce, I arranged for an assistant to work in my office whenever I felt the symptoms of avoidance. Having a "babysitter" during those months made my life a lot easier.

This is a rather subtle idea, that another person nearby can calm an anxious inner elephant and enable us to focus and concentrate, whether the other person knows it or not. But the idea is not uncommon. Support groups are enormously popular because of collegial support to change behavior. AA is probably the most famous and successful support group, and there are groups for just about every physical illness or behavioral issue with which people want support to cope or change. The comfort and emotional warmth provided by a group may seem trivial to a rational observer, but comfort is exactly what reduces your inner elephant's anxiety or fear, thereby strengthening the intention of your inner executive to do what you have been resisting. Research at Vanderbilt, for example, found that when members of a weight-loss group have a lot in common, they feel safe and lose more weight. Being around like-minded people with a similar goal is an important part of successful personal change.

Helping your inner elephant feel calm and safe increases your focus and forward movement. Involving other people is an important way to guide your inner elephant toward behavior that is new or that you have been avoiding. A connection to others can also inspire and sustain hope, give you guidance, and reinforce progress. For example, a regional manager for a brokerage firm asked for my thoughts about a "bullpen" arrangement for brokers. He said a big problem in his offices was the difficulty new brokers had making cold calls. Once hired, they soon ran through family and friends, and cold calls were essential for building a book of business. The cold-call rejection rate was above 98 percent, and over time brokers would start avoiding cold calls. He had heard of brokerages that used bullpens and wondered if that would help. Brokerage sales managers typically did not provide emotional support to calm a brokers' anxiety; the more macho managers expected new brokers to survive cold calling on their own. I was enthusiastic about the bullpen idea. Placing the cold-calling brokers in a conference room where they could see and hear one another sounded like an ideal solution to help calm their fears of rejection. I encouraged the regional manager to try it and let me know what happened. I called two months later, and he said two offices did try the bullpen for cold calling with some success. He could not yet verify increased sales, but he knew of two salespeople on the verge of quitting who changed their mind and were showing progress. Retaining salespeople was his primary goal.

Given the obvious help of other people for managing oneself in the face of felt resistance, I tried an experiment in my Leading Change MBA class. Each student selected some change to make in himself or herself over the next three weeks (eat healthy, lose weight, go to bed earlier, stop drinking sodas) with the help of a fellow student coach. The coach had two responsibilities: to call and ask a few questions each evening and be very supportive and encouraging. The coaches were not to be analytical, rational, or critical as if an authority figure. Roughly 80 percent of the students reported solid progress over the three weeks, several with lapses, but progress nevertheless. The written papers at the end of term showed that the partner system helped most of the time, and forward progress stopped when the partner's calls did.

One student felt great resistance to tackling an exercise regimen.

> As I interacted with my partner on this project, having to voice my feelings to another person was more difficult than simply rationalizing excuses in my mind. The days I was able to convey a success to my partner were eye opening. It felt good to be accountable to another person, and his support had a resounding effect on other areas of my life. I made unexpected progress toward realizing my vision of living a healthier life.

Another student added,

> The calls with my partner helped me be accountable to monitor my progress. It helped me face reality. At first I didn't want to look like a fool to her. However, as time went by the calls became more personal and I reported failures as well. The calls helped in a way I don't fully understand, but my progress was better than when I tried to make progress alone.

To accelerate forward motion in your behavior, sustaining a partner relationship for three months or more would be enough time to make the new behavior fairly permanent. The major point is that one way to overcome the anxiety that causes avoidance is to have the help of a partner whose presence will calm the underlying fear or anxiety and thereby strengthen the intention of your inner executive.

Remember This

Get Connected

When you are feeling fragmented or unfocused, or when you are caught in avoidance behavior,

- Do not stay isolated.
- Sit near others who are calm and focused.
- Find a partner to work with.
- Join a compatibility group.

Let It Happen

Why does the presence of one or more supportive people help our inner executive gain control over our inner elephant? It works because these people can often calm and soothe a distressed inner elephant, and a calm, peaceful inner elephant is easier to work with; it accepts guidance and direction. When emotional or scared or traumatized, an elephant is hard to manage. If so-called support people appear as negative, critical, or attacking in some sense, the elephant's natural instinct is to resist and fight back, which agitates and strengthens the inner elephant's resistance and avoidance.

What this adds up to is that when you notice avoidance, *calm down* rather than add pressure on yourself. The avoidance is caused by unconscious anxiety. Giving up pressure rather than adding pressure may seem counterintuitive. The underlying philosophy is opposite to the way many people think, which is to use brute force rather than calmness to control themselves. Calming down rather than pushing and forcing reflects the philosophy "Let it happen," rather than "Make it happen," when dealing with a recalcitrant inner elephant. You are behaving as though you are being kind and gentle and making friends with your elephant and with the task you are avoiding. Trying too hard to mentally push or force yourself to do something is typically a mistake. Don't become a "critical parent" and waste mental energy berating yourself, which only agitates the elephant and strengthens its resistance. Force and resistance balance out to maintain the status quo. If this inner struggle sounds all too familiar to you, learning to calm down and let things happen may be more promising than trying to force yourself to do something.

People too often try to pressure themselves, which is often the opposite of what works. Recall from Chapter Four that the inner elephant exaggerates the threat associated with something it fears or does not like. It sees a snake instead of a rope. This exaggeration is part of the reason for resistance. One trick to stay calm and let it happen is to remember that the dread is always worse than the thing dreaded. Your inner executive knows this. You can help calm the inner elephant the same way you eat a whale—one small bite at a time. You can break a big, threatening-looking task into *tiny, tiny bites* that are not threatening at all, as mentioned in Chapter Six. For example, if I feel overwhelmed about writing a book, which I do, I break it down and focus on one chapter. If I'm overwhelmed with the chapter, which I am, I break it down to a single paragraph, or even a single sentence to write. If writing a single sentence overwhelms me, I can break down that task to reading a single sentence of source material. When the task gets ridiculously small, my inner elephant can no longer resist. The work then just happens with no effort on my part. Once I read the first sentence, then I can read one more sentence, and so on.

The point of relaxing to let it happen is that you allow your inner elephant to get started, perhaps by choosing a small piece within the elephant's comfort zone. This is similar to a Japanese technique called *kaizen,* which calls for tiny improvements rather than big changes. Pressuring yourself to do too much may activate fear in the emotional part of your nervous system, which triggers a flight response, and your elephant will run away from what you are trying to do. We all hear about stretch goals, which work well in some settings, but they are not the way to guide your elephant through its anxiety. If you resist exercise, try it for one minute only to "let it happen." After a few days of easy one-minute exercising, you'll likely find yourself expanding the time with no felt resistance. It will happen naturally, without pressure. Doris aspired to run at least three miles three times a week, but she was not running at all when she asked for my help. She ran three miles regularly when employed, but graduate school offered few respites. I suggested she try one mile, or even half a mile. Once she got used to the idea of a short distance, soon she was running again without forcing herself. Poppy did the same thing with her goal of drinking sixty-four ounces of water each day. Going from drinking little water to two quarts was a big change, so we broke it down to one twelve-ounce bottle of water a day. She found that amount easy, let it happen, and built up from there.

• TRY THIS •

Let It Happen

- Calm down your inner elephant.
- Do not try to force yourself to engage in the task you are avoiding.
- When ready, start with a tiny piece of the task.
- Aim low, not high, to "just get started."
- Then let it happen.

Aim low, not high, to psych out your inner elephant's anxiety or tendency to be overwhelmed. Then, let it happen. Here is a quote from Mother Teresa that captures this idea from another perspective: "If there are 100 children hungry, and you can feed only one, feed one. Don't worry about the ninety-nine you can't feed. If you did, you'd end up doing nothing. And do it today. Tomorrow the child will be dead."[1] Don't let big eyes block your forward movement. Stay calm by selecting a tiny part. That is enough.

Sit by Your Problem

Another idea for calming down is to "sit by the elevator," which means to move forward gradually and gently to keep the elephant's anxiety low. An executive from a utility company approached me during a break in a program for his company. He asked if I had seen a video in which a man had a phobia about elevators, which caused many problems because he worked on the eighth floor of a building in the city. The man did not want to spend thousands of dollars on psychotherapy to unravel the cause of his condition, so he found an adviser. The adviser told the man to meet him at a specific address on a Saturday morning and to bring a folding chair and card table. They met, and the adviser took the man inside the building and set up the chair and table near the elevator. He told the man to sit there and let nature take its course. Oh yes—the charge for curing the phobia was $10.

How did the adviser earn the $10? As the man sat near the elevator, he became more comfortable. When nothing bad happened, his anxiety diminished. As his anxiety diminished, he moved closer to the elevator. This increased his anxiety, and he sat still again until he calmed down. The man was motivated to use the elevator, and his inner elephant was gradually reducing its fear and getting used to the elevator. Each time he calmed down, the man moved closer to the elevator, eventually stepping in and out, and finally riding it to upper floors.

Anxiety can be controlled through graduated exposure. In psychology, this is called *exposure therapy*. You can pay to have someone with you if you have a serious phobia, which is called *supportive exposure therapy*. Or you can do it alone in cases of less intense feelings of avoidance or resistance to a task or object. Just take one small step at a time toward the fearsome object to keep anxiety low. Whenever the man's inner elephant was peaceful and calm, the inner executive took a step toward the elevator, and soon the man was on the elevator. You can do the same thing.

I use this approach with MBA students. I ask them to find something toward which they feel resistance and then to "sit by the elevator." If they are avoiding a project in marketing, just go sit by the book and papers. Don't try to do anything, just sit there and calm down. The students reported that from two to ten minutes is typically enough time for them to calm down and pick up a book. Then they take the first tiny bite from their work. Soon they begin flowing into the resisted task. You do not need to force yourself to do anything. Just relax. As your inner resistance declines, you will calmly begin work on the project. Again, the trick is to find a way to just get started. After you are immersed in a task, the pleasure is the same no matter the task.

• TRY THIS •

Sit by Your Problem

1. Identify a task, materials, or an object toward which you feel resistance.

2. Sit close to these materials.

3. Do not take action; just sit until resistance fades away.

4. When calm, slowly approach the material.

5. Go slowly to just get started, then immerse yourself in the task.

For example, Wanda was in an enormous fight with herself over writing a final operations paper. She didn't want to face the task. Finally, she took all her materials and her computer to the library, set them in one of the small carrels, and closed the door. There were no distractions, so she just looked at them for fifteen minutes. She was calming her inner elephant. Then she found herself going through the papers, and before too long she was ready to write. "Sitting by the elevator" helped her finish that paper on time. The next time you are in a struggle with yourself over some task, find a way to sit by the project and calm down rather than try to make it happen.

Relax Your Body

The body and mind are connected, so you can calm your mind by relaxing your body. Indeed, I think relaxing the body is easier than relaxing the mind. Your body is tangible; it is easier to find. The advantage is that when you relax your body, your mind will follow. The more relaxed your body, the quieter and more peaceful your mind. You might develop a regimen to use at the end of the day, during breaks, or when you face a daunting task.

However, most people don't know how to relax. It has to be learned, like cooking or playing tennis. The muscles of the body carry tension throughout the day. Your inner elephant wants to take action, to do things, rather than to sit quietly and just "be." Tension in muscles is a readiness to respond. Thus relaxation of muscles can bring about a peaceful, relaxed attitude. Your body is not used to being relaxed. If you sit quietly, you may feel anxious and impatient, and your mind may start to race. One exercise I give students is to relax for ten, twenty, or thirty minutes. Relaxing is difficult for some, so they get up and move before their time is up.

Relaxation takes intentional and focused effort. William James, dean of American psychologists, wrote an essay about relaxation in 1899. He observed that modern people were too tense and anxious, and that tension arose from the egoistic preoccupation with results. He cited many examples of people who spent years trying unsuccessfully to rid themselves of anxieties, inferiorities, and guilt feelings, to no effect. The way to success, he argued, was through surrender and passivity, not activity; through relaxation and not forced actions. James said to give our compulsive self a rest.[2] Techniques such as meditation, which focus on relaxing the mind, are described in later chapters. Techniques for relaxing the body are discussed here.

There are many excellent techniques for relaxing your body, including yoga, tai chi, massage, biofeedback, and exercise. You have to choose one and use it. Each involves learning to let go of the body's tension. Siri Hustvedt wrote a blog for the *New York Times* about living with migraine headaches. At first he thought of his condition as "the enemy," and fought it with all his personal resources. He did not want to be passive or a quitter. When he moved away from his aggressive approach, he started to get better. With biofeedback, he practiced letting go. He learned to relax physically. He learned to stop fighting and forcing. He still has migraines, but when one comes on, he does relaxation exercises, which eliminate the most severe pain and nausea.[3]

Simple Techniques

A technique you can use anywhere is progressive muscle relaxation. Sit quietly and then alternatively tense and relax each muscle group in your body in a sequence that makes sense for you. You might start with the feet (or one foot) and then move to the calves, upper legs, buttocks, abdomen, chest, hands, forearms, upper arms, shoulders, neck and tongue area, and head. Your mind's eye can concentrate on or "see" each muscle group during tension and relaxation. Tensing followed by relaxing provides for clear definition of the muscle group and deeper relaxation.

As I mentioned in Chapter Four, several years ago I had a complex year taxwise, and avoided doing my part for my accountant. Days were passing, and the more pressure I felt, the more I resisted, creating internal conflict. I vividly recall clearing a Thursday on my calendar just for taxes. On Wednesday night I piled all the receipts and forms on the dining room table. In the morning, I didn't even want to sit next to the materials. For some reason this had become a major block to my inner elephant. So I went to an upstairs room and lay down on the bed. Not knowing what else to do, I just went through progressive muscle relaxation to calm myself down. Then, after about twenty minutes, I felt a swift internal shift. The resistance simply disappeared. I actually *wanted* to go down and do the work on the taxes. Suddenly my inner executive was in charge of my relaxed elephant. Taking advantage, I ran downstairs and started to work. Sooner than expected, the tax work was complete. I took it to the post office, with a note of apology to my accountant, wondering why my inner elephant had resisted so hard for so long.

If you have time, lying down is a great facilitator of relaxation. Let your body release its tension. Let your thoughts fall away like autumn leaves. The world can get along without your help for a few moments. Let go of your need to control things. My favorite method of relaxation is to just let go, let go, let go of the physical tension in my body. I learned this from a *Sanyasi* (spiritual Hindu itinerant) passing through Nashville. Start by lying down, and intentionally *let go* of the tension in your body.

Or sit comfortably in a soft chair, close your eyes, and just *let go* from within your body. Let go from the inside out. Let go from within your chest, from within your jaw and tongue, from within each leg and each arm. Until you get the hang of it, it will take focus and effort to let go of tension, because your muscles are tight. Focus on letting go of *all* muscle tension for fifteen seconds. Then try again for thirty seconds. Then try for as long as you can. Repeat until you are totally relaxed for a few minutes. With this method, I become so relaxed that the muscles of my body seem to expand as the muscles let go. I'm surprised when the expansion doesn't pop the buttons off my shirt. Best of all, my mind becomes quiet and calm. With a little practice you can completely relax for a few minutes by physically letting go while in your office, watching a movie or TV, or even working on the computer.

Sports

Sports psychology provides a store of knowledge connecting relaxation to higher performance, whether on the putting green or in the batter's box. In competitive sports, tensing up and trying too hard to force the action usually cause lower performance. Stan Utley, a putting guru on the professional golf tour, has advice for players who miss a lot of short putts: they should relax and free up the tension in their shoulders and arms. "When people get tense, they try to guide the ball rather than let the putter head swing itself through the ball."[4] Tim Corbin, head coach of Vanderbilt's successful baseball team, teaches his players systematic physical routines to stay calm during a game. If the batter starts to feel rushed and his mind starts to race, he is coached to step away from the batter's box and follow a routine to calm down and regain focus and intention. If a pitcher feels an uptick of emotion, he steps off the mound to regain composure and the focused intention to throw the best pitch. Having a set physical routine is a good way to slow down a racing mind. Jim Fannin teaches players to unhinge their jaw and take a few deep breaths to help them relax. Tension is stored in the tongue and jaw area, and opening the jaw allows tension to escape. When Michael Jordan stuck out his tongue when driving to the basket, it was a sign of his body's relaxation.

Hatha Yoga

Yoga is an ancient Indian practice that has achieved popularity in Western culture, even on Wall Street. The *Wall Street Journal, Fortune,* the *New York Times,* and *Inc.* have reported on the infiltration of yoga into the testosterone culture of Wall Street banks and hedge funds. For example, Diane Shumaker-Krieg, global head of research at of Wachovia Securities, said, "Yoga is my little vacation each day. It makes me happy, which gives me energy." Even if she just has time to stand on her head for fifteen minutes, "it's amazing the clarity that gives me—and the chance to connect to the nonmathematical side of my brain."[5] At Karsh Capital, about a third of the thirty-three employees took yoga classes at the company's offices each week. Michael Karsh had practiced three years, and he knows to "take a step back, have a breath and stay focused."[6] D. E. Shaw, another New York hedge fund, offered hour-long yoga classes at the office. Many companies offer yoga instruction to employees for its emotional and physical health benefits.[7]

Yoga as known today in the West is mostly hatha yoga, known for its slow-paced stretching and physical postures, often combined with a focus on breathing and mental relaxation. Historically, hatha yoga was a holistic practice from ancient India that included strict moral discipline, purification procedures, and controlled breathing as a prelude to serious meditation. I recommend hatha yoga because of the combination of mental concentration with physical relaxation. It brings the body and mind into harmony. I think of it as reaching the mind through the body, which is ideal for people who like to reduce stress and tension with physical exercise.

Here is writer Laraine Herring's description of her experience with yoga:

> Yoga is slow. Mindful. It cultivates a relationship between body, mind, and spirit. . . . As I've worked with yoga, I began to listen, for the first time, to my body. Yes, that feels good. No, that stretch is too deep, pull back. I noticed sudden tears surfacing during a spinal twist and the incredible, surprising unburdening (of what?) that occurred in pigeon pose. I began to welcome conversations between me and this form of flesh that carries me.
>
> When I truly began to listen to my own skin, I could hardly contain the din. It was like a mother coming home from work to a dozen kids all talking at once. It panicked me, being this close to my skin. No wonder we distract ourselves from it in every conceivable way. This skin, this body, held everything I'd ever done. Through showing up on the mat, I learned to show up for my body. My ability, not just to listen, but to hear, surfaced. And as I learn how to hear, I learned how to write in a new way.[8]

Hatha yoga brings together active masculine energy with receptive feminine energy. Yoga training enables you to balance opposing energies, embracing power and flexibility, hot and cold, positive and negative, mind and body. The physical positions require strength and balance, while at the same time keeping your mind focused and breath smooth. Each pose brings different parts of the body to your mind's attention. One intention of hatha yoga is to increase your conscious awareness in the present moment. Physical strength and flexibility are by-products. The slow pace combined with physical awareness promotes a calm and meditative state of mind. People who practice yoga learn to be more relaxed under otherwise stressful situations in which they might overreact. During a posture or stretch, you can let go of aggression and force, learning to let go in stress situations. Stretches clear tension from the muscles and help your mind feel relaxed for a long period of time. Participants say that their muscles are more flexible and their bones are stronger; the mental benefits they cite are greater willpower, concentration, and self-containment. I think of yoga as a supportive way to relax your inner elephant and strengthen your inner executive, because you can attend classes with other students and learn from a teacher.

• TRY THIS •

Relax Your Body

- Try this relaxation technique to see how it feels.
  1. Sit comfortably or lie down; close your eyes.
  2. Progressively tense and relax each muscle group in sequence.
- Alternatively, you can "let go" from within your body:
  1. Let go from within muscle groups simultaneously for fifteen to thirty seconds.
  2. Repeat until you completely let go of muscle tension for several minutes.
- Another way to calm your inner elephant is to develop a physical routine, which might include stepping away, that you engage during stressful situations.
- A yoga class is excellent for relaxing the body and calming the mind.

Calm Your Elephant by Acting the Part or Making a Gentle Request

The e-mail from Lois asked if she could see me to talk about an avoidance issue. Lois had taken my leadership course, so she was familiar with ideas about how to lead herself. Concerning avoidance behaviors such as procrastination, I typically do not teach the practices from popular books, such as to set goals, prioritize, remove distractions, aim for excellence, prepare thoroughly, identify constraints, and so on. These ideas are good, but the people in my classes and programs already do most of these things. I tend to recommend ideas that take advantage of their understanding of the inner executive and inner elephant. I made a list of ideas to discuss with Lois.

Her issue was how to use free time. If she had a week off between classes, her intention to work on papers and projects would be undercut by her inner elephant doing other things. If she had free time on the weekend, she would avoid starting on a paper due two weeks away. She would end up on Sunday night before classes with nothing accomplished. Lois was not a perfectionist making a high demand on herself. She just wanted to spend a few hours getting a head start when she had the time to do so. Lois said she typically did not avoid work when she was under the normal pressures of daily tasks, class, or study group deadlines. We reviewed a number of options from class, none of which resonated for her. Soon I reached the last two items on my list—"acting the part" and having a conversation with herself.

Lois was not familiar with either, so I explained that acting the part means behaving "as if" you are playing a role rather than behaving for real. A professional actor is fully engaged in her role, often behaving in ways she would never be comfortable with in everyday life. An actor knows she is not the character, but can play the part. So instead of pressuring yourself when your elephant is resisting something, relax and let yourself behave as if you are acting. Just pretend. Start by sitting for a few minutes and letting your inner executive visualize yourself acting the desired behavior. You might also visualize what you will feel when the desired behavior is completed. Picturing the behavior in advance is an important step. You can also physically rehearse the required movements to see how they feel.

• TRY THIS •

Act the Part

1. Sit quietly and visualize yourself performing the desired behavior.
2. Visualize what you will feel when the behavior is successfully completed.
3. Try going through the physical motions to see how the role feels.
4. Initiate the desired behavior as if rehearsing or playing a part.
5. Remember, it is just pretend. Your elephant can stay calm because there is nothing to lose.

Acting the part means that it is not really *you* executing the behavior, which reduces the pressure on your inner elephant. Once you have a visual script, just play the role. There is nothing to lose. It may take two or three times to get the hang of it, but once you can detach from your elephant's fears, acting the part becomes easy. For example, one MBA student acted the part of a host to prompt himself to reach out to many people after failing to do so as himself. Another told me that he acted the part to ask a new girl for a date. He made a game of it rather than be held back by his fears.

I asked Lois, "How about if you play the role of someone using her free time wisely?" Lois answered, "That sounds okay, but what about your final idea?"

The idea of talking to her elephant might sound weird, so I raised it cautiously. "How would you feel about having a conversation with your inner elephant, asking why it avoids work when it has free time, and asking if it would be willing to do some schoolwork over the break?" I said. Lois seemed quite open to the idea, so I explained the theory behind this approach, which I had learned in a workshop. "This idea may strike some people as silly and childish, but it works," I told her. One key assumption is that every thought or behavior of the inner elephant originally had a positive purpose. Everything we do was learned as a way to cope effectively with a specific situation, even if the behavior annoys you now. So if you ask the inner elephant directly about the purpose of its resistance, it may be able to answer, which will provide insight into why the seemingly dysfunctional avoidance occurs. Your inner elephant, in its own way, is trying to do what is best for you when it avoids work during school breaks.

The second assumption is that if our inner executive speaks gently and soothingly to the inner elephant, asking if it would please do something, then the elephant is likely to respond in a positive way. Remember that while growing up, it had to contend with criticism and negative judgments, and it may get more now from bosses, professors, and family members—not to mention the judge within. The elephant often resists because it is upset. You are helping it calm down. A kind and nurturing attitude toward your inner elephant can yield a surprisingly positive response. If instead you yell at or criticize your inner elephant, it will shrink into itself and resist even more.

Lois seemed excited about this idea. I explained how she could role-play by having two chairs facing each other, one for the inner elephant and one for the inner executive. She could move from chair to chair as she spoke to the other self, asking first why it wants to put off working over the break and, second, if it would consider putting in a few hours on schoolwork. She could switch chairs to answer each question. Switching chairs did not appeal to her, so I explained that I used this approach simply by closing my eyes and speaking downward into myself as if there were another entity inside me. If the feeling of resistance can be identified in the body, it is best to speak directly to that feeling. I recalled an incident where I had some free time to work on my annual performance review but was feeling psychological resistance. I couldn't get started. I spoke directly to that resistance and said something like, "Would it be okay if we work on the annual review now?" I waited a few moments. I did not get a verbal yes or no. The answer came by the resistance falling away. I assumed that this was a yes and promptly did my annual review. The internal resistance felt a bit like a balky child who needed some nurturing attention. By speaking nicely to it and asking its permission, it said yes. It was as if the inner elephant wanted to cooperate, but needed to be asked in a nice way.

I saw Lois in the library a few weeks later and asked whether she had tried having a conversation with her inner elephant. She said it was the best thing she had ever tried for her avoidance behaviors. She completed a lot of schoolwork over the school break by asking her inner elephant each morning if it minded working for a couple of hours. She said she spoke to it as if she were soothing a cranky child. "Why, just a few minutes ago my inner elephant wanted to play a computer game as I sat here rather than prepare for an exam I have tomorrow. I turned inward and asked sweetly if it would be okay to go ahead and work on the exam now. It agreed. Asking my elephant nicely has worked for me every time."

Having a conversation with the inner elephant to ask permission is related to the idea of autosuggestion. Both techniques involve speaking to the inner elephant—one makes a suggestion; the other asks permission. The difference is that the request speaks more directly to the unhappy, childlike inner elephant to calm it down and relax its anxiety and resistance. Both strategies work for gaining control of your accelerator so that you can move forward despite feelings of avoidance.

• TRY THIS •

Make a Gentle Request

1. Close your eyes and focus on the location of internal felt resistance.
2. Speak gently and softly to this resistance.
3. Ask permission to proceed with the avoided task as if soothing a fearful child.
4. Wait until you sense that your inner elephant is ready to proceed.
5. Get started and complete the avoided task.

Lois is an example of how to make practices in this book work for you. So long as the elephant and executive are in harmony, we feel no distress as we plow through the day. Inner distress arises when your elephant wants to avoid something that you want to undertake. The inner elephant and inner executive then are at odds, and managing yourself means changing your inner elephant. Lois had a great attitude that will work for you—willingness to try something, just a little willingness to apply ideas from this book that may seem strange or different.[9] Let go of your skepticism. If you are avoiding a task, there will be some underlying anxiety, so try something new: acting the part, talking to your elephant, autosuggestion, calming down your anxious elephant by consciously relaxing, or engaging with other people. Learn what works for you. All you need is enough willingness to try one or more of the suggested practices in this and other chapters. Relax and let the rest take care of itself. Reading the book is easy, but reading is not enough. Does reading a menu satisfy your hunger, or do you order and eat the meal? Try a few spoonfuls of this material. Practice is required for you to change yourself even a small amount.

8
·

Slow Down to Stop
Your Reactions

*No matter what has happened, always behave as if nothing
had happened.*
—Arnold Bennett

*We are not troubled by things, but by the opinion we have
of things.*
—Epictetus

IRIS WORKED HARD FOR SEVEN YEARS to build up her service business.
She employed fifteen people, and the business was finally earning solid
profits. One of Iris's employees, Adele, asked to speak with her privately.
They went to a conference room, which offered some privacy, but other
employees could see them. Adele asked for a raise, delivering an "I
deserve a raise" talk about her increased responsibility and low salary
for several years. So far, so good. Well, maybe not. Iris freaked out,
going from listening mode to tirade in about ten seconds. Iris lost control
and shouted about people who are like family trying to take advantage
of her generosity, along with all the things she does for Adele . . . Iris
overreacted and vividly demonstrated how *not* to respond to a request.
Adele was crushed and later talked with others about quitting. Iris

missed an opportunity to have a thoughtful discussion about salary. Her impulse toward anger and overreaction was not to be denied.

A young manager, Forrest, was in trouble with the boss, his uncle, who had appointed him a manager in the family business. "It sounds like the problem is that you don't stop and think," I suggested after he told me how he impulsively started projects and did not finish them. He claimed that he did stop to think. It was just that the ideas felt so promising and urgent—why not strike quickly? In a major case of overoptimism, each business project looked great to his inner elephant at the beginning, but he seldom finished the projects, and they failed to make money. He would become bored, abandon them, and move onto something else. By slowing down his impulse, he might get a clearer, more objective picture of costs and benefits before undertaking a new business deal. His emotions were too strongly identified with each new idea. Slowing down would provide time for emotions to weaken, to think things through, and to consult with others. Forrest was acting out of impulse rather than thoughtfulness.

• • •

Speed is exciting. Speed is fun. Slow is boring. Waiting is boring. Urgency is exciting. An adrenaline rush feels good. Your inner elephant has a short attention span. Often it overreacts to issues to which it feels sensitive, and often it wants to jump ahead to the next new thing that looks more exciting than the current thing. Most managers work at a hectic pace, make snap decisions, and love it. Rapid-fire problems and solutions are the nature of management. This is well and good so long as you hold back your unthinking impulses, particularly the negative reactions that could do harm. For example, Mark Andreessen, the whiz kid who started Netscape and ignited the dot-com blaze, tended to overreact brutally to any implied criticism. "This is why I should not run a company," he said.[1] Chapter Seven explored ways to calm down so that your inner elephant can move forward on projects it wants to avoid. Chapter Four described the opposite problem of reacting too quickly. This chapter will consider strategies for how to put on the brake to prevent your inner elephant from acting on impulse and in haste when your inner executive's slower thoughtfulness would yield a better response.

Stop and Think

In an interview with *Fortune* magazine, Michael Bloomberg said, "The worst advice that people can take is to react before they've had a chance to think. I think we all say things and wish we hadn't said them. Ready, shoot, aim is not the smartest policy."[2] Speed is not good when it involves blind reaction to a colleague, direct report, spouse, or child. Why not provide an intelligent response that contains insight and wisdom? The thoughtful response means using your brakes to stop your reaction for a moment. Give yourself some time to think. Instant reactions, especially when expressing anger or issuing a sarcastic putdown, nearly always detract from your social effectiveness. Have you ever written an e-mail and pushed the Send button when angry? If so, you know what I mean.

Many managers have to learn patience, learn to control their emotional reactions. Richard Anderson, CEO of Delta Airlines, said, "I've learned to be patient and not lose my temper. And the reason that's important is everything you do is an example, and people look at everything you do and take a signal from everything you do. And when you lose your temper, it really squelches debate and sends the wrong signal about how you want your organization to run."[3] Restraining yourself takes some practice and honest self-appraisal. Dany Levy, founder and head of DailyCandy.com, said that sometimes she doesn't slow down enough to walk someone through why she made a decision. She sees herself as a fairly anxious person, and has learned that as a boss she cannot be impulsive and irrational. "I've learned to sort of slow down, take a deep breath." Carol Bartz, CEO of Yahoo, said that to lead others she learned to hold back. "I have a bad habit—you get half your question out and I think I know the whole question, so I want to answer it. And so I actually had to be trained to take a breath. . . . I have to shut up."[4]

Managers can learn to slow down, sometimes with a nudge from the boss. Greg Brenneman, chairman of CCMP Capital, said "One thing that I have very rigorously reacted to is absolutely no nasty e-mails from executives back to employees or back to franchise owners. Or to each other. If I intercept one of those, it'll be a bad day."[5] Brenneman understands the negative impact of harsh words on people and the culture. Everyone gets angry from time to time or feels the impulse to say something hurtful, but good leaders do not verbalize those thoughts. A manufacturing manager told me that slowing down his response during intense times when lines are down was transformational for him. Instead of reacting while overheated, he "walk[s] away" and cools down to make sure he's not offending people, who then refuse to cooperate. The conscious effort to slow down before speaking has meant "fewer toes stepped on and better responses to my suggestions."

During difficult times, the heart and body tense up. When revenues, activity, and stock price are down, pressure for performance can be enormous. Your mind may be racing faster than normal. Tightness and pressure are associated with negative emotions, such as resentment, anger, jealousy, revenge, or contempt. For example, the founder of a textile manufacturing company was so upset about the state of the world and of his industry that he felt "angry nearly all the time. I'm lashing out at my employees, vendors, and clients." Here are some ideas for slowing down your inner elephant to prevent overreaction.

o *Count to ten.* Remember what Grandma said: "If you're angry, count to ten before saying something." Just slow down your reaction time. It is often as simple as that. Wait for the emotional rush to pass before speaking. Many managers use a mechanism of some sort to encourage hesitation or delay before reacting.

o *Remember the 8Ts.* One business owner told me that he used the "8 Ts"—*take the time to think things through thoroughly*—whenever he was upset and reactive. I consider that good advice and have used it myself.

o *STOP.* A colleague of mine noticed a woman looking at her wrist and could see something unusual on her watch. He asked her about it, and she showed him the STOP on the watch face. The letters stood for *s*tep back, *t*hink, *o*rganize your thoughts, and *p*roceed. What a great mechanism for training her elephant! Stopping for a moment before reacting gave her time to see a bigger picture and consider other options before responding.

o *Use autosuggestion.* Chapter Five described how to change behavior by repeating an autosuggestion phrase. You might slow yourself down by repeating several times a day, "I am taking the time to think things through thoroughly" or "I am slowing down to listen." An insurance company manager who rushed through his meetings slowed things down by repeating to himself, "I am slowing down to engage." He would write the statement on his pad so that he could see it during that meeting and would repeat it several times in his mind before the next meeting. I have had students use such autosuggestions as "I am slowing down to love others" to great effect. Others are "I am slowing down" or "I am waiting until my impulses pass before deciding."

o *Wait one minute.* Another manager told me that he uses a one-minute rule. He started it at home and now uses it at work. Whenever he felt an urge to snack, he would look at his watch and wait one full minute before heading to the kitchen. During that one minute, the craving would peak and begin to decline. Just one minute was enough that sometimes he would not have the snack at all. He said he was rarely reactive at work, but if he did feel a sharp reaction to someone, he always waited at least one minute to respond.

○ *Wait for reaction 2.* The regional sales manager of an auto supply company told me that he taught himself always to wait for his second reaction. He described to me his reaction 1 and reaction 2, especially when he received bad news. His instant reaction (1) often did more harm than good, so he learned to distrust it. He would not respond verbally until a follow-up reaction came into his mind, which could appear a minute, an hour, or a day later. He told people he would get back to them. Reaction 2 was nearly always smarter than the first one. Sometimes it would be the same. Jeffery Katzenberg, CEO of DreamWorks, loved to speak first in meetings and voice criticism of what he didn't like. After receiving advice from a colleague that Katzenberg's "different" did not always mean *better,* Katzenberg slowed down to hear other people first, and now self-edits with his equivalent of a five-second tape delay for his negative reactions.[6] The key in both of these cases is that the leader has developed good awareness to see the immediate reaction in his head and know not to express it—a great use of the inner executive.

○ *Take three deep breaths.* If you feel yourself filling up with emotional reaction you don't want, another good way to slow yourself down is to take three conscious breaths. Focus on the air coming in and going out. Breathe in and out more deeply than normal to bring your awareness away from your impulse and into the present moment, which will pull you into your inner executive, enabling you to think more clearly and from a bigger picture. You can also visualize breathing in calmness and breathing out your emotional tension. An EMBA student told me that she was upset when her manager asked her to be responsible for a training program. She took three deep breaths. As her emotions cleared, she could see the bigger picture of why the boss had picked her. During a televised golf match, a commentator mentioned that Tom Watson took four deep breaths whenever he felt his emotions rising and pressuring him to rush a shot. The breaths quieted his emotions and slowed his reaction. I sometimes feel impatience to rush through and finish a project just to get it done. I can finish quickly, but quality plummets. Deep breaths bring me back to the present moment to stay immersed in what I am doing.

○ *Write it down.* Another way to get rid of an emotional impulse is to write it down. Abraham Lincoln took a huge amount of unjust criticism and handled it with patience, forbearance, and determination uncommon to most people. He felt the distress deeply, but did not react outwardly. If he did express his harsh sentiment, it was to get rid of his negative feelings. As noted in another chapter, he would write a harsh letter venting his anger, but then would not send it. Lincoln knew how to manage his emotions.[7] I have certainly typed a few memos and e-mails over the years that I did not send. After getting out all the ire, sending the message no longer seemed urgent.

○ *Remember that this too will pass.* There is a story from ancient India wherein a retired warrior sought a way to remove his mental anxieties and achieve peace of mind. He summoned his guru, Lord Krishna, to request a solution. Krishna wrote a note that the man was to read whenever affected by anxiety or strong emotion. The note read, "This will not last." Today a more common variation is "This too will pass." This is powerful advice because emotions really are temporary, like the shifting currents in a large river. In the moment, your emotions seem urgent, but that urgency is an illusion. If you can wait a few moments, your emotions will change. They always clear away. Your inner executive knows this, so you can repeat something like "This will not last" to prevent your reacting out of negative emotion. Slowing down allows you to be in charge of your reactions rather than having the reactions be in charge of you.

○ *Follow the twenty-four-hour rule.* This is an extension of the previous ideas, to be used when emotions are very strong and need time to clear. My daughter, an assistant principal, uses this rule with teachers and parents. If someone is upset, she schedules a meeting for the next day so that strong emotions will have passed and the discussion will be rational. If you are really upset, don't speak to a subordinate or send an e-mail. Your inner elephant is feeling pain and wants to blame someone. Avoid the temptation. Cool off. You are caught in a protective animal-type reaction. Action now will trigger upset in others. The things you do or say will destroy peace, harmony, and the positive culture around you. You might make something happen, but no one will feel good about it. Moreover, outbreaks are contagious. You will reinforce anger, resentment, or fear in others. They will pass it on. You may have heard the story of the boss who bawled out his direct report, who went home and fought with his wife, who spanked her child, who then kicked the cat. You can do better. Waiting twenty-four hours won't kill you.

○ *Observe your behavior.* If you ever act impulsively or react too fast or too strongly, an important step is to become conscious of what you are doing. Once you see yourself doing something objectionable, awareness has arrived. You have to see what you are doing before you can stop it. Once you see it, you can begin to manage impulsive behavior. For example, Ellis, an MBA student, liked to jump in and argue for his own way. If someone suggested lunch at Satco, he would propose South Street. If a friend argued for Satco because of a cheap beer, a deck full of cute girls, and a sunny day, Ellis would respond that it might rain, that one of their guests was tired and would not want to sit outside, and that other friends would rather talk than look at girls. Ellis tried to out-lawyer everybody over things big and small. He was a great guy in other respects, although immature in always reacting to get his way. Then suddenly he "saw it." As he told me, after he won an argument about where to eat, "I suddenly felt small. It was as if Mac was big enough to avoid upsetting me in order to preserve a fun afternoon. I began to worry how often I push back on trivial matters. I fear I do it way too often." Ellis is now aware of his impulsive behavior, the first big step in holding himself back.

o *Find your reaction pattern.* What triggers your reactions? What type of reactions do you have? Try this exercise to help you stop and think. An excellent way to increase your awareness is to make a list of the situations or triggers that set you off in some way. Start the list right now and add things that you think of over the next two days. Check the list each evening and add to it until you feel that it's fairly complete. Then take one item from the list and visualize that event occurring. Feel the reaction within you, and just be with it. Watch it weaken and drift away. Take the next item on the list and do the same. As you get comfortable sensing the emotion, your awareness expands, and you are less likely to act on the impulse when the trigger event occurs. By rehearsing mentally before the event happens, you will be able to stop and think to bring your reaction under your control.

Remember This

Ways to Stop and Think

Rather than react too quickly, consider using one of the following ways to stop and think.

- Count to ten.
- Think the 8 Ts: take the time to think things through thoroughly.
- STOP: step back, think, organize your thoughts, proceed.
- Use autosuggestion—for example, "I am slowing down."
- Wait one minute.
- Wait for reaction 2.
- Take three deep breaths.
- Write down your distress.

- Think and say, "This too will pass."
- Obey the twenty-four-hour rule.
- Observe your impulsive behavior.
- Find your impulse pattern:
  1. Make a list of reactions.
  2. Identify the triggers.
  3. Imagine a triggering event and visualize letting go of your impulse.

Stop Interrupting

A seemingly small but annoying habit of many managers is to interrupt when someone is speaking. It seems as though they want to speed up the conversation or rush to make their important point. Interruptions can be annoying and disrespectful. They are the opposite of executive presence. Interrupting is a symptom of a deeper issue. It reflects a focus on self rather than on another person. What happens when a child gets excited? He or she wants to tell someone about it. The same thing happens with the inner elephant. If we become excited, upset, or emotional, the inner elephant wants to talk and be heard. It wants to dump out its feelings. It wants its point of view to be known. The underlying desire to have one's own view dominate creates a problem, of course. Interruptions usually mean a lack of presence in the moment, and the interrupter is not hearing the other person. The interrupting manager is imposing his impulsiveness on others. If you are guilty, the solution is to slow yourself down. Remember this rule: *do not interrupt*. If you do interrupt others,

- Pull yourself together and be patient.
- Act like a leader.
- Use executive presence.
- Don't be a reactive child.

Your inner executive can help you apply the brake to slow down your reactions.

Here is an exercise I use to help managers stop the habit of interrupting. It starts with a Zen story.

The Zen master instructed a student to bring him some tea. The student dutifully went to the kitchen and prepared the tea. Soon the student returned with a teapot and saucer on a tray. The master picked up the teapot and poured tea into the cup. Soon the cup was full, but the master kept pouring. The tea spilled onto the saucer, then onto the tray, and then onto the floor. "Master, Master, what are you doing? You're spilling the tea." The master responded, "Yes, so I am. What is the lesson?" The confused student stammered that he did not know. "Okay, then. Return the tea to the kitchen and clean up this mess. Then I will give you the lesson." The student returned and sat cross-legged before the master. Soon the master provided his lesson: "a full cup will hold no more tea."

Most managers are not sure what this story means, so here is my explanation. Your inner elephant wants to talk and tell, tell and talk. It is like the excited child who wants to be heard. It wants its point to be heard. It wants to pour tea. But the other person's cup is already full. The person with whom you are talking is filled with beliefs, opinions, skepticism, worry, fear, defensiveness, and things to do, along with distrust and distraction. And your interruptions are not helping. If you really want that person to hear what you have to say, shut up! Let that person "empty her cup" before you speak. Put the brake on your inner elephant. Once the person empties on the topic without interruption, there is space for her to hear what you have to say. Indeed, she will want to hear what you think. So to be heard, stop interrupting.

Your assignment as leader is to listen until the other person empties. You are much more likely to be heard and effect a change in his behavior if you slow down and allow him to empty his cup. If you interrupt, argue, want to be right, and want to have your way, the other person can't hear you because his cup is not empty. It is more important for you to shut up and listen. To slow down, it would help to mentally rehearse letting the other person empty her cup before the conversation. Or you can repeat "I will empty her cup" or "I am staying quiet" beforehand to get your mind right. By slowing down, not interrupting, and letting the other person's cup empty, he will want to hear you. During the conversation, use whatever techniques you can to engage the other person in speaking, such as asking questions. A manager from Dell told me that he was taught to begin conversations with "Help me understand . . ." to induce the other person to speak first. Otherwise, his own inner elephant might empty first in the conversation.

A specific exercise I use with students and managers is to undertake three conversations in a row during which they deliberately empty the other person's cup without interrupting. After three conversations, you will definitely have the hang of it. After six conversations, you will be a master and use this technique much of the time. You will probably still interrupt others when you are agitated, excited, or upset about the topic. With practice, you will get to perfection, which is to *never* interrupt.

A manager at a health care company said, "I introduced a personal topic with one of my direct reports. I listened as he talked somewhat at length about his challenges at work, along with family and evening classes. There were several instances when my inner elephant was prompting me to interrupt and interject my experiences, but my executive helped me to hold back my comments until he finished. I thought the conversation was very successful, partly because it felt good, and partly because he really heard my suggestions." An MBA student noticed that he frequently interrupted his wife. He resolved to do better one night when she was "venting" about a bad day. I warned in class that an upset spouse was not an ideal person on whom to practice, but he tried it anyway.

> I interrupted and disagreed with her, which escalated into a fight. I waited until morning and decided to try this experiment again. I tried to empty her cup without interrupting by asking, "What did I do last night to make you angry?" When she spoke, I started to get defensive and things escalated. I figuratively put my hands around my throat to stop my elephant. I stayed quiet no matter how much she ripped into me. After she finished, I just apologized (using my executive to simply let go of the insults hurled at me). It was hard but I finally did it, and she was no longer angry.

A giant advantage of emptying someone's cup is that it acknowledges that you simply can't know what another person is thinking. If you assume you do know, that will close your mind. An IT executive from an equipment company told me the following story:

> One of my managers came in to question me about a project assignment. This guy is more creative techie than manager. I get pretty frustrated because he meanders, and I typically cut him off. I started to roll my eyes and repeat my previous instructions about what to do, when I remembered this assignment. So I asked a question and gave him time to empty his cup. His point finally got through to me. He had found a much better way to organize the project to resolve technical issues. I had been too rushed to hear it. Your assignment saved us time and money.

Another manager loved talking about work, politics, and football. On these subjects, he immediately jumped in wanting his views to prevail, so emptying people's cups was really hard for him. Because it was an assignment, he decided to open the conversation by asking a question first. To his surprise,

> I was able to hear several insights on each subject that I might otherwise have missed. By letting the other person empty his cup,

I believe he was more receptive to my thoughts. Afterward, I realized that most of my conversations are just a competition in which everyone is trying to make a point. My strategy has been to strike first to gain advantage. The conversation was richer when I slowed down and first drew other people out.

Listening adds more value than interrupting, and, equally important, a delayed response will project an image of you as more thoughtful and wise. The second response that comes into your mind a few minutes or seconds after your first reaction is typically better. To respond with wisdom, wait and hear your own deeper thoughts from your inner executive rather than react on impulse. The deeper thoughts form while you are listening. Initial reactions often arise from a fight-or-flight instinct. Let that instinct pass. Practice staying calm and collected, and respond out of a calm and rational presence. The thoughtful response is nearly always a better answer. And even if it's not better, nothing is lost by listening and waiting a few minutes. At the very least, no damage will be done by holding back the impulse.

Remember This

Stop Interrupting
To be heard, shut up.

1. First, empty the person's cup.
2. Don't interrupt.
3. Speak only after the other is empty. You will then be heard.

And you will hear.

Detach from Your Emotions and Impulses

People often believe that medical decisions in the emergency room are made instantly, but according to Jerome Groopman, in *How Doctors Think*, that is a "misperception." To think clearly in hectic circumstances, doctors slow things down to avoid impulses and mental errors. A skilled emergency room physician works with "studied calm," by slowing his thinking and actions so as not to be distracted by the chaotic atmosphere.[8] Being quick and shooting from the hip earn no points and are indications of less skill and maturity in the emergency room.

Danny Meyer learned how to manage people from a consultant, Pat Cetta. Danny was in a state of anger and upset, bemoaning to Pat the fact that his waiters and managers at Union Square Café were not getting his message. They seemed always to test and push him to the limit, driving Danny crazy. Pat insisted that getting upset was not the answer, and was more likely part of the problem. Pat told Danny to put a saltshaker in the middle of a bare table, exactly where he wanted it. Then Pat pushed the salt shaker a few inches off-center. "Now put it back were you want it," he said. Then Pat moved it off-center again, and Danny slid it back. They repeated the cycle a few times. "People are always moving your saltshaker off-center. That is the job of life. Until you understand that, you're going to get pissed off every time someone moves the saltshaker off-center. It is not your job to get upset. You just need to understand: that's what they do."[9] Pat was teaching Danny to detach from his emotional reactions. Danny's job was to patiently move the shaker back each time and explain why it needs to be in the center. Danny's mind needs to be above the emotional give-and-take, seeing what is happening, and teaching and coaching people toward correct behavior. Getting upset helps not at all. The leader's job is to *not* be upset or arguing with people. Stay above petty reactions and provide appropriate correction. That is the saltshaker theory.

• • •

How do you learn to detach from impulses? An exercise I often assign to people is Be Bored. It is very simple: sit in a chair for thirty minutes and don't get up. If thirty minutes scares you, try a slightly shorter time, such as twenty minutes. You don't have to meditate or concentrate on anything in particular. Shut off any outside distractions, such as the TV; close your eyes; and just feel the next impulse that arises. Spend the thirty minutes feeling impulses and letting them pass to know what nonreaction feels like. For busy people, many impulses come up in a short time. Seeing and feeling the impulses without acting will strengthen your inner executive's control over them. One manager reported, "My first attempt at sitting for thirty minutes left me anxious and unfocused. I could not help but think about the things that my elephant thought I should be doing. On my next few attempts I got better at letting go of my impulses. Now I use this technique at work each day. Letting go of the impulses seems to weaken my elephant. And it is amazing how it leaves me refreshed, in control, and ready to go."

Another manager told me of her experience: "The first wave of impulses made me want to scribble notes of the things I was not getting done and things I needed to do. As these impulses boiled up, I focused on letting them go. As I renewed my commitment to not responding, the impulses slowed and ultimately stopped. I found the exercise to be relaxing and energizing. Training my elephant by empowering my executive has paid tremendous dividends in my self-control. I come back to this whenever my elephant becomes unruly."

If you can master the Be Bored exercise, you can gain control of your impulses by not reacting to them. Learn to see your impulses and just let them go.

Remember This

Detach from Emotions and Impulses

- Stay above the fray, not in it.
- Detach from inner impulses as a way to slow your reactions.
- Be bored.
  1. Sit for thirty minutes with your eyes closed and with no distractions.
  2. Let your impulses arise and pass.
  3. Do not get up or take action.
  4. Your impulses will weaken, and your inner executive will strengthen.
- Detach and just "act" emotional for positive impact.

What about having an emotional reaction, such as anger, just to get someone's attention? I often have managers argue that sometimes displaying anger seems the right thing to do. What if someone needs a fire lighted under him if he is to realize his potential? I agree that there are times when strong emotion seems like the correct response. So my answer is this: be an *actor*. Don't express rage when you are really angry. Don't chop someone's head off when you are upset. Let it pass. Then you can psych yourself up to *pretend* to be angry, while staying under control. That is the key to expressing emotion: be in control of the emotion. Be in your executive and not your inner elephant. Acting is a good leadership quality to develop. This is similar to the "acting the part" exercise in Chapter Seven. Acting as if you were upset keeps the inner executive in charge; your executive is selecting a wise action for a distinct purpose. In contrast, your inner elephant won't stop to think. It will express anger on impulse, and reap the negative consequences.

Just Say No

Dorothy and I were with a group of people at a friend's house for a Thanksgiving Day dinner. A couple of guests commented that I looked trim, which I appreciated because I had lost seventeen pounds. In the course of the conversation, I asked whether anyone ever felt food cravings. Nearly everyone admitted yes. I asked whether anyone ever took just a small amount of the desired food, hoping that this would satisfy the craving, and then couldn't stop eating. To my surprise, several stories unfolded. One person had tried to eat a single cookie and ended up eating the entire sleeve of cookies. A woman said she loved to bake bread, and if she ate a single slice, she would end up consuming half a loaf. A man said he ate one snack cracker he craved, then consumed the whole box. He also said that one time he drove to the store to buy a box of those crackers because the craving was so strong. He ate one, then half those in the box, while sitting in his car. The common theme in these stories was that taking a small amount of something did not help control the urge. Indeed, the inner elephant's cravings got stronger with a single bite, resistance collapsed, and the person stuffed himself or herself, not exactly what the person had in mind.

Sometimes you can change your inner elephant's behavior by saying "No!" and meaning it. In other words, deny the inner elephant's impulse completely. Don't give it a single bite. There should be no quarter given, no effort to appease the inner elephant with a small amount or with any aspect of the unwanted behavior. This means to stop cold turkey. Lock your brakes. Not giving in to your elephant for short periods reduces its strength and hold over you.

The reason for my conversation at Thanksgiving dinner was that a few months prior I had explored the concept of intermittent fasting. I had gained some weight. I had heard people talk about fasting, and thought maybe it would work for me. I read a couple of books and was intrigued by the idea of simply not eating for a day or two as a way to gain control of my inner elephant's indulgent eating habits. Although the books described fasting as a way to purify the body, it seemed to me like a way to strengthen my inner executive's intentional behavior. People can quite easily live on water or juice for up to three weeks, so could anything bad happen by fasting only a day or two? Intermittently fasting for short periods supposedly has benefits similar to calorie restriction diets. I became very clear about my intention, deciding to go without food the next Saturday. That would be a thirty-six-hour fast, from dinner on Friday until breakfast on Sunday.

On Saturday morning, my inner executive was prepared to deny all food, no matter how much my inner elephant protested or how hungry I felt. I drank a lot of seltzer water that day. I became aware of hunger sensations in the early afternoon, the first time I had felt physical hunger in a long time. I realized that normally I eat out of habit rather than hunger. I just sat with the hunger feeling, "watched" it, but felt no need to satisfy it. Before long, the hunger feelings went away. My inner executive felt in charge. Moreover, I decided to do aerobic exercise for thirty minutes. My inner elephant seemed to be surrendering on matters it normally resisted. The day of fasting was pretty uneventful, except that when I thought of something I should be doing, such as a household task I disliked, I did it readily. The power balance between my inner executive and inner elephant seemed to have shifted a bit in favor of my inner executive.

Sunday morning I weighed myself and was down four pounds. (Of course I can't lose four pounds in one day by not eating, any more than I can gain four pounds in one day by overeating. I assume that the weight reduction was from the temporary loss of salt and water.) The interesting part of the fast happened over the next six days. I was much more conscious of what I was eating. My old eating habits seemed weaker. My food choices came from my rational executive more than from my impulsive inner elephant. I felt stronger and more in control of my eating. I found it easy to skip a meal. I was not "afraid" of being hungry. I tended to eat when I felt hunger in my gut rather than when my inner elephant felt an impulse to eat. By the end of the first week, I was down two pounds, which felt about right. I continued the Saturday fasting for about three months until I reached my desired weight. The value of the intermittent fast continued to be less in the Saturday fast and more in the daily control it gave my inner executive over my food intake. Over the several months after I stopped fasting, I regained a couple pounds, but that was all. I have felt more inner executive control over my eating ever since. If I detect a slight gain, my inner executive can again take charge by fasting on a Saturday.

Mike Hyatt, CEO of Thomas Nelson Publishers headquartered here in Nashville, is one of the most intentional leaders I know. He has the capacity to think things through and then choose a behavior that will have positive impact, even if the behavior is not part of his habit pattern. He told my class that he had decided to go on a media fast for sixty days. Wow! That seemed like a challenge to me. Mike's reasoning was compelling. His job was to think about the future. He couldn't keep his eye (or mind) on the future when constantly checking current events. If something was really important to his business, he would learn about it.

Indeed, as it turned out, the people around him would quickly tell him anything important. By going cold turkey and shutting off his exposure to media for two months, his mind was free. His mind got a vacation to rest and refocus. He felt less reactive. The temporary fast provided time to look forward.

The point is that there are times to completely deny your inner elephant's impulses, if only temporarily, to gain control over them. You may have noticed that intermediate fasting is similar to the Be Bored exercise. Gradual change sometimes is not the best option. If you habitually interrupt people, for example, then you could let people "empty their cup" in every single conversation for an entire day to gain control of that impulse. Lock your brake on dysfunctional impulses. Make denial your single focus. As your inner executive gains strength, you can relax into spontaneous interchanges and will not interrupt so much. If you have a habit of making sarcastic or destructive comments that you want to stop, or if you are constantly judging things and making negative comments or always wanting to have the last word, why not stop cold turkey for a day to strengthen your inner executive's control? You will become a better leader for doing so. If denying something to your inner elephant completely for a short time resonates as an option for you, I encourage you to try it. It worked for me.

Remember This

Just Say No

- Sometimes it is most effective to completely renounce an undesired behavior.
- Eliminate the behavior for a defined time period, and repeat the practice to keep impulses weak.
- Enjoy a stronger inner executive.

Employ Punishment

Marshall Goldsmith told a story about how he stopped himself from making impulsive destructive comments. His problem was that he made nasty comments about people when they were not in the room. This was a problem for him as a manager because it completely opposed his espoused value of teamwork. So he admitted to his staff that he wanted to quit making destructive comments. "If you ever hear me make another destructive comment about another person, I will pay you $10 each time you bring it to my attention."[10] Goldsmith really wanted to break that habit.

Goldsmith's staff was happy to help. They would mention names of people who would bring up his bile, and he took the hook each time. By noon he was down $50. The next day, his nasty comments cost $30. The third day, $10. His policy stayed in effect for several weeks, and it cost him money. The result? For his next 360° feedback about his behavior, he moved from the 8th percentile on "avoids destructive comments" up to the 96th percentile. He doesn't make destructive comments anymore.

Immediate punishment (being dinged for $10) works great in the right circumstance. A few years ago I, along with many other drivers, would take a side road to avoid the backup at the stoplight for the exit of a popular shopping area. There was a clear No Left Turn sign that everyone ignored. One day, feeling pleased at circumventing the traffic at the light, I made the illegal left turn from the side road. After driving two blocks, a policeman waved me into a vacant filling station. About twenty cars were waiting to get tickets. There was no escape. The ticket was $100. Now I remember that ticket each time I leave the shopping center, as I wait patiently at the traffic light. The punishment left a mark on my memory. Other drivers must have learned the same lesson. Very few cars now make that illegal left turn.

Everyone knows the power of positive incentives for reinforcing good behavior. Ho hum. You can read about the power of rewards anywhere. The point here is that it can be just as important to use mild punishment that your inner elephant does *not* like. This inhibits bad behavior rather than rewarding good behavior. It attacks the impulsive behavior directly, which Goldsmith did so successfully. There is also something powerful about feeling a sting after bad behavior occurs. Like the traffic ticket, a financial penalty may provide that sting. Research shows that the pain of losing $1 is several times greater than the good feeling associated with receiving $1. Why not take advantage of the principle that the pain of loss is an effective inhibitor of your bad behavior?

Another way to use punishment is to collaborate with a partner to provide a financial incentive for your inner elephant. For example, if you are trying to go on a diet or exercise regularly, you might make a bet with a friend for $500, of which you lose $20 every day you fail to diet, exercise, or both. This will provide a negative incentive to give up your old habits. If you miss your target completely, or if your friend does better than you, your friend could keep the $500 or donate it to a charity, perhaps one you don't want to support. That would double the pain, providing even more incentive to stop indulging yourself. Or you

can try the Web site stickk.com, mentioned in Chapter Six, to arrange a
financial disincentive if you fail to achieve your goal of holding back.

If a punishment makes unpalatable some bad habit that you want to
stop doing, this approach may provide some benefit. One ingenious idea
is to use mental imagery to create punishment by association. Consider
Raul's solution to a food craving:

> At night, after the kids were asleep, I would walk into the kitchen and
> find something full of chocolate and sugar. I wasn't hungry but could
> not shake the craving. Standing there I would repeat in my mind that
> I was not hungry and didn't need to eat anything. That helped, but
> often I would have something anyway. What really worked was to
> imagine that I could smell fish and could even taste raw, spoiled fish in
> my mouth. It made me feel like I wanted to throw up. When I mentally
> mixed the fish thoughts with the chocolate craving, the craving went
> away. I then switched to happy thoughts of how good I felt during
> a happy time in my life. This was a reward for not snacking. These
> thoughts helped me overcome food cravings.

Raul was using a technique of pairing an aversive mental stimulus with
a craving in order to weaken the craving, making it easy to control the
impulse. You can plan and practice a mental scenario in advance.[11] To see
how it works, right now think of a food you crave. As you feel that desire,
visualize the food in the most disgusting form imaginable to you—such
as covered with worms or maggots or rubbed into a dirty ashtray or
spittoon. Then visualize tasting and swallowing this disgusting mess.
Remember, visualization sends the same signals to your inner elephant
and body that actual behaviors do. You might try this for any obnoxious
behavior that offends other people. It is cheaper than paying $10 a pop.
Just think of your bad behavior along with a noxious image, and watch
your impulse shrivel. With intention and some mental effort, you can
create aversive stimuli to hold back your reaction in a work or family
situation. A visual stimulus can be almost as strong as the real thing, and
makes it much easier to slow down and stop the unwanted behavior.

Remember This

Employ Punishment
- Identify an undesired behavior.
- Select a penalty for each display of the unwanted behavior.
- Engage others in the process of assessing penalties.

Another option:

- Visualize an aversive mental stimulus.
- Summon the visualization when an impulse arises.
- Watch the impulse disappear.

PART FOUR

Become Aware of Your Inner Resources

9
.

Get to Know Your
Inner Elephant

*Resolve to be thyself; and know that he who finds himself,
loses his misery.*
—Matthew Arnold

*It is wisdom to know others. It is enlightenment to know
one's self.*
—Lao-Tzu

JOHN BEARDEN SOLD HIS REAL ESTATE business in Canada and came
back to Nashville to reflect. He observed that he often got to the finish
line "dragging people with him." He recalled when a consultant told him,
"John, you have so much potential, but you're running over everybody
. . . you turn people off." Bearden decided that now was the time to learn
what made him tick.

Before restarting his career, Bearden hired a personal coach. He completed the Myers-Briggs Type Indicator questionnaire that revealed his
"field marshal" (ENTJ) leadership style. Field marshals have essential leadership qualities of vision, drive, and decisiveness. However, the
downside is their tendency to be hasty, insensitive, and overbearing. With
these new insights, Bearden accepted an offer to become chief executive

of GMAC Home Services. His increased self-awareness enabled him to be less overbearing and to spend more time considering hard data and listening more carefully to colleagues' opinions. At a presentation by his most senior executives, rather than interject his own opinion early to bias the outcome toward what he wanted, he allowed other positions to be articulated and discussed with creative tension. Just sitting and absorbing was a satisfying outcome.[1]

Let's face it: your elephant has been running your life. For better or worse, everyone is on automatic pilot more than they realize. It makes sense to get to know your inner elephant. Systematic self-inquiry enabled Bearden to discover the patterns and preferences of his inner elephant, key parts of which he had been unaware. Now he could take advantage of his strengths and change his weaknesses. He saw his inner elephant clearly—both good and bad. Inner elephants have many negatives, but their behavior patterns can also reveal strengths. This is important because if you are frequently fighting with yourself to do things differently, you may be in the wrong business. It may make sense to find another situation that aligns better with your elephant's automatic behaviors. It may also make sense to discover the weaknesses you don't see—your blind spots—so you can know and fix them. With specific knowledge, Bearden redirected his inner elephant away from an overbearing attitude to develop his patience and facilitation skills. Your inner elephant no doubt has many parts of which you are unaware. So an important step for improving yourself is getting to know the positives and negatives of your own inner elephant.

Know Yourself

Have you ever tried to "groove" a stroke in tennis or golf, or put in your "repetitions" to get a sport movement correct? Tim Gallwey suggested a groove theory of habits in *The Inner Game of Tennis*.[2] Each time you act (swing) a certain way, you increase the probability that you will act that way again. Patterns or grooves build up and become more likely to repeat themselves. It is as if each action deepens the groove on a record disk, which is analogous to the nervous system of the body. After repeated similar actions, the needle falls into the groove automatically—your new behavior occurs automatically. Your inner elephant's lifestyle, tendencies, preferences, and mental patterns are all grooved. And you have more and deeper grooves than you think.

Before you can start to change yourself, one job of your inner executive is to understand your extant grooves so that you can put yourself in a situation that uses your automatic grooves, your natural potential. Self-assessment is an important part of self-management.[3] There is a lot to be said for learning your habits and talents, as well as your shortcomings, and putting yourself in situations where you can work smoothly and automatically. Why spend time fighting your inner elephant's grooves and patterns unnecessarily? Understand and put yourself in the place to do well. A survey of seventy-five members of the Stanford Graduate School of Business's advisory council revealed the nearly unanimous answer to a question about the most important capability for leaders to develop—self-awareness.[4] Self-awareness of your inner elephant is achieved by recognizing your needs, traits, patterns, and preferences, much as John Bearden did in his consultation with an executive coach. Then put yourself in a position to employ your automatic behaviors and enjoy a life of fewer struggles and more enjoyment. Find and go with the flow of what your inner elephant does well. If you are a natural at counseling people and dislike math, you are not taking advantage of your grooves by pursuing work as a financial analyst.

Each year, Warren Buffet, the legendary investor, hosts about 160 business students from many universities worldwide. He answers whatever questions the students ask, one of which is typically about how to know what career to pursue. How did the great man know that investing was the right work for him? Buffet answers in two parts. First, he says his natural "wiring" was made for capital allocation. If he had been born in a country such as Sudan or Cambodia, without abundant private capital and a system of capital allocation, he would never have gotten to use his natural talents. Nor would he have succeeded in a different era when there was no capitalism. Buffet is very clear in recommending that people need to do what fits their natural mental makeup. How did he know that his wiring fit investing? Buffet says the key was his love for it. He tried other work that was unsatisfying such that he would not do it for any amount of money. Investing, however, was so much fun that, paradoxically, he would do it for free. That was the vital rule for Buffet: find a work situation that you really like and enjoy, and it will fit the pattern of your mental wiring.

One problem, as described in Chapter Three, is that many people are in denial, especially about themselves. Leaders often have an inflated or distorted view of themselves that is propped up by the magician, attorney, or judge within. A good first step is to use questionnaire-type instruments to gain self-insight. John Bearden used the Myers-Briggs Type Indicator. Other popular and effective questionnaires are the Herrmann Brain Dominance Instrument and the DISC profile. There are instruments for optimism and pessimism and for self-confidence. They all work, and I recommend them. I typically ask my MBA students to start their self-inquiry by completing the VIA Signature Strengths questionnaire at Martin Seligman's Web site, Authentic Happiness (www.authentichappiness.org), or by completing the questionnaire at the StrengthsFinder 2.0 Web site. The Signature Strengths questionnaire is free; the StrengthsFinder questionnaire requires a code obtained with the purchase of one of the books based on Gallup research (for example, *Now, Discover Your Strengths, StrengthsFinder 2.0,* or *Strengths-Based Leadership*).

In 1998, Martin Seligman founded positive psychology. Much of the recent explosion of interest in college classrooms and in the popular press on the importance of strengths began with his work. Positive psychology represented a significant shift from psychology's historic focus on negative aspects, weaknesses, and the dark side of the human psyche. As a place to start, Seligman joined with Chris Peterson of the University of Michigan to map out a list of human strengths and virtues. They surveyed every list they could find (major religions, the Boy Scout Oath, and so on) to see which strengths were common across lists. They boiled it all down to six higher-level virtues that embodied twenty-four personal strengths.[5]

o Strengths of wisdom and knowledge
  1. Creativity
  2. Curiosity
  3. Love of learning
  4. Open-mindedness
  5. Perspective
o Strengths of courage
  6. Authenticity
  7. Bravery
  8. Persistence
  9. Zest
o Strengths of humanity
  10. Kindness
  11. Love
  12. Social intelligence
o Strengths of justice
  13. Fairness
  14. Leadership
  15. Teamwork
o Strengths of temperance
  16. Forgiveness/mercy
  17. Modesty/humility
  18. Prudence
  19. Self-regulation
o Strengths of transcendence
  20. Appreciation of beauty and excellence
  21. Gratitude
  22. Hope
  23. Humor
  24. Religiousness/spirituality

What, exactly, does one of these strengths feel like, if you happen to have it? The criteria for a signature strength, such as creativity or persistence, would typically include

A sense of ownership of the strength ("This is the real me")

A feeling of excitement while displaying or using it

A rapid learning curve when using it

A yearning to use it

Invigoration rather than exhaustion when using it

A feeling of motivation to use the strength[6]

Data have been gathered about these signature strengths from people around the world. The rankings of strengths from nation to nation are very similar from Azerbaijan to Zimbabwe. Which strengths do you think would rank highest and lowest across all the countries? Kindness and fairness rate highest, and *self-regulation ranks lowest*. Yes, self-regulation ranks lowest all over the world. I was surprised and relieved when I saw that statistic, because it means I'm not the only one who has trouble controlling my inner elephant.

Another exercise I have used successfully with MBA students is to find their high-performance pattern. This is based on the work of Jerry Fletcher.[7] Rather than start with a predefined list of strengths, you analyze your past high-performance experiences to see what worked. Think back over your personal history for experiences when you performed extremely well, when you felt in the flow and especially successful in your activity. This could have been a high-performance job assignment, such as a special project or other work activity. High-performance experiences also occur in the arenas of relationships, volunteer work, recreation, family events, and crises. The experiences should be important to you, but need not be seen as extraordinary by the world at large. Try to identify a handful of experiences and then narrow them down to two or three that reflect you at your best. Think about each experience as a sequence of stages, with a beginning, middle, and end. How did you learn about it? get drawn in? get rolling? bring other people in? keep it going? How did you handle ups and downs? bring it to a conclusion?

Write the stories out in detail and then analyze them to see which actions or processes were common denominators of your success. You may find that when you perform best, there is a distinct unfolding of events that includes ten or more steps. Show your pattern to people who know you and ask for feedback. Because everyone has blind spots, a good idea is to have someone else analyze the stories and say what themes he or she sees. This process can produce major insights and show you how to put yourself in positions to perform at your very best. You can seek those opportunities in which your inner elephant performs naturally and well. For example, one person discovered, "My high performance pattern is about unblocking complex organizational processes that are creeping along and causing gridlock, by obtaining up-front authority, gaining the trust and cooperation of those involved, and putting in place a new process that is much better."[8] Now she knows the projects and work assignments in which she can be a star without changing herself.

One neat thing about understanding strengths is the philosophy behind it: concentrate on your strengths, not your weaknesses. You excel in life by maximizing your strengths, not by fixing your weaknesses. When you live and work from your strengths, you are more motivated, competent, and satisfied. The judge aspect of your inner elephant is superb at finding your faults and weaknesses, and it ignores the good things, such as your strengths. People can enumerate their weaknesses much more quickly than their strengths. You may have to think carefully and intentionally to identify your strengths, or use one of the previously mentioned instruments or exercises. Information on your strengths opens an important horizon for your inner executive. You can put yourself in the place of greatest potential for your strengths.

Once you are clear about your strengths, it is fun to develop and refine them. Use periods of practice to improve yourself and find ways to deepen a groove for your strength rather than struggle to overcome a weakness. If curiosity is one of your strengths, for example, enhance it by attending a lecture you want to hear on a topic about which you know little, or enjoy a restaurant featuring an unfamiliar cuisine. Take time to discover a new place in your locale and study its history. If leadership is a strength, organize a social get-together for your friends, step up and take personal responsibility when something goes wrong, complete an unpleasant task that others are avoiding, or make a newcomer feel welcome.[9] These activities will be relatively easy and enjoyable for you, and will deepen the groove that makes you excellent.

Strengths are fun, but you should not ignore your weaknesses. The theory of constraints is very clear that the weakest link in any system limits performance, and correcting the weakest link will have a big payback.[10] Jack Welch told a Harvard class how some managers were afraid to roll the dice and take a chance, and others rolled the dice way too easily. Both types faced limited leadership opportunities unless they fix their "constraint." John Beardon received huge benefit from removing the dominating style that turned people off. You can overcome weaknesses too, by using the practices in this book and putting yourself in situations that help overcome your weaknesses. For example, psychologist Timothy Wilson told of how he took baby steps toward becoming more extroverted by making more of an effort to chat with people he did not know at social get-togethers.[11] When I dropped out of college for a year and tried to sell life insurance, I found that I was not suited to that job and did not do well, but the expectations helped me become much more outgoing. Selecting situations to develop aspects of yourself can have a big impact.

But before focusing on fixes, there are other ways to spot weak links that may restrict your effectiveness.

Remember This

Know Yourself

- Warren Buffet believes that you will be good at what you love to do.
- Learn about your extant grooves and strengths via the Authentic Happiness or StrengthsFinder Web sites. A signature strength is one you are excited to use and are invigorated by.
- Your high-performance pattern is a factual indicator of your strengths.
- Organize your life around your strengths more than your weaknesses.
- Identify and correct weaknesses that limit your performance.

Solicit Feedback

When then-CEO Kevin Rollins was upset with Dell's management culture, he asked every Dell manager to submit to periodic evaluations by underlings and other people with whom they worked. Thanks to this process, Rollins learned about himself. One senior vice president proclaimed that Rollins was "aloof, a poor listener, and a leader who at times could seem unapproachable." Another senior VP said that Rollings could be argumentative, maybe even bullheaded. Rollins endured the sting of people telling him that "He could be so supercilious and icy cold that his personality should be stored in a meat locker." He was facing reality when he said, "I could give the cold, calculating answer, but I really wanted to be a more inspirational leader." He saw that he was too much like Alexander Hamilton—efficient but short on people skills—and aspired to be more of a motivator like George Washington.[12]

You are two people who are quite different—the one you think you are and the one other people think you are. To "know thyself" is a lofty ambition of the inner executive that may strike fear in the heart of your inner elephant. Your inner executive gets stronger as you increase your awareness of the way you come across to others. Increased awareness can break through illusions held by the inner elephant. Direct feedback from others is a great step toward reality by integrating what you perceive with what others perceive about your patterns, style, and behavior. If your organization has a 360° feedback system, that is a good start. You'll get feedback from peers, direct reports, and your boss.

I think that helping students or managers get 360° feedback is the most anticipated and most feared activity that I do. It is anticipated because managers are intensely curious about how they come across to others. It is also feared, because inner elephants do not want to hear unpleasant truths. As discussed in Chapter Three, the inner elephant often sees what it wants to see, or needs to see, to maintain its self-image. It may unconsciously twist data to support its viewpoint. Our internal judge may jump to exaggerated negative conclusions about ourselves and others, our magician will cook available facts to make us look good in our own mind, and our attorney will defend the distorted view to the death. David Pottruck, former CEO of Charles Schwab, for example, had a difficult journey to self-awareness. A star in athletics and business, it was hard for him to hear that people didn't trust him and that he was a lightning rod for friction. Breaking through Pottruck's denial involved extreme feedback from his boss, two divorces, and losing the top job.[13] Without feedback, we typically are not accurate observers of ourselves or how we affect others. Facing reality is not easy.

In an organization perfectly designed for learning, every action would be followed by immediate feedback about its impact. Learning has three essential elements: action, feedback, and synthesis (making sense of the action and feedback). With instant feedback, managers would quickly identify strengths as well as barriers to success in their own personalities and strive to change as needed. For example, if a thoughtless statement hurt someone's feelings, or if an employee has evidence that your proposed initiative probably won't work, it would be great to learn these things immediately. Psychologists say that increased awareness takes you 50 percent of the way toward personal change—a huge step. Feedback is a great vehicle through which to face reality.

But the world of organization management typically does not provide immediate feedback. It conspires with your inner elephant to keep you in the dark about your impact on others. Before Anne Mulcahy became CEO of Xerox, she did a stint in human resources. She quickly discovered how little honest feedback people get in companies.[14] Terry Lundgren, chief executive of Macy's, is willing to give feedback, and it can be hard to break through. "I look 'em in the eye and tell 'em, 'You got an issue,' you know, they don't even realize it until you just hit 'em over the head with a frying pan"[15] Unlike Lundgren, most people won't volunteer feedback, except possibly during a formal performance review or through anonymous feedback given during an HR evaluation. Because ongoing feedback is important to growth and improvement, you probably have to take the initiative to face reality about your inner elephant's shortcomings.

A great approach is to create a structured system for written feedback gathered by others. When Stephen Kaufman was CEO of Arrow Electronics, his feedback from the board was cursory and unhelpful. Board members were cordial and did not deliver bad news. His solution was for independent directors (seven of the nine directors) to meet with executives outside formal or social functions. Each independent director met with three executives individually to discuss strategy, culture, competitive position, and operations—indicators of CEO performance. The directors met to share insights and organize their feedback to Kaufman under five headings: leadership, strategy, people management, operating metrics, and relationships with external constituencies. Then Kaufman wrote a two-page memo recounting what he heard to make sure of agreement about key points.[16] Kevin Scharer, CEO of Amgen, seeks feedback to face reality by having the head of human resources conduct an evaluation of him and his team, which they write up and present to Scharer and the board. The process can be a bit uncomfortable because there are usually three or four key things that need to be done better.[17] John Donohue, head of eBay, appreciated the twenty pages of written feedback distilled from the assessment team's half-hour interviews with forty partners, which he received every six months in his previous job as CEO of Bain.[18]

Professors typically use a formal system to obtain feedback from students. Their feedback is collected anonymously, so students feel safe that there will be no grade retribution. The formal systems are limited to the predefined questions. When I started giving talks to executive groups, I found the best feedback to be a videotape of my presentation. The same was true of classroom teaching. By simply watching myself on the videotape, I could see exactly how I came across, and it was easy to improve my technique once I saw the picture. The videotapes were far more effective than numerical scores. The videotape is factual, nonjudgmental feedback—the best kind. You can videotape yourself in meetings, for example, to get a direct view of how you come across to others.

If you don't have a formal system for feedback and are not in a position to design one, there are other options for soliciting feedback. When I was associate dean of the business school, I came up with the idea to ask students to meet in small groups to discuss points not covered in the formal feedback systems. For example, a group of three to five students (or direct reports) can discuss among themselves answers to specific questions, and then provide feedback and discuss it face-to-face with the professor (or manager). Although the discussion is face-to-face, each person's opinion is anonymous. I found the feedback from groups to be highly accurate and free of negativity. People appreciated being asked, and they provided feedback that was thoughtful and helpful. Face-to-face meetings allow the receiver of feedback to ask questions to clarify issues.

You can also solicit feedback one-on-one if you have a good relationship with the other person and the questions are well designed. Carol Bartz, Yahoo's CEO, asks simple questions like "How am I doing? What should I do differently?"[19] She keeps probing and makes it safe for people to answer honestly. Marshall Goldsmith, the executive coach, suggests using the question "How can I do better?" to solicit one-on-one feedback. That is a great question, but people have to feel safe in their relationship with you in order to answer honestly.

Your direct reports may also respond well to questions, such as "What would you like me to start doing to help you be more effective?" and "What would you like me to stop doing to help you be more effective?" Most direct reports can answer these questions without fear because the information is about making them more effective; the questions don't ask for critical judgments. When you approach a direct report or colleague with your sincere interest in honest feedback for improving the performance of yourself and others, these questions will provide good results.

With some trepidation, an EMBA student decided to try a feedback conversation with her fiancé. "How can I do better as a partner and future wife?" The answer was hard for her to hear: "Be more direct and less dramatic in important conversations." She told me it took all of her will not to interrupt and defend herself. She reported that as she let her fiancé empty his cup, "My mind opened to his point of view that my overemotional elephant makes important discussions (new house, wedding) more difficult. Hearing this feedback, I now approach each important conversation in a more direct, thought-out manner. My emotions are still there, but they don't take control. The important conversations are now much more fulfilling."

A bigger step for gaining unvarnished feedback is to work with an executive coach. As people move up the organizational hierarchy from individual performer to manager and enterprise leader, social skills and social intelligence become far more important than technical knowledge. Turning people off with a hurtful put-down or a disdainful look has huge consequences. So the challenge of coaching is to change your behavior and to change other people's perception of your behavior. A coach can help you learn about yourself and change enough to convince others about the new you. Eric Schmidt, head of Google, resented the advice to engage a coach. He got over it when he experienced the value of another set of eyes. The coach helped Schmidt think bigger picture and take the long view.[20]

Coaching has become popular because personal change is difficult to accomplish by yourself. Until your inner executive is strong enough to manage your inner elephant, an outside coach is a big help. An executive coach is not a clinical psychologist who wants to understand "why" you act like a jerk. The coach cares only about helping you face the reality of your dysfunctional behavior and then changing it. A coach will typically collect 360° feedback from everyone who knows you, or at least works with you, and then present you with the brutal facts to break through your illusions. Your boss, peers, or subordinates typically will complete numerical rating scales about such behaviors as how you treat people and whether you listen to others, communicate purpose or vision and engage people in it, encourage others, and so on. The coach will collect facts and examples as evidence to support perceptions. After you wake up to the truth, then change can begin. There is nothing mysterious about this process, and you may have experienced it already. Feedback is a key part of helping you see yourself accurately and without bias. If you are a hard case who has damaged others on the way to the top, you may be asked to apologize to people and make amends for your previous behavior.

Vinita Gupta's employees were quitting in droves, and she believed it was partly due to her stiffness and awkwardness. She hated touchy-feely stuff, lacked patience and humor with colleagues, and did not take criticism well. She disdained small talk and had problems with perfectionism. Gupta hired a coach to help her see her shortcomings and do something about them. She learned that she was so focused on the next task that she rarely said hello to anyone in the hallway. As she became aware of her constant frown and understood its impact on employees, she opened to new behaviors. She let herself be videotaped during meetings and presentations. She learned how to approach and sit with employees in the lunchroom, making idle conversation or soliciting information about the company—something she had never done before. Later on, the coach sought feedback from colleagues to see if they noticed a change. They did. Meetings had freer discussions, and Gupta's more frequent social efforts were appreciated. She made enough progress to build a positive corporate atmosphere and sharply reduce turnover.[21]

Keen executives know that coaching feedback works. At YUM Brands, for example, managers are taught to be spontaneous coaches. They are trained to be feedback providers who are direct and to the point to show junior executives how to build teams of enthusiastic participants. When people see, through feedback, that they are ineffective at building a team, YUM will provide a coach to follow the person around and brief him or her on the behavior observed and its effect on people.[22]

Remember This

Solicit Feedback

- Other people see you differently than you see yourself.
- Corporate 360° feedback is a valuable self-awareness tool.
- You can create your own system to provide candid performance feedback:
  - ◻ Videotape yourself or ask for group feedback.
  - ◻ Ask "How can I do better as a _____?"
  - ◻ Ask "What would you like me to start or stop doing in order to help you be more effective?"
- An executive coach will collect realistic feedback and help you change.

Take Advantage of a Setback

Walt Disney once said, "It's important to have a good, hard failure when you're young."[23] He was speaking from experience. Disney reportedly was fired by an advertising agency early in his career for a "singular lack of drawing ability," and an early business venture went bankrupt before Disney experienced a major success. Such business titans as Oprah Winfrey, Martha Stewart, and Ted Turner say that a reversal or two paves the way to success.[24] Bennis and Thomas reported in *Geeks and Geezers* that the common theme among successful leaders was a big failure.[25] The redemptive element of these failures was the personal learning, which made the experience worthwhile. Failure provides remarkably clear, unblemished feedback about you. What better way to face reality and accelerate your leadership growth?

If you are taking risks, a setback will arrive in time. The trick is to learn from it. It has been said that people learn more from failures than from successes. Success reinforces the inner elephant's mental illusions. Pain has a purpose. It is a call to change our attitude, behavior, or thinking—to wake up and know ourselves better. A setback is irrefutable feedback that a behavior is not working. Try as they might, the internal attorney and magician within cannot explain away the reality of a stark failure. I experienced a setback in my first academic job when I was turned down for an early promotion I believed I deserved. The turn-down was analogous to being fired. I was stunned and humiliated. After my anger faded, I had to swallow the bitter pill that I had screwed up. I gradually "got it" that I was the problem, not my colleagues or the system. I was living an illusion of false assumptions that my teaching and research were superior, when in fact they were inferior in the eyes of others. I learned a lot about my shortcomings. Part of my inner elephant died in that humiliation. I never again made naïve assumptions about my work performance. Being forced to face reality was a huge gift.

In my experience, managers abhor setbacks about as much as they abhor death. The inner elephant typically despises anything resembling failure. Only success counts. Do not have a blotch on your record. Keep your nose clean. Chris Argyris said that professionals today rarely experience failure, "And because they have rarely failed, they have never learned how to learn from failure."[26] Yet a person who has a long string of successes may get puffed up. A setback shines the light of a new reality, helping us see facts and ourselves more clearly, and helping us not take ourselves too seriously. One senior executive who got fired twice says it helped him change his brusque, know-it-all management style. He refused to be interviewed by *Fortune* magazine for a story about comebacks because he didn't want to brag about his current success.[27] Ego shattering is one of the gifts that come with a setback.

In recent years, there has been much research on the benefits of adversity, indicating that most people undergo a positive transformation in their values and perspectives after experiencing a trauma or victimizing event. It isn't the event but the suffering and emotional pain that batter and weaken the distorted views of the inner elephant. At some deep level, trauma may actually be good for us. Although the idea that people experience beneficial personal growth (often referred to as posttraumatic growth or paradoxical growth) from such experiences as losing a child, being diagnosed with cancer, or losing their house in a hurricane may seem controversial,[28] there is evidence that life difficulties, challenges, crises, and setbacks can be "engines of wisdom."[29] Rather than return to the previous level of psychological functioning, many victims experience a higher level of functioning. The event enables them to rethink priorities and to be more present in their lives.[30] The inner executive can gain strength and the inner elephant can lose strength during experiences of suffering and adversity. Adversity is a test, the purpose of which is to learn and grow by facing reality.

Spiritual traditions teach the importance of setbacks in helping you see and weaken your inner elephant's illusions and awaken your inner executive. A Zen teacher said, "Having many difficulties perfects the will; having no difficulties ruins the being."[31] The poet Kahlil Gibran wrote that we must know fear and failure to enjoy success: "Your pain is the breaking of the shell that encloses your understanding. Even as the stone of the fruit must break, that its heart may stand in the sun, so must you know pain."[32] Sathya Sai Baba, the spiritual teacher in India, said for us to be like the sugarcane and "welcome the cutting, the hacking and the crushing, the boiling and the straining to which it is subjected; without these ordeals, the cane would dry up and make no tongue sweet. So, too, man must welcome trouble, for that alone brings sweetness to the spirit within."[33]

Shantanu Narayen, head of Adobe Systems, sees failure as simply learning: "someone might look at it and say, you know, that start-up was not successful, and I look at it and I say, 'I learned how to build a team, how to raise money, how to sell a vision, how to create a product.'" The failed start-up was a great stepping stone for him.[34] Anne Busquet lost her job as general manager of American Express's Optima Card unit when some of her employees were found to have deliberately hidden $24 million in losses on Optima Card accounts. As general manager of the unit, she was held accountable. Busquet eventually restored her reputation and worked her way up to executive vice president of consumer card marketing. One of her most significant realizations after she lost the Optima job, Busquet says, was that she expected everyone to be like her—a perfectionist. Busquet learned to face herself realistically by actively soliciting bad news and letting everyone know that mistakes were okay as long as people were open and honest. Her former boss says that the failure helped Busquet become much more patient, a better listener, and more tolerant of people with different work styles.[35]

The inner elephant mistakenly assumes that failure leads to failure and must be avoided at all costs. Not true. In the bigger picture, the pain of failure breeds success, and the feeling of success breeds failure. When you have a failure of some sort, after the pain clears, step back and review what happened. Just remember that you can recover from anything. So why not benefit from the experience? In their book *Firing Back: How Great Leaders Rebound After Career Disaster,* Jeffrey Sonnenfeld and Andrew Ward examined leaders who faced dramatic setbacks in the form of prison time, bankruptcy, public derision, and all sorts of other defeats, yet managed to make a comeback. In every case, the leader made a conscious inner-executive choice to move ahead in a positive fashion rather than to wallow in self-pity or remain stuck in the inner elephant's pattern of resentment and despair. Now that seems the right way to face a setback.

Remember This

Take Advantage of a Setback

- People hate setbacks and typically don't know how to learn from them.
- A setback is a friend to help you learn about yourself.
- View a setback as undistorted feedback and a call to change yourself.
- Terrible setbacks produce profound personal growth.

10

Expand Your Awareness

Wisdom flashes like lightning amidst the clouds of the inner sky—one has to foster the flash and preserve the light.
—Sathya Sai Baba

The first rule is to keep an untroubled spirit. The second is to look things in the face and know them for what they are.
—Marcus Aurelius

ANISH MANAGED AN ENGINEERING GROUP. He had a strong analytical mind and came across to me as thoughtful and gentle. However, he had an edge with employees that sometimes cut deeply. He didn't tell me exactly what he did or said that caused the problem, but he received incisive feedback and was determined to change his behavior. His method was to spend fifteen minutes each evening reviewing the day, searching for moments when he may have said something hurtful to another person or brushed someone off. He was able to get himself into an easy chair each night and think carefully about all his daily transactions. At first it was hard, he said, because he couldn't remember anything. He persevered, and after a few days, he found it easier to remember most things that happened during the day. The interesting thing, he said, was that after three weeks, he was reflecting on incidents a few minutes after they happened, which made the end-of-day routine seem superfluous. After four weeks, he was aware of behavior—especially potentially troublesome behavior—as it happened. He saw the words or actions as they happened. After five weeks, he was aware of the impulses before he acted, so he edited out the negative comment or action. His edge no longer made an appearance. He believed he was cured of the offensive actions that used to upset others.

Review the Day

Anish's focused approach produced a great result. What happened? Anish expanded his self-awareness—his inner executive—by systematically reviewing his day and holding himself accountable. As his awareness expanded, so did his executive presence, which was his ability to be in the present moment during the day rather than act from his impulsive inner elephant. His procedure seemed just right. Anish reviewed the day with no sense of guilt or recrimination. He was an objective observer, almost as if he were watching a video playback of the day in his own mind. He simply faced the reality of his behavior and placed responsibility for it on his own shoulders. He did not judge or get down on himself. As his awareness expanded, he reached the point where he was present enough during the day to see undesired actions before they happened. It seems so simple. You can bring about important behavior change simply by reliving each day in your own mind. The end-of-day review is like resting your oars in the water and looking back over the distance covered. Anish called himself to account objectively for things he had done.

Sinan was a professional athlete before he came back to graduate school. As an athlete he had learned to put failures behind him and move on without regret. Now back in school, he said he was not learning as much as he could. He said that his mental habit of putting "failures" behind him was preventing the examination of why things turned out badly on a paper or exam or during group meetings. He already had the habit of praying silently for a few minutes after he got into bed, a great place to start. After we talked, he decided to add to that prayer time the question "What have I learned today?" When we talked a few days later, he felt good that he remembered to do his mental review each and every night. "The first night was definitely challenging, since my thoughts were all over the place and I could not concentrate on my day. After a few nights, I was able to focus my attention on my day and visualize everything." This took about five days. "Then I was able to take lessons, both positive and constructive, from my day, and apply them to my next day."

I talked to Sinan after a couple more weeks. "I have been performing this exercise every night for over two weeks now, and the results are astonishing! I have definitely taken a number of lessons, both academic and personal, from my daily happenings and applied them to my next day." He was excited about how much he was learning. Hearing his enthusiasm about it was convincing to me.

As another example, a physician colleague would go home frustrated and upset about the ridiculous paperwork requirements of his practice. His cure? After work, he would stop and picture one patient he helped during the day. That brought his stress level down and shifted him into the present moment and out of the negative mood.

Judy, an EMBA student, told me that she had a difficult time relaxing at the end of the day, so she tried this tool of reviewing the day. After sitting still, she at first used a notepad to track thoughts that entered her brain. That really helped her remember episodes, tasks, and feelings that she might have otherwise forgotten. After several days, she built up to a thirty-minute review. She received a benefit she had not expected: a calm and quiet mind. Judy's ability to focus and stay present for thirty minutes weakened her monkey mind. After about six weeks, in a note to me she said,

> I find it invaluable and will continue this. Taking an evening break was not something that I initially enjoyed, but it was a great exercise in teaching me to quiet my mind. Bringing me to account is something that I hope to continue throughout life. It centers my focus and forces me to be honest about my own thoughts, actions, and the reactions of others.

How do you develop the evening habit to review the day? You have to carve out the time. Schedule the review for the same time and place each day, and find a quiet place where you won't be disturbed. Evening works better than late afternoon because the evening mind is quieter. Focus on the day's events starting with early morning, and review the positive as well as negative occurrences. If this is a completely new behavior, it may take some resolve. Perhaps schedule it on your calendar. You may feel resistance from your inner elephant. Pairing your review with another daily activity really helps. Sinan fit his review with a daily prayer habit he had already established.

Nate, a retail store manager, coupled his review with a similar evening exercise he did with his six-year-old son, with benefits to both. Nate and his wife called the evening exercise "high-low." The son would tell the parents about the best and worst parts of the day. They would talk through these experiences and what he might learn from them. So

Dad reviewed his day too. After a couple of weeks, Nate discovered that his own "highs" occurred when he made a more conscious effort to reach out to people on an emotional level. This was new behavior for him, thanks to the daily review. Nate was finding ways to connect with people to develop better relationships. The main pattern of his "lows" related to his mind's persistent habit of finding fault and judging people negatively. However, his wife noticed a change, which was that he voiced fewer criticisms of individuals, although he was still critical toward their behaviors. Nate considered the shift from judging people to judging their behavior a positive first step toward becoming more open minded.

Dante found an evening review of his daily positive and negative actions helpful for achieving his goal for self-improvement, which was to become more "intentional." He concluded that the negative actions during the day were closely associated with the behavior of his inner elephant, and his positive behaviors were closely associated with his inner executive. Some of his positive, executive-type behaviors included the following:

Took time to play with children even though he had pressing work

Cleaned up after dinner so that his wife got a break

Listened carefully to an upset employee

Initiated a difficult conversation with a peer he had been avoiding

Presented a process improvement idea to his general manager

Successfully used listening techniques with colleagues and family

His negative, elephant-type behaviors included the following:

Hit the snooze button and had to rush his kids to school

Had an argument with his wife about taking the kids to school

Overreacted to a schedule change made by his secretary

Arrived late to meetings

Failed to submit a status report on time

Forgot to pay a credit card bill on time and incurred a penalty

Jumped to a wrong conclusion about the actions of two direct reports

Dante claimed that his heightened awareness and presence strengthened his inner executive and his positive behaviors. He said, "It is easy for me to remain immersed in work all day and never bring my head above water to see what is happening. The daily review helped me see and do the right things."

Rick concluded that he suffered from unrealistic optimism because he never achieved everything he set out to accomplish during a day. Rick used the evening review mainly to review negative actions he had taken each day. One recurring theme "was not allowing conversations with my direct reports to play out. I would interrupt and give advice prematurely." Another theme was his "focus on action and execution and failing to recognize the need to communicate the big picture of vision and direction. Even when I tried to listen, my elephant would have me thinking about next actions. On the positive side, I stopped doing e-mail when listening to others."

What happened with Rick's unrealistic optimism?

> After reviewing the day for several days, I feel good about how hard I am working, avoiding procrastination on difficult tasks, and building a disciplined schedule. My expectation of constant action was indeed unrealistic. I am trying to do less, and accomplishing more, because I feel more present and seem to be working from a bigger picture. I am also more relaxed in the evening to spend time with my six-year-old daughter.

Brenda had a different idea for her end-of-day review—she used it to plan the next day. Brenda enrolled in the EMBA program while running her own business, the equivalent of two full-time jobs. As she tried to review the day, her mind would fret about unfinished business and start worrying about the next day. So she went ahead and started a to-do list for the next day, or even several days ahead. Emptying her mind onto a to-do list "alleviated my stress. I was no longer worrying about all the things I was unable to accomplish that day. Accordingly, I focused my time on making a to-do list every night before bed. After just one week, I found myself going to bed earlier with less stress." The end-of-day review can serve the additional purpose of planning the day ahead, relieving stress, and calming your mind.

So, what happens if you are drawn to the idea of an evening review, but your inner elephant will not cooperate? Maybe it wants to do other things and won't sit still, or it keeps forgetting about it. You can use any of the tools and techniques described in other chapters. All it takes is to find a quiet spot and allow yourself to relax and think about your day. If that does not work, an especially effective trick to get yourself to review the day every day is to use a partner, which was mentioned in Chapter Seven. Marshall Goldsmith, author of *What Got You Here Won't Get You There,* suggests developing a list of review-the-day questions about behaviors you want to change or sustain, and asking your partner to call and ask those questions each evening. The partner's phone call overcomes the potential resistance or forgetfulness of your inner elephant. The calls should be brief, and ideally you would ask each other a short list of questions, be supportive, and get off the phone after five minutes.

As discussed in Chapter Seven, I assign student partners to ask daily review questions in my Leading Change class for MBAs. I ask them to change something about themselves as a metaphor for trying to change an organization. To help overcome their resistance to change, I assign everyone a partner to call and ask review questions each evening. As an experiment, I have asked students to try to change their behavior without a review-the-day phone call for a week or two, and then with a partner's phone calls for three weeks. The difference is clear. Most students tell me that having a partner to ask questions helps them review and be aware of daily efforts; otherwise they don't change behavior at all. The daily questions also help them feel accountable to themselves and to their partner.

Reviewing the day requires a dose of intelligent will from your inner executive. Until your inner executive is stronger, your own willpower can be supplemented with a partner. Goldsmith's questions are a great place to start when you review the day and hold yourself accountable. They reflect Goldsmith's focus on constantly improving his own sense of well-being, getting enough exercise and eating healthy food because he is on the road so much, showing positive affect toward others, making sure he spends some time writing, and dropping habits that annoy others. The following are some of Goldsmith's short-answer questions he asks of himself:[1]

> How happy are you?
>
> How much walking [how many push-ups, sit-ups] did you do?
>
> Did you eat any high-fat foods?
>
> How much time did you spend watching TV or surfing the Internet?
>
> How much time did you spend writing?
>
> Did you do or say something nice for your wife?
>
> How many times did you try to prove you were right when it wasn't worth it?

It is smart to follow a similar tack with your own daily review. Choose questions that will serve to increase your awareness about the key events of the day, especially with respect to desired changes. Here are some questions my students have used to review their days:

> Did you work out today? For how long?
>
> If not, what prevented you from working out?

Did you meditate (or pray) this morning?

How did you feel afterward?

Did you prepare a meal at home today?

How many fruits and vegetables did you eat today?

Did you phone or e-mail friends today?

Did you participate in a class discussion today?

Did you reach out to someone at work today? How?

Did you participate in a non-work-related networking activity today?

The best questions are simple and factual, and typically suited to yes-no answers. Goldsmith's point is to use the questions as targeted reminders about the day, which increase awareness of what you were doing and thereby hold you accountable. If it takes more than a few minutes to respond to questions from a partner, you are unlikely to continue the calls because they take too much time. With a partner, there is not time for a deep, soul-searching inquiry. When reviewing the day alone, however, you can take time to focus on and visualize events, which trains your mind to concentrate and will also increase your awareness of events as they happen during the day.

• TRY THIS •

Review the Day

1. At the same time each evening, find a quiet place to sit comfortably.

2. Close your eyes and relax.

3. Recall the day; see the events in your mind.

4. Notice events that went well, and those that you want to improve.

5. Dwell a bit on situations you would like to improve. See details of what transpired.

6. Ask yourself, *What are recurring themes in my day?*

7. If you need some support, work with a partner to help maintain daily review discipline.

8. Provide your partner with specific questions to ask.

9. After your review, consider planning and visualizing the next day.

10. Notice how your behavior changes each day.

The point of reviewing the day is to identify a few things that will improve your behavior and performance, things you know to do that you are not doing, and things you are doing that you prefer not to do. Arrange for a partner to help if you can't review the day on your own. With or without a partner, reviewing the day is a powerful exercise. You can break free from your elephant's bad habits and sharply increase your self-awareness and hence strengthen your inner executive.

I consider reviewing the day one of the most powerful techniques I teach people. There are multiple benefits, from changing a specific behavior to quieting your mind and relaxing your body. It increases your self-awareness and your presence in the moment. If you start the habit of reviewing your day every evening, you will soon notice a change. Other people will notice the new you.

Contemplate Creatively

At a dinner party one evening, I asked the Nashville songwriter sitting beside me where his songwriting ideas came from. He responded immediately, "the space in between my thoughts." A pretty deep answer, I thought. Another songwriter said his ideas often came during quiet moments when his mind was doing something else. I think they both were saying the same thing.

When do your "aha" moments occur? Think about times when you had a good idea. When or where do you get your best ideas? When I ask a roomful of managers this question, the most common answer is "in the shower." Other popular answers are while driving, exercising, or upon waking in the morning. The point is that good ideas most often appear in your mind during *pauses* in your day, when your mind is not filled with racing thoughts. The morning shower was often a creative time for me, but recently it is has been when I exercise. Over Christmas break, I managed to exercise on my elliptical every day for two weeks when working on this book. I had new ideas every single day while exercising. Ideas popped up unexpectedly—a new way to organize material, a better name for a chapter, adding something I forgot, a new insight—that were important enough to write down so I wouldn't forget.

Many managers are not wired for quiet time or reflection. Their temperaments are suited to fast action and decisiveness. Do you try to use every single moment of every day? Most managers do. They are crazy busy, as in a boot camp. The performance pressures are so great, the deadlines so near, they can't slow down. And they love the fast pace. Reflection may sound like wasteful navel gazing when there is real work to do. Who wants to be a monk contemplating a flower?

Well, the whole point of reflection is to slow down for a moment, focus your attention on an issue or experience in need of a creative response, and discover an answer within yourself. When you slow down and have space between your thoughts, you will find better, more creative answers. You can expand your awareness, and your creativity, by making more space in your own mind.

Most managers see themselves as below average in creativity, but with a little practice, anyone can increase his or her creativity through intentional reflection. Matt was a senior IT manager and was serious about finding time during the heat of daily battles with IT users to "reflect." "When moving to Chicago, I resented the thought of a forty-minute commute. Now I use that time to think through the problems on my mind and the ideas that come to me in the morning. The drive lets me do a quick sort of the good from the bad. I may retrace my thinking when I can snatch a few minutes during the day, such as walking to get a cup of coffee or even going to the bathroom." Matt uses the time before work, and pauses during the day, to look within, generate ideas, and probe more deeply into his thinking.

John Donohue, CEO of eBay, takes a periodic day away. He takes few calls because it is a "thinking" day. "It's a day to just get away and step back and reflect. And I find that very hard to do in the office or in a familiar environment. I find that if I don't schedule a little bit of structured time away, where there's no interruption, that it's fairly hard to get the kind of thinking time and reflection time that I think is so important."[2] Anne Mulcahy, when CEO of Xerox, was at the gym by 6:00 A.M. and in her office by 7:15, giving her an hour before meetings to get organized for the day. Although executives complain about the amount of travel, "time on planes probably is critically important to doing our jobs. It's time to be reflective. It's time to catch up. It's time to really be thoughtful and communicate."[3]

Wendy Kopp, founder and CEO of Teach For America, says that she reflects an hour each week on her overall plan for herself: "What do I need to do to move my priorities forward? And then there are the 10 minutes a day that I spend thinking about, 'OK, so based on the priorities for the week, how am I going to prioritize my day tomorrow?' I don't know how I could do what I do without spending that time." In a world that is moving faster and faster, Kopp uses quiet time to clarify her intentions and stay proactive rather than become reactive.[4]

Things move so fast that often you may not know what you really think or feel about an issue. Reflection makes your mind proactive rather than reactive, engaging and developing the inner executive. Reflection is often a mental examination of your own thoughts and feelings, your own experience. A reflective mind can look at itself as an observer. Reflection is easier in a slower moment where you can create space in your mind to focus on a single issue. You can explore the hard drive on your inner computer that stores your values, goals, predicaments, and life experiences. Reflection seeks connections, discrepancies, meanings. The inward focus allows new ideas and answers to arise into your awareness, and adds new meaning to observations, facts, ideas, and experiences.[5]

Reflection is also a choice: that of thoughtful wisdom over instant reaction. The idea of reflection is to find deeper understanding of cause-and-effect relationships, because organizational problems often are more complex than they look. For example, manager Rick Smith resisted the advice of his boss, Jack Welch, to look at risks similar to those at another division, which had unexpectedly lost much of its value. Confident and certain, Smith charged ahead without contemplating the risks, and learned a year later there were indeed many similar issues—a costly mistake.[6] Greg Brenneman, chairman of CCMP Capital, places a lot of emphasis on whether his CEOs think things through. He asks CCMP's CEOs how they would increase earnings 20 percent: What levers would they pull? "Some CEO's will say, 'I'm going to do one, two, three, four, five.' And you listen and say 'Yeah, that makes sense.'" He said some top managers look at him as though he came from Mars, and others filibuster him with thirty minutes of buzzwords.[7] These are people to worry about because they haven't taken the time to reflect or are not able to think through their business.

Reflection is an interesting collaboration between your inner executive and inner elephant. Your inner elephant has a lifetime of experiences stored within. Yet it typically responds to immediate situations with fast reactions, it welcomes distractions, and its impulse is to move on to the next new thing. The elephant has no way to consciously sort out the themes and lessons from all that experience. The key is to use your inner executive to intentionally focus on a single issue or topic and stay focused until an answer bubbles up from the experience stored within. This is using your executive to awaken your creative intuition. It requires both focus and a "pause." The pause allows space between thoughts for the new idea. The creative idea will not arise when your mind is racing about other things. Your mind has to stay focused on the topic.

One student in an MBA program at another university disliked all the required group work. Her assignment was to spend time reflecting on the issue. "My whole perspective has changed now. I see group work as, first, a great opportunity to meet people; second, an opportunity to develop trusting relationships; third, an opportunity to become a better person; and fourth, an opportunity to gather the talents and resources others have to create something that I would never have been able to do on my own."[8] Her experience with reflection helped transform her thinking about group work.

A tough personal decision, such as whether to accept a transfer overseas while children are in high school, can lead to sleepless nights. An inward investigation, in which you weigh alternatives and get in touch with your deepest feeling, is a source of a better personal decision. Reflection awakens your deeper intuition. You can engage in a similar reflective inquiry when your gut tells you that something is wrong at work. Focusing inward to listen and discern the source of the negative feeling can bring the cause into the light.

Another time when reflection has great value is when you need to learn from an experience, especially a difficult one. Reflection can unlock the deeper meaning to be taken from a setback or failure. T. S. Eliot wrote, "We had the experience but missed the meaning."[9] Don't miss the meaning of your experiences. You learn more as a leader in difficult times than in good times. Taking the time to reflect back over an experience is worthwhile to make sense of the event and understand its higher meaning.

• • •

A simple exercise I use to teach reflection to managers is to ask them to focus on a specific issue for which they do not have an immediate answer. The pause required is only a few minutes for quiet focus and reflection. For example, I might ask, "What does it mean to manage by letting things happen rather than by making things happen?" I ask them to turn over that idea in their mind slowly and repeat some form of the question: What . . . does . . . it . . . mean . . . to . . . let . . . things . . . happen? Repeating it slowly in the mind keeps the focus on the idea. Leaving some space between words gives room for an answer to arise. The trick is to be patient and wait for the answer to bubble up from within.

> One manager had a revelation that he could manage his people more like he plays golf. His golf game improved when he learned to "let it happen" rather than force each shot.
>
> Another manager realized that rather than assign duties to people, he could ask what people are interested in and let them work according to their natural motivation. He would not have to push people so hard and supervise so closely.
>
> Yet another manager said he could let things happen by just slowing down his reactions. His challenge was in knowing how to interact

with Brazilian businesspeople. "I can react in a fraction of a second and then realize, wait a minute, they think completely different. Give their ideas room. Let me try to understand where they're coming from and encourage where I can, rather than shoot down everything different from the United States viewpoint."

Another manager discovered a farm analogy in her mind—the farmer can't make corn grow, and a manager cannot make people grow. She has to provide opportunity and support just as the farmer provides water, fertilizer, and weed control. She decided to focus more on providing the right conditions to develop desired outcomes rather than expect people to work based on command.

In these cases, each manager's inner awareness expanded to awaken new solutions. Just thinking before responding can make a huge difference.

Another reflection exercise you can try is to contemplate one of the following questions until you receive an answer. "What is my relationship to solitude?" Think about what solitude means to you. "How do I spend time alone?" "What distractions do I use to keep myself away from solitude?" I have assigned reflection time to MBA students to use however they want. One of the top students in our program started scheduling time weekly, on Sunday morning, during which he said the reflection strengthened his intention to do his best. As another student's awareness expanded during the exercise, he suddenly saw that he had not been a very good husband. During the quiet time, he was able to step back and appreciate his wife's contributions and sacrifices. He used that discovery to get out of his head and demonstrate his heartfelt appreciation to her, which he said relieved both his stress and the tension in their relationship. Another student discovered she had skipped the contemplation phase of a project while rushing to the action phase. She had lost motivation because the project was not producing results. More reflection on the front end would have produced a better result.

You can also reflect on things outside yourself, which is great practice. One student strengthened her reflection while reading a book by pausing frequently to think about what she had just read. It took some practice, but by the second book, the reflection became part of her reading experience: "The new ideas that came up stayed with me and helped me remember the material." Another student used reflection time to expand his awareness outward. He was able to see patterns on mosaic tiles and hear a gentle humming sound at night while walking past a light pole. He heard the sound of his feet on the sidewalk and noticed the deep green of the grass. He felt a breeze on his cheek and heard the joyful shout of someone in the distance. He spent only five to ten minutes a day with this expanded awareness, and he claimed that he was much more alert and focused from the practice.

• TRY THIS •

Contemplate Creatively

Reflection is proactive rather than reactive. Use your intention for the following steps because your inner elephant may resist.

1. Schedule a break somewhere in the day; allow five to ten minutes.
2. Focus on the topic, repeating the thought slowly in your mind.
3. Stay focused on one topic or thought, allowing fresh ideas to arise.
4. Make note of creative insights, meanings, and solutions.
5. Welcome thoughtful wisdom in place of instant reaction.

The point of contemplation is to expand your awareness to allow your imaginative insights to arise; to find your deeper wisdom; and to inspire creative responses to solve a problem, make a decision, set direction, interpret an event, or give advice. The process is simple enough: find a quiet moment to keep your mind focused on the topic or issue at hand. You can slowly repeat a question to yourself to reflect more deeply and thus draw out your buried intuition. This will awaken the best of your creativity and wisdom. With periodic reflection, your mind's awareness expands, your executive presence increases, and your intention sharpens.

PART FIVE

•

Reach for the Heights

•

11

•

Sharpen Your Concentration

A man's mind may be likened to a garden, which may be intelligently cultivated or allowed to run wild.
—James Allen

Love the moment and the energy of the moment will spread beyond all boundaries.
—Corita Kent

WARREN BUFFETT ACCEPTED AN INVITATION from his good friend Katharine Graham of the *Washington Post* to spend a weekend with some of her friends at a remote vacation home. Several successful people from the Seattle area, such as Bill Gates's parents, were to be there, as was Bill Gates himself. Both Gates and Buffet had reputations for being impatient with idle talk, and they hit it off with each other, spending several hours in conversation. At dinner Bill Gates Sr. posed a question to the table: What factor did people feel was the most important in getting to where they had gotten in life? Warren Buffett said it was his "focus." Bill Gates gave the same answer.[1]

Warren Buffett understands focus. He spends long hours focused on financial statements, the *Wall Street Journal,* and digging into other data that give him insight into the financial workings and value of corporations. Bill Gates has the same quality. This is a Thomas Edison–type laser focus that can be concentrated on a topic for hours, days, weeks, and months, until a problem is solved or an issue resolved, a book is written, or a new advertising campaign is completed. Whatever these people do, they do with every ounce of their attention and energy.

The Warren Buffet–Bill Gates capacity for focus or concentration is not the norm. Many managers I work with say they are too easily distracted by e-mails and phone calls. They find it hard to hold their focus on individual projects. They tend to be poor listeners because their minds do not stay focused on the person across from them. In meetings, they often want to shift the subject to talk about whatever comes into their mind rather than stick to the agenda. When writing up a project, they may break away frequently to walk around, check the Internet or their e-mail, or find a snack. They may put off writing reports that require focus and concentration until the very last minute, preferring instead to welcome every interruption, e-mail, phone call, person, or problem that pops up during the day, which of course happens a lot.

The typical inner elephant is not built to stay on task. It is conditioned to respond to stimuli in the environment, which is why it loves distractions. A study by the business research firm Basex said that workers lose 28 percent, more than two hours, of an average day to distractions.[2] Someone who works at a computer will click on favorite Web sites an average of forty times a day. There is incredible opportunity for personal distraction with PDAs, phones, e-mails, projects, problems, and employees, all of which want attention. Indeed, it is easy to blame these intrusions for one's lack of focus. Surely the reason for our short attention span lies in increased external temptations, brought on by electronic media as well as food, drink, television, and anything else our mind has a hankering for.

Don't believe that the problem lies outside you. That is your inner magician making up a logical explanation to justify your behavior. Your inner elephant wants these distractions. It yearns for something new and different in order to escape from the present moment. The inner elephant dislikes the here and now, preferring immersion in thoughts or fantasies about the future or past where it is more comfortable, particularly when facing a difficult task. How long can you sit quietly at home without turning on the television; reading a report, magazine, or book; or engaging in conversation? How much time do you spend in a hotel room without watching TV or going online? The distractions we face in the physical and electronic world do not have eyes to see us or hands to grab us. The inner elephant notices and grabs at distractions.

It chooses distractions. It cannot sit still. If there is not a distraction, your mind will create one. It keeps switching radio stations trying to find a better song. We are prisoners of our inner elephant's desire for distraction.

Whatever catches our attention is the master of our attention. The inner elephant has no will except to pursue its likes and avoid its dislikes, which makes it something of a slave to our senses and outer distractions. If you have ever tried to resist a strong impulse or craving, you know what I mean about being a slave. When our attention is drawn to whatever has the strongest pull, we are not in control.[3]

But there is hope, because focus and concentration can be learned, with guidance from your inner executive. The idea of focus or concentration is to take control and be master of your own attention. Then you can achieve extended focus despite the so-called distractions. The frozen gaze that Tiger Woods uses on the golf course is an example. Woods has issues off the golf course, but on the course he can mute the chatter in his head with intense concentration. When walking close to fans reaching out to touch him, he doesn't reach back, maintaining a fixed gaze. Woods can stay focused for hours doing practice swings or physical exercise. He is said to rest his mind during competition by fixing it on flowers, plants, or birds. When Tiger was a child, his father would disturb him midswing by pushing over a golf bag, throwing pebbles at him or the ball, or jingling his keys to build his concentration and imperturbability.[4]

Focus Your Attention

When I speak of focus or concentration, I really mean the intentional focus of your attention. William James defined attention as "taking possession by the mind, in clear and vivid form, of one out of what seem several simultaneously possible objects or trains of thought."[5] Focusing your attention means to shine the light of your consciousness on a subject for an extended period of time. Your attention is always occupied with something, such as when you are lost in the thoughts streaming through your mind. Think of it this way: whatever occupies your attention is *where* you are and *what* you are at that moment. The inner elephant's attention is typically captured and driven by what it likes and dislikes in the external world. It often roams unconsciously until it strikes on something that attracts or repulses it. Then it is caught there until it shifts to something else.

Concentration is one-pointed attention on an item or task. For practice, some people sit quietly and focus on one item such as a flower or an image on the wall. Learning to concentrate takes conscious effort, some force or willpower to bring your attention to bear on one thing. This is building the muscle of your inner executive. Moreover, concentrated focus on one thing puts up a barrier of sorts so that other thoughts and distractions are less likely to intrude. Without concentration, your mind will be drawn here and there haphazardly. With concentration, it can be undisturbed by external distractions or random thoughts from within. The object of your focus fills up the mental space, so there is less room for random thoughts or obsessing about desires, problems, and difficulties. For an example of focus, imagine yourself in a blacked-out room in which there is a poisonous snake. Your attention will be focused on that one thing.

I am talking about intentional concentration, which is concentration *on purpose*. Watching an engaging movie or reading a favorite novel for an hour is not the concentration we want to achieve. This is the inner elephant's concentration because it is pulled toward an attractive and interesting stimulus. The concentration of the inner executive is based on *intention* rather than attraction. You are training your mind to pay attention. Concentration means you can stay focused even if the object does not attract you.[6] This is similar to the concentration required by military personnel in Iraq who stay alert to small roadside bombs. The effort can be exhausting until the mind gets in shape with repeated practice.

Remember This

Focus Your Attention

- You can achieve great success through prolonged focus of attention.
- Focus directs your attention on purpose.
- Your inner elephant welcomes distractions.
- Whatever has your attention is where and what you are.
- Intentional focus will block out distractions from within and without.

Focus on Means, Not Ends

During a personal coaching session, Olaf described to me his ability to set and achieve personal goals. I was amazed. He achieved many things, such as running a marathon, reading all the great books, buying a house, climbing a mountain, racing cars, getting good grades, and so on. He was equally focused on achieving goals at work. But, he said, "You know, these accomplishments don't last. Once it's over, the satisfaction disappears. I sometimes wonder, 'what's the point?'" Despite all his accomplishments, Olaf felt empty inside soon after achieving each goal. I thought Olaf's insight was significant. Goal achievements didn't provide the deeper satisfaction he was seeking. We talked about shifting his exclusive focus away from the goal outcome, which he achieved with grit and determination, and learning to enjoy the process of the journey. He was charging through activities he didn't particularly like just to reach a goal. The key to increasing his satisfaction lay in where he placed his focus. Could he focus on something he liked doing, regardless of the outcome?

A good way to improve concentration is to shift your attention away from future goals to the present moment. Recall from Chapter Four that the elephant prefers the reward at the end of a task rather than enjoying the task itself. One way to practice concentration is to focus attention on what is right here, right now, and to immerse in that. The inner elephant is constantly jumping around in hopes of finding new rewards or fulfilling itself in some way. It is constantly changing channels in the hope of finding a TV program it enjoys. But lasting satisfaction does not arrive in the future. Your inner executive is able to be in the now, and can sustain focus because it is less concerned with future rewards.

Managers often become obsessed with their goals, forgetting that engagement with the present moment will hold their attention. It is good to have a goal or purpose in the back of your mind, but as a secondary rather than primary focus. Too strong a focus on the goal means that achieving the goal is more important than the quality of the process through which the goals are reached. To the extent that we are more interested in *having* than in *being*, and in *what* we achieve rather than *how* we achieve, we can easily fall into excessively goal-oriented thinking and lose the focus and enjoyment of performing a task. You can enjoy performing your job well regardless of external rewards. Richard Anderson, CEO of Delta Airlines, gave this advice about careers: "If you just focus on getting your job done and being a good colleague and a team player in an organization, and not focused about being overly ambitious and wanting pay raises and promotions and the like, and just doing your job and being part of a team, the rest of it all takes care of itself."[7] Colin Powell would give this advice to a second lieutenant who aspired to become a general: "Doing your best in the present moment has to be the rule. You won't become a general unless you become a good first lieutenant."[8] You are more likely to achieve a long-term goal like "making it" if you focus on the quality and enjoyment of doing rather than on the reward.

Many spiritual traditions teach followers to engage in actions without expecting rewards, as if the actions are in service to a higher power. In other words, stop worrying so much about the goal. The focus on means is not the inner elephant's way, but is an effective way to learn to concentrate on the task at hand. The reward, if any, is left up to a higher power, which could be the organization or a divine entity. In sacred art, for example, performance is an offering to the Divine; it is not intended for personal enhancement. In a perfect scenario you do not worry about the fruits of your action—you just give your attention to the action itself. The fruits will take care of themselves.

The mind can handle only one thing at a time. Detachment from the reward is actually your detachment from the inner elephant's selfish want, which frees the inner executive to concentrate intensely by immersing in performing the activity fully and completely. Focusing on *how* you do the activity in this moment enables greater concentration than thinking about what you may obtain in reward. When only the end goal counts, you may have to force yourself through the means, which increases resistance and reduces focus and performance. When you focus on the means, your attention flows into the activity on its own, requiring less effort and sustaining itself for a longer period. The satisfaction from the goal result is short lived, as Olaf discovered.

You can build up to your focus on the means in steps. With practice, not only will your concentration be sharper but also your enjoyment will be high and your performance better. For example, professional athletes are trained to keep their mind focused in the moment, which is the next play or the next swing. If a golfer is thinking about how making or missing the putt will affect the final score, her concentration is gone. The best results come when an athlete focuses on nothing but execution in this moment and letting the results just happen as they will.[9]

Remember This

Focus on Means, Not Ends

- The inner elephant tends to focus on rewards.
- Improved focus occurs in the present moment, when we pay attention to the means instead of the ends.
- Build up your ability to focus through repeated practice.
- Let go of focusing on outcomes; they will happen on their own.

Slow Down, Look, and Listen

A Sufi teacher using the Diamond Approach taught a group of us how to "sense, look, and listen," or what I think of as "slow down, look, and listen." The idea is to stop and pay attention to what is going on around you, or to slow down and watch carefully whatever you are doing. A good place to start is with a simple task you have to do routinely but find tedious and uninteresting. Perhaps it is a task you rush through to get it over with. The task could be grocery shopping, preparing or eating a meal, cleaning the garage, fixing something around the house, folding the laundry, filling the dishwasher, or taking a shower.

The trick to increasing your focus is to slow down your physical actions. One example is the golf instructor who asks students to practice taking ninety seconds to complete their swing. This enables the golfer to be aware of every aspect of his swing and for the instructor to see any flaws. Another example is martial arts. To help people master the defensive moves to use under pressure of attack, Richard Machowicz makes people move in slow motion.[10] Slower than normal physical speed helps keep the mind focused. Slow-speed rehearsal helps condition the body to ignore flight-or-fight impulses in an emergency.

For your activities, slow down to the three-quarter or even one-half speed and focus on what you are doing, what you see and feel, what you hear. If you are walking upstairs in the morning to wake up a child, walk slowly and feel the touch of your foot on each step, feel the muscles contract and loosen in your legs, feel your hand on the banister, feel the movement of your body. What do you see around you? What do you hear from within or without? Maintain the slower speed for a several minutes. Do you still feel in a hurry to complete the task? What is your level of satisfaction when you slow down and pay attention?

Practice focus and concentration when eating a meal. This means eating alone so that conversation will not distract you. It also means no reading, television, or iPod. Eat slowly and consciously, paying attention to what you are doing. Feel the touch of the fork in your hand. Look at the fork carefully. Look deeply into your food. Notice its color and texture. What else do you see? Sense the touch of the food or fork in your mouth. Try to sense saliva being produced; the food disintegrating in your mouth; the chewing motion; the smell, taste, and texture of the food. How many flavors do you recognize? Bring the same level of concentration to each bite and to each sip of drink. Try closing your eyes while chewing. Try to sense the hunger feelings in your stomach. When does the hunger end? At what point do you feel full?

Try bringing the same level of focus to folding the laundry or washing your hands. Slow down and sense everything you feel, taste, see, smell, and hear. Practice focus while sitting at your desk by doing the following exercise. Look forward. What do you see? Perhaps a chair, book, phone, cup, or papers? Engage your curiosity. Look carefully at the color, shape, and context of the object. See one or more objects on or near your desk with fresh eyes of focus for about thirty seconds. Now turn your head to the right. Again, focus on an object with fresh eyes. Can your mind see beneath the surface of the object within your focus? What is the shape and color? Persist for about thirty seconds. Now turn your head to the left and repeat for thirty seconds. Now just sit quietly for a few minutes, with eyes closed, and *listen*. What do you hear around you that you did not notice before? Listen carefully for several minutes.

One of my MBA students reported the following:

> I took time to practice concentration in several ways. One example is when I focused on just brushing my teeth slower than usual. I focused on the movement of the brush against my teeth, the feeling of toothpaste on my teeth, and the work of my hand as it moved the brush in and out. What I found is that at first it was hard to push away other thoughts that wanted to crowd my mind. But as I continued to focus on the task I was able to truly recognize the details of what I was doing. I become more curious about the task at hand when I completely focused on it.

Another student said,

> I thought about every motion that went into taking a sip of water from my cup. I became aware that my mind sends signals to every part of my body to work in unison—my arm brought the glass to my mouth, my mouth opened and my hand tilted the cup. My tongue filtered the water through my teeth and my throat controlled the amount of water that passed through. When thinking about this routine yet complicated process, I had no time to think about anything else.

It is paradoxical that slowing down and spending more time doing an uninteresting activity increases both your ability to concentrate on it and your enjoyment—a pretty good deal. Shifting your attention from finishing to being present in the doing is the key. As an experiment, pick a simple task that you have been putting off, such as washing a pile of dirty laundry or sweeping the garage. Use your inner executive's intention to bring your attention to the present moment's "doing." That is the secret.

Slowing down helps you focus and get into the moment. The doing will take you to the completion of your goal, but your concentration is on the now and how rather than on getting it over with. The more minutely you can focus on every sensation associated with doing a task, the stronger and more persistent your focus will become. Every task is equally enjoyable when your mind is fully engaged.

• • •

Another way to improve your concentration is to relax. If your body and mind are tense, tight, nervous, annoyed, restless, upset, fearful, or angry, then your mind is agitated; thoughts are flooding in, ruining your concentration. The inner elephant is in charge during moments of agitation and is difficult to control. It will have its way rather than focus on what you want. Try performing an important task after a period of relaxation. Perhaps start writing a report first thing in the morning upon awakening. A good mechanism is to perform an important task during the first ninety minutes in the morning. This is your most intentional time because resistance is low, so don't waste it on e-mails and the Internet. Undertake a new initiative after returning from vacation relaxed and refreshed.

People relax in different ways. I discussed progressive muscle relaxation in Chapter Seven, which works for many people. Sit comfortably and tighten and relax each muscle group. The more relaxed your body, the fewer thoughts flooding in, and the easier to concentrate. Another approach I recommended was to just "let go" for several minutes. Sit comfortably in a chair, close your eyes, and try to let go from within your body and mind. Let go from the inside out. Just feel like you are letting go from within each leg and each arm, and from within your torso. After a brief period of relaxation, your mind will be refreshed to concentrate on the task at hand.

The blood pressure of my friend Ben, a consultant, is above normal. He lives with a high level of tension. When his blood pressure reads too high at the doctor's office, he asks for a moment and shifts his concentration down into his body to let go of internal stress and tightness. When the doctor retakes his blood pressure, it typically squeaks into the normal range. As your body relaxes and your mind focuses, the thoughts jumping into your mind will slow down. When the inner elephant is relaxed, concentration is better. Your inner executive can assert purposeful concentration more easily. Try closing your eyes and letting go right now for five minutes and see what happens.

> ## Remember This
>
> ### *Slow Down, Look, and Listen*
> - Practice focus by slowing down routine tasks to three-quarter speed.
> - See every moment of the activity.
> - An uninteresting activity becomes interesting when you are focused on the present moment.
> - You can focus better when you are relaxed and rested.
> - Perform important tasks first thing in the morning.

Focus on People

Carlos was a big hulk of a man, a regional manager of commercial sales for a tire manufacturer. He understood relationship marketing and the importance of listening carefully to customers. He encouraged his people to build relationships with customers, but admitted to personally having a difficult time with listening. Carlos told me that his mind jumped around while a customer or direct report was speaking. He admitted that sometimes he missed key points. Carlos was in an international executive program in which I gave instruction on how to increase focus when communicating with another person.

There are two times when we are most likely to revert to unconscious and unfocused attention with other people: when we first meet someone and when the other person is talking. There are a couple of easy rules to follow to maintain focus when first meeting someone. The first is to practice identifying the eye color of the person whom you are meeting. Narrowing your focus makes it easier to pay attention. The second step is to repeat the person's name in the first sentence you speak. This additional action will keep you present during the initial conversation. You are more likely to remember key details about the person.

When you are meeting a person you already know, such as a spouse, employee, or child, use the thirty-second rule. Rather than fall into your normal mode of casual interaction, use your inner executive to focus completely on the person for thirty seconds. Give him or her your full attention. Make eye contact. Ask questions. Listen. Be interested. You can maintain this intentional focus for thirty seconds if you fix your resolve ahead of time, perhaps while you are driving home or to work. Set your intention and then try it with the next person you meet. See what happens when you really focus on someone. You can do anything for thirty seconds. After thirty seconds, move on to your normal behavior. These simple elements of personal focus are fun to practice in the classroom, and they are relatively easy to try on your own. With a little intention, you will increase focus on the first meeting and develop a new habit.

Staying focused while listening to another person talk can be more challenging, especially if your inner elephant has heard any of it before. When the conversation is familiar, the inner elephant's habit is to start thinking about a response, or it skips to something else entirely. I teach and practice how to keep the mind focused, but there are times when my mind drifts. If my wife and I are having a conversation, the familiar voice and a familiar topic may trigger my mind shifting to another thought. When that happens, my eyes glaze over (a dead giveaway), and Dorothy immediately says, "Dick, are you listening to me?" "Yes, dear, I heard what you said," I respond, and try to paraphrase something. An unfocused mind can jump away at any time.

The three exercises I use to help managers improve concentration and keep their mind from drifting while listening to another person are to (1) narrow their visual focus, (2) paraphrase, and (3) ask five questions. In the classroom, managers choose a partner for these exercises and later try them outside the classroom on their own.

Narrow Your Visual Focus

As noted earlier, to narrow visual focus, I coach people to focus on the pupil of the speaker's left eye. Focusing more narrowly helps concentrate your attention more than looking generally at the face, nose, mouth, or whatever is your habit. The more precise your focus, the easier it is to maintain. I took tennis lessons while in graduate school. My eyes would see the ball coming over the net, but my mind would jump away prior to the ball's contact with the racket, causing a few bad hits. The tennis instructor said, "Tell me which way the ball is spinning as it comes over the net." I had to focus more narrowly to see direction of the spin, and lo and behold, I was able to watch the ball into my racket. When I watched for the spin, the mistakes declined sharply. Gazing into the left eye while listening provides the same increased focus. Your mind is less likely to jump away.

Narrowing your focus on the pupil may take a little getting used to. I encourage people to sit a comfortable distance from one another and to just maintain a steady gaze. Do not use eye contact to assert dominance over the other as if you were a prizefighter in the ring. Just maintain eye contact by focusing on the pupil of the left eye. If direct eye contact is uncomfortable because of your cultural background, then I recommend focusing on the bridge of the nose between the eyes. Also, you may focus on the right eye if you want. The left eye is supposedly the path to the right brain, which is better for relationships. I learned this technique from actors who get incredibly bored repeating their lines after a hundred performances. To prevent their minds from drifting, they are taught to focus intensely on the left eye of the person speaking on stage. It helps their concentration.

Some people gain substantial focus from using this technique. One EMBA student said,

> The most obvious of my deficiencies is listening to others in conversation. My monkey mind is evident as my attention shifts rapidly from one area to another during conversations. For me, the most effective technique for maintaining attention is to focus on the left eye of the speaker. With friends, colleagues, and family, I have been able to greatly improve my focus.

Another student gained similar benefit:

> This method of looking at someone's left eye works great for me in meetings. My mind is focused, and I feel more alert. I recently realized that I misunderstood a subordinate's comment because I was writing an e-mail at the time. I took the wrong action. I now make it a point to stop and look in the left eye whenever someone interrupts me. It forces me to pay attention to them, thus preventing mistakes.

Paraphrase

I am sure you are already familiar with how to paraphrase, which is to repeat back your interpretation of what someone has said, using your own words. But how often do you paraphrase in normal conversation? It requires intent from your inner executive. When I teach managers in an executive program, I assign conversations in which they must practice paraphrasing in their own words what they are hearing. Knowing they have to repeat back something they heard helps sharpen their concentration. For example, one manager told me he started using a phrase he picked up from IBM, which is to close conversations with "To clarify and confirm . . ." He explained, "This phrase is incredibly useful. I have to pay attention to be able to summarize. It helps both parties commit to memory the topics that were discussed and ensures expectations are clear. The phrase also gives the other party assurance you have been listening and provides a 'warm fuzzy' to them. It saves me all the work and problems that arise from misunderstandings."

When I talked to Vera, she had the look of stress on her face. During high-stress periods, she said that she frequently got off-track in class and during conversation. Her biggest wish was to refine her ability to focus her full attention on what was going on in front of her and to self-correct if her mind drifted. I suggested some ideas, and the one that worked best for her was a rule to paraphrase every thirty seconds.

> When comparing my previous week to my week of paraphrasing, there was drastic improvement in my ability to stay on track with people and to get much more out of my day. I was able to see how a more focused day translated into taking away more in both my professional and personal life. Paraphrasing every thirty seconds is a mechanism for my success.

Vera's experience with better focus reminded me of a phrase from Jon Kabat-Zinn:

> Each moment missed is a moment unlived. Each moment missed makes it more likely I will miss the next moment, and live through it cloaked in mindless habits of automaticity of thinking, feeling, and doing rather than living in, out of, and through awareness.[11]

Ask Five Questions

For the asking-questions exercise, during a simple assigned conversation, the listener must ask five questions to draw out deeper understanding. This is fairly easy to do, and with a little practice becomes natural during conversations outside the classroom. An MBA student who was extremely distracted grew to hate saying "What?" all the time during conversations. Her elephant mind was constantly jumping, so she missed what was said. She tried the mechanism of asking questions in every conversation. The five-questions exercise works as a way to train the mind, but sometimes is a bit much in a casual conversations. She opted for trying to ask three questions in every conversation for one week. She counted the number of times she asked three questions and the number of times she said "What?" each day for two weeks. Retraining her mind was a challenge, but by the end of two weeks, the number of "Whats" decreased by 60 percent, and the number of conversations in which she asked at least three questions tripled. She was pleased. "I have reduced the embarrassment and negative impression from constantly saying 'What,' and the frustration to everyone when my answers did not make sense."

• • •

These three listening exercises—focus on the pupil of the speaker's left eye, paraphrase frequently, and ask questions—all increase focus, but have different effects. Several managers said they like the asking-questions exercise best because they feel more engaged with the other person. They tell me that the paraphrasing exercise requires greater concentration on what is being said. Managers in cross-cultural conversations rate paraphrasing the best way to focus to understand each other when one person is less fluent in the language spoken. Focusing on the left eye requires the greater stretch from their normal listening habit. It takes practice to focus on the left pupil and also hear what the person is saying. The major impact of focusing on the left eye is on the person speaking. Maintaining eye contact makes the speaker feel cared about, because he or she perceives the listener as interested and concerned. Select the practice that helps you stay focused on the other person. When you learn to focus, you become very good at listening.

As for Carlos, whom I mentioned at the beginning of the chapter, practicing the exercises during his company's program and trying to increase focus back at his office seemed to pay off. About looking in the left eye and asking questions, he said in his e-mail, "I feel a difference in me. When I talk to someone I feel myself looking into them with more focus, and I sense I am giving them a lot more attention than previously. My mind pays better attention to what is being said."

Listening is a form of love, communicated by eye contact. I recall speaking with a CEO about the business he built into the largest in the industry. I asked about his father, who had started a similar business and at one time was in competition with the CEO. He started to answer my question, but then he choked up and began crying. Talking about his relationship with his father brought up deep, unresolved pain. His father started him in business and then turned on him and tried to drive him out of business. He and his father were estranged during most of the CEO's career, and they never reconciled prior to his father's death. What do you do when a CEO sitting across from you starts to cry? In my own training, I learned to let people have their emotions. In other words, it is better not to say, "Don't cry" or "Don't be angry." Emotions are natural and will pass soon enough. Be patient. All I could think to do was to maintain eye contact by focusing on the pupil of the CEO's left eye. I maintained a steady gaze toward the left eye, not feeling embarrassed and not looking away. The CEO recovered after a few minutes, and we completed our conversation. As I got up to leave, he came around the desk and grasped my hand with both of his. "Thank you so much, Dick," he said. Puzzled, I asked, "For what?" "When I went through those difficult moments concerning my father, it felt like you came right over the desk to be with me. I appreciate your concern." To me, that is the power of focus and eye contact. Staying focused on his left eye conveyed my concern.

Remember This

Focus on People

- Maintaining focus on another person is difficult.
- Use the thirty-second rule to maintain focus during normal interactions.
- Practice with these mechanisms to stay focused:
  - Focus on the pupil of the other person's left eye.
  - Paraphrase every thirty seconds. Paraphrasing is especially valuable in cross-cultural conversations.
  - End business conversations with "To clarify and confirm . . ."
  - Ask three to five questions during each conversation.
- Listening shows caring about another person. Stay focused.

12

Develop Your Witness

The end of all our exploring will be to arrive where we started
And know the place for the first time.
—T. S. Eliot

And the day came when the risk it took to remain tightly closed
in a bud was more painful than the risk it took to bloom.
—Anaïs Nin

"DURING FIVE OUT OF SEVEN conversations yesterday I gave advice," said Jeremy, a twenty-eight-year-old finance student. "I must think I'm master of the universe. My elephant tried to solve other people's problems, even when they didn't have problems. I listened just long enough to interject my view. The thoughts just seemed to jump into my mouth."

Jonathan, an operations student in the MBA program, had a similar experience. "I could see myself trying to top other people with a better comment, both in the hallway and in class. It happened several times. I could see the thoughts clearly. I even imagined other opportunities to top people on the walk to my apartment."

Rachel commented on driving home during rush hour. "I could feel the tightness and frustration in my chest. My mind seemed to fill up with critical thoughts about other drivers, the city, the roads, whatever. When

I saw the slightest deviation from what I considered efficient driving, up popped a criticism, clear and predictable. Part of me knows those were normal people driving in a normal way, but I was still critical."

These students were experiencing an aspect of their inner executive called the *witness*. In Eastern spirituality, the witness is a significant facet of the higher consciousness. The witness is the mind's eye turned inward to see the thoughts, feelings, and other sensations that arise. The witness is that part of Rachel's and Jonathan's minds that could see their critical thoughts and perhaps question whether those thoughts were valid. In contrast, the inner elephant is preoccupied with the external world through the five senses. Virtually all automatic thoughts, feelings, desires, and fears that arise in the mind are concerned with the external world. The witness, however, is able to observe these thoughts and feelings. Although you may already be aware of your witness aspect, it can be specifically developed by shifting your focus of concentration from external objects to within your physical form. The witness is the nonattached and dispassionate awareness that observes your thoughts and sensations, without judgment or reaction.

Turn Inward to Develop Your Witness

The witness may also be called the watcher or observer, an element critical to the management of your inner elephant. In the physical world of science and philosophy, the observer and the observed must be different entities. If you observe a book, then that book is necessarily separate and different from you. The book is not you. The scientist is separate from the experiment. The doctor is different from the patient. The subject cannot be the object; the seer is not the seen. Understanding this separation between the knower and the known is key to understanding the value of the witness for managing your inner elephant. The witness can see and know the activities of the inner elephant, which means the inner elephant is separate from your witness.

Most people, through their childhood conditioning, come to believe that they *are* their thoughts, emotions, attractions, fears, and so on. This is the process of identification through which you believe you are something and feel attached to it. We see ourselves as separate from other people. We also assume that we are the mind and body we occupy, with all its habits, reactions, and thought patterns. There is no doubt that we are a part of the mind-body package, but the assumption in this book is that we can see and assert some influence over the actions of our inner elephant. If you can begin to directly see your thoughts, desires, and dislikes, then you can start to feel separate from them. This is called *disidentification*. You can learn not to identify with the stuff going on in your head. You need not be the man who was washing his car at 10:00 P.M. because he felt the impulse, using floodlights to see the car.[1] Not following his impulse did not occur to him. He assumed that he was the thought and had to obey the impulse. You will discover that you don't have to identify with everything the inner elephant likes, hates, believes, or wants. Being able to see your thoughts as separate means you can *decouple* from them as needed. It is like getting disentangled from a swarm of insects. You can experience nonattachment toward unwanted thoughts and desires. Mental images come and go without your having to act on or fulfill everything that comes up. Recognizing your thoughts as just thoughts can free you from their distortions and help you manage your life. You can let thoughts pass, especially the dysfunctional ones that are not constructive to your leadership.

For example, Harris saw the pattern of his thoughts, and that awakened in him a new perspective:

> I saw myself craving to interrupt people and to interject my thoughts into anything they were trying to communicate. So I focused on the number of times during each conversation that I felt the urge to offer advice. I also found myself being mentally critical of someone who spoke negatively about other people, yet I became aware of myself doing just that. By becoming more aware, I have been able to control these impulses to some degree at home and work. Seeing my thoughts, I am less likely to simply say something without thinking. Simply being aware of my pattern has helped considerably.

Wendi had a similar experience with how she thought about social interactions.

> I saw that my inner elephant was avoiding social/personal conversations with colleagues at work. My mind judged these conversations as simply a waste of time. What a mistake! By avoiding conversations, I may come across as impersonal, cold, and stand-offish with coworkers. I am ignoring the critical thoughts and using my inner executive's intention to invite colleagues to lunch and to start up occasional informal conversations.

The witness can observe thoughts in the mind just as you can stand and watch cars pass on the road without feeling attached to them. Most minds are like a busy street with rush-hour traffic. As you strengthen your witness, more of your energy shifts to watching the traffic, and less energy feeds the thought flow, or acts on the thoughts that arise. If you become 20 percent aware of your thoughts, then only 80 percent of mental energy is left to keep the traffic moving, especially the thoughts or actions that you want to eliminate. Just seeing your thoughts will give you some power over them. There is a story about the king who sat in on a talk by the Buddha. His foot was wiggling, and the Buddha asked him about it. Once the king was aware of the moving foot, it stopped. His awareness of his foot stopped the unconscious wiggling.[2] Likewise, as your witness becomes aware of the traffic in your head, the rush hour may slow down, giving you more control and choice over your thoughts and actions. Your witness can grow and expand as you exercise it, thereby strengthening your inner executive. You will free yourself from compulsive thinking and are less likely to act on thoughts that don't add value to your life.

Most of us take our thoughts for granted. Thoughts are always rushing through, and we hardly notice, just like the king that did not notice his wiggling foot. We identify with thoughts and believe they are real and true. Taking our thoughts for granted works just fine most of the time. Only the dysfunctional or unhealthy thoughts get us in trouble or diminish our leadership. Those are the thoughts and impulses we need to see in order to do something about, just as Harris and Wendi did.

Look around the room you are in. There are many objects and perhaps people and movement. The same thing is going on inside your head and body. There are internal objects (thoughts) and sensations to see that can be observed by the witness. A similar shift in perspective can also happen in a movie theater. If you watch an Indiana Jones action movie, one of the *Halloween* scary movies, or a sweet movie like *Enchanted*, you will likely get drawn in and lose yourself as if the movie events were real, and you feel part of it. You identify with the movie. This is just like being immersed in the images flowing through your mind. The images seem real and true because you identify with and feel yourself to be a part of them. What happens at the theater when you realize you are watching a movie? Your mind is suddenly detached, and you see there are visual images on the screen that you can observe and enjoy, but you know that you are separate from them. Now you are a "witness" to the movie. You can take the movie less seriously. The action on the screen is not you and not real. It is a succession of flickering images. You can use your witness in the same way to observe your inner movie's images while realizing they are playing on the screen of your mind. When you observe your own mind, then you are the witness. You are a detached observer of the movie within yourself.

You can practice using the witness by focusing your attention on your breathing, body, thoughts, feelings, internal discomfort or resistance, physical sensations, and impulses, thereby seeing your inner elephant directly. Learning to focus your concentration inward will help you detach from the random chatter, automatic thoughts, and impulses that typically flood your mind. Here is a simple exercise concerning your breath, for example.

○ *Focus on your breath.* One place to start is to focus on your breath, which is part of your body. Close your eyes and first focus to feel the touch of your breath on the tip of your nostrils. Then try for a more refined focus to feel the subtle touch of the breath on the skin between the nostrils and the upper lip during your slow, natural inhalation and exhalation. Holding this focus will help calm your mind. This touch of breath is light, and sensing it takes good concentration.

Inward focus is not natural for most people, so effort is needed. There are a number of exercises that will help you shift your attention from the external to the internal. When you have a few minutes, try one or more that appeal to you. Each time you try one of these exercises, your witness will expand. A single trial will give you a flavor, but regular practice is needed for a major shift toward inward awareness.

○ *Focus on your saliva.* Sense the saliva in your mouth. When you are aware of the saliva, you are in the present moment. Now increase the flow of saliva. A dry mouth is a sign of fear or tension, and you can bring your mind into the present moment to achieve calm by increasing the flow of saliva. Second, close your eyes and focus on the area of your tongue and jaw. Many people carry tension in the jaw area. While focusing on this area, consciously relax your tongue and jaw to let go of any tension.

○ *Scan your body.* Another internal focus is the body scan, which is recommended by Jon Kabat-Zinn and colleagues.[3] Sit comfortably with your eyes closed. The idea here is to look inward into your body. Don't rush. Take your time. Can you sense any feeling where your body is in contact with the chair? with your clothing? Now shift your mind's eye to exploring your tongue and jaw area, as described before. Can you sense and release any tightness or tension? Now shift to the area of your belly. What sensations can you detect in your abdomen? Sense its movement when you breathe and detect any feeling within. Once aware of sensations in the abdomen, move your spotlight of attention down your left leg and into your left foot up to the toes. Investigate any sensations you find. When ready, move your examination into the right leg, ankle, and foot. Continue your investigation of each part, lingering on the shin, the knee, the thigh, the pelvic area, buttocks, and through your arms, hands, torso, face, and head. With repeated body scans, as your concentration improves, explore each square inch of skin surface and any sensations beneath. Further, where are your lungs, heart, kidney, liver? Focus your attention internally on those areas. You won't be able to sense organs directly, but you can put your attention in the area of each. Can you sense your heart beating?

o *Write down current thoughts.* Can you see your thoughts right now? Spend a few minutes writing down your thoughts exactly as you notice them. Sit quietly at a desk or table and try to see the next thought that arises. Write it down. The content of the thought does not matter. Don't judge your thoughts; just try to be aware of the next one and write it down. Continue until you have recorded ten thoughts. The importance of the exercise is not to learn what you are thinking, but to strengthen your witness to see each thought. Do this periodically and see what happens.

A similar exercise is to read the words on this page slowly and use your witness to directly observe the words passing through your mind. Take a few minutes to try this. Read the next sentence slowly and see the words in your mind. Close your eyes and repeat the sentence in your mind. Can you see or hear the words?

Another approach is to trigger some thoughts to watch, such as from your judge. To witness your judge's negative evaluations, look at your face closely in a mirror. Look at your eyes, your wrinkles, your colors and finer physical details. Do self-critical thoughts emerge? What are those thoughts? The more thoughts you can see internally, the stronger your inner executive's witness is becoming.

Engaging your witness may seem a stretch if you are just beginning. But you use your witness without realizing it anytime you are aware of your thoughts or feelings. It has been an unobtrusive observer. With the increasing strength of your inner executive, you can see your inner mental dynamics and decide what to act on and what to ignore, just as you decide in the outer world. As your witness develops, you can achieve distance from the persistent and often compulsive mental chatter inside your head. One woman told how learning to "see" her whole body and detach from tension and negative thoughts about her son was like "when you come back from a vacation and the house is a bit musty, so you open all the doors and windows to let the air blow through."[4] You are like a fish becoming aware of water for the first time. With awareness comes space and freedom from your inner elephant's issues to choose appropriate thoughts and actions, just as you can choose which movie you want to watch at the theater.

Your witness is like a scientist or physician that is completely objective in its detached observations. As part of my meditation training, I was taught to use minor pain as the object of inward focus. Watching the pain developed my witness as I learned not to fear or react to the pain.

○ *Watch a pain.* Pain can be generated by sitting in a slightly uncomfortable position, such as cross-legged on the floor, and then not moving. I have students sit in a chair, lean forward, stretch their arms out, and hold a book. Soon a muscle will feel sore, and the mind's eye, like a physician examining someone else's body, can focus on the exact location, size, and feeling of pain with keen observation. Normally the inner elephant would react to pain with a desire to escape. The witness, however, is simple awareness and can observe pain with detachment. Indeed, with some practice, you will find that minor to moderate pain is easy to tolerate when you observe it as a detached witness. It is just another sensation within the body. You can also observe other sensations, such as hunger or an emotion, without reacting to them, to develop your witness.

You can also practice by watching an intentional repeated thought, such as an autosuggestion (Chapter Five).

○ *Watch an intentional thought.* Repeat slowly a phrase that has appeal to you and concentrate fully on its presence in your mind. My recommended autosuggestion for this task is "I am thinking only of this thought." Repeat it slowly to yourself and watch each word in your mind. Another autosuggestion for holding your internal focus is "I am focusing on this moment."

During a coaching session with Janet, we decided on the phrase "I am focusing on this moment" to improve her inward concentration. Focusing on repeating that thought produced some unexpected results.

> I felt a sense of calm and noticed that some of the negative feelings I was experiencing seemed to drift away. This practice has enabled me to significantly increase my overall level of concentration on a variety of tasks, as well as reduced stress levels associated with self-criticism. Whenever I notice self-criticism come into play, I simply state the phrase. Whenever I become agitated or have trouble focusing on a friend, colleague, or loved one's conversation, I state the phrase. This practice seems to awaken more positive feelings toward myself and others.

Janet's inward focus was strengthening her witness and weakening the traditional dynamics of her inner elephant. Travis had a similar experience:

> Frequently repeating the phrase about focusing on this moment, I have noticed that I can manage my monkey mind/elephant/judge in a much more efficient and gentle manner. Previously I had become frustrated when I had difficulty concentrating, but I now am aware of these distracters with a useful tool to address them when they pop up. To continue to develop my level of concentration, I will continue to employ this and perhaps other phrases.

Something else happens as well. Some philosophies teach that you can look at your thoughts and emotions as the surface of the lake. When you are agitated, thoughts and emotions are like high waves. If your inner witness can directly observe these waves and notice that "you" are the one looking and are not the waves, then the agitation will gradually subside. The light of your attention is powerful when focused on your own thoughts and feelings. Learning to see the internal disturbances will calm the surface of the lake. Indeed, the underlying nature of the inner executive and witness is tranquility. When you can focus on your elephant's mental agitation, unease, tension, or racing thoughts, the agitation may calm down into a more happy state.

As the witness gains ascendancy in your daily life, your inner executive will have more influence over your elephant's thoughts and moods. With increased concentration, you will be aware of your thinking and thereby can guide it constructively. You may no longer need to believe or act on undesired thoughts that may arise in response to the situation around you. It all starts with one-pointed focus. David Brooks, columnist for the *New York Times*, after reading books on why some people are phenomenally successful, commented that it was their ability to concentrate: "Control of attention is the ultimate individual power. People who can do that are not prisoners of the stimuli around them. This individual power . . . leads to self-control, the ability to formulate strategies in order to resist impulses."[5]

You can develop your concentration to see your inner world and thereby formulate strategies to guide your inner elephant. Moreover, by turning the light of your attention inward, the disturbances on the surface of the lake of your mind will quiet down. Intentional thoughts and actions will gradually replace automatic mind chatter and visceral reactions. You can learn to watch your internal movie and even to be the director. This is the ultimate way of leading yourself to be the best leader you can be. Enjoy the show.

Remember This

Turn Inward to Develop Your Witness

- People identify with their thoughts, but are not their thoughts.
- Turning inward means to focus your attention within your physical frame.
- The observer is necessarily separate and different from the observed; you are the observer.
- Your witness can observe the involuntary thoughts, mental dynamics, and physical sensations of your inner elephant.
- Exercises that focus the mind within will strengthen the witness and help you detach from unwanted thoughts or impulses.

Use Radical Self-Inquiry

With pointed concentration and your witness's inward focus, you can adopt specific techniques to deal with intrusive thoughts that negatively impact your life. A clear example of dysfunctional thought is obsessive-compulsive disorder (OCD). OCD is characterized by highly intrusive, involuntary, and repetitive thoughts that result in compulsive behaviors that a person feels driven to perform to prevent some imagined dreaded event. A person with OCD may have an irresistible urge to wash his hands even if it is the fifth time washing his hands in the last ten minutes and he is late for an appointment. If ever the assistance of a witness with internal focus were needed, this is the time. OCD is an extreme form of automatic thought described in this book as arising from the inner elephant. A striking solution for people afflicted with the condition has been to teach them to develop their witness to focus inwardly to "see" this habitual and compulsive thought.

Neuropsychiatrist Jeffrey Schwartz understood inward focus and meditation-type practices and the potential of teaching patients meditation as a way to cope with insistent and intrusive thoughts (obsessions). People identify with an instruction appearing in their mind, so a strong thought is difficult to ignore. Schwartz understood that people could be taught to strengthen their capacity to see, detach from, and resist specific thoughts. "I felt that if I could get patients to experience the OCD symptom without reacting emotionally to the discomfort it caused, realizing instead that even the most visceral OCD urge is actually no more than the manifestation of a brain wiring defect that has no reality in itself, it might be tremendously therapeutic."[6] Can patients be taught to focus precisely on a compelling thought, just detach and watch it, without feeling the need to act? And if so, would the thought weaken and go away? These questions were addressed in the research Schwartz conducted with his colleagues.

OCD sufferers were taught to cope with an insistent thought by concentrating inwardly to see it directly and reinterpret what it meant. They were taught to think of the thought as random garbage thrown up by a faulty mental circuit in the brain. Once a patient could see the thought, interpret it as the result of a faulty system, and know that it was not real, he or she had a powerful tool with which to resist acting compulsively. Subjects would see the thought not as an overwhelming desire to wash hands or check the stove or lock the door, but as a result of faulty brain wiring they happened to possess. Patients could learn to disidentify with the OCD thought; it was no longer "I" having the thought, just a false signal from a faulty brain circuit.

Within a week or so after patients learned to observe and relabel their urges as a signal from a faulty brain process, they reported that the disease was no longer controlling them. Perhaps more important, they started to believe they could do something about their condition. To provide objective evidence to confirm the subjective experience of the patients, Schwartz and his colleagues did brain scans on eighteen OCD patients before and after ten weeks of meditation-based therapy. Twelve patients improved significantly as revealed by the brain scan after the meditation training, which showed reduced activity in the OCD brain circuit.[7] In other words, teaching the witness to observe and not react to the brain's signal, and to redefine it as a faulty circuit, actually rewired the brain circuit to send a weaker signal or no signal at all. These patients were free of these persistent intruding thoughts. This finding is phenomenal! The higher consciousness actually changed the brain chemistry. This would mean that a concentrated effort can change the signals in the brain to eliminate unwanted thoughts. People can change the brain signals rather than be trapped receiving unwanted signals. In essence, the ability to look inward, see one's thoughts, and redefine them is a solid basis for learning to change debilitating thought patterns in one's personality.

• • •

Another approach to changing your thoughts was developed by Byron Katie, a self-help guru listed as one of *Time* magazine's spiritual innovators for the twenty-first century. She uses the technique in her work with patients. Katie works with thoughts generated by the critical internal judge, the predictable tendency of the inner elephant to be highly critical of self or others. These critical thoughts are associated with negative emotions and some level of inner distress. When people learn to see the critical thought associated with their inner distress, they can undo its damage by asking and answering a series of questions about the thought:

1. Is it true?
2. Can you absolutely know that it's true?
3. How do you react when you think that thought?
4. Who would you be without that thought?
5. Can you turn around that thought to its opposite?

I have recommended these questions to a number of people who had overly active internal judges. To sharpen their concentration, I asked them to keep a log of the judgmental thoughts that arise about themselves or others. Keeping the log sharpens their witness. Once they became aware of judgmental patterns, they could pause and ask themselves the five questions. For example, one MBA student reported the following inner dialogue, which started with the thought, "Jamie is such a jerk!"

> *Is that true?* "Yes, obviously."
>
> *Can you absolutely know that it's true?* "Well, maybe not. Maybe it is just me reacting to something that annoys me. Maybe someone else would not feel that way."
>
> *How do you react when you think that thought?* "I feel miserable. I am angry and upset."
>
> *Who would you be without that thought?* "I would be someone who did not feel miserable, annoyed, or upset. I would feel more peace."
>
> *Can you turn around that thought?* "Hmmm. Maybe he's not a jerk. Maybe it's just my elephant-self reacting. [Continuing to think] Maybe I am the jerk. I am having the harsh thought toward another person for something he can't help."

You can see how this line of questioning changes the interpretation of the critical thought, just as the OCD patients changed their interpretation of obsessive thoughts. As your witness is able to focus on distinctive individual thoughts, you can ask the questions to change your interpretation, and the thoughts will calm down, as does your inner distress.

One of my MBA students, Ellen, had a continuous inner dialogue about the faults of other people. As a coaching assignment from me, she agreed to keep a log of her critical thoughts toward others so that she could tune in to and see her judge. The constant critical thoughts felt natural to her. She had had them as long as she could remember. In a group meeting, Ellen would think about a colleague, "Are you lazy, or are you just dumb?" Watching an overweight lady order a salad, she would think, "Nice try, but it won't help." Listening to a professor talk about his glory days, "You're talking about yourself again." These critical thoughts were as natural as water flowing down a mountain stream.

The next step of Ellen's assignment after keeping the log was to pick one critical thought and ask the questions, such as the thought about her professor. So she asked, is it true? "Yes, it's true." To the second question, she said, "No, I can't know that with absolute certainty." To the third question, "I am not aware of any reaction to this thought." To the fourth question, "I would be a person with fewer critical thoughts, which would seem to be a good thing." To the fifth question, "Does this mean the professor is not talking about himself? No, that's not it. The turnaround is that I am annoyed by what you say. I am annoyed and didn't realize it. I must be assuming I don't do the things of which I am critical about others. The turnaround is that I am the problem, not the professor." Ellen got it, particularly the part about becoming aware of her own negative feelings associated with her negative thoughts. I am happy to report that after two weeks Ellen told me that she kept a log again for two days, and her negative thoughts had decreased by 50 percent. By using radical self-inquiry to see and question her thoughts, her lifelong critical judgments were quieting down.

An IT team leader found self-inquiry helpful with handling a direct report. Gene saw himself as an overly judgmental person toward himself and others, so he wanted to try radical self inquiry.

> I judged one of my team members, Larry, as an incompetent slacker. *Can I know that thought is true?* Absolutely, as shown by his job performance. *Can I know absolutely?* Maybe not, because I am not on the floor with him to see the obstacles he faces daily. *How do I react to my thought?* I get angry that we allow that person to continue to work for us while harder working people run circles around him—but my managers keep telling me I'm wrong. *Where would I be without that thought?* Every time I walk past his workstation I would not be focused on his incompetence, nor would my mood suffer. *How would I turn this thought around?* Maybe it is not Larry, but what we are expecting of Larry or the tools we have given him to do his job.

Gene's learning was more than he expected:

> After answering these questions I took the time to find out why Larry did not do his job. I went to show him how to properly execute, and I found his computer profile incorrectly set up. He was missing

an entire screen to do a secondary task. I had been doing this task for him thinking he was incompetent. It was quicker for me to do it than explain it. It turns out the incompetence was on my part because I control computer security. I am going to ask more questions and make fewer judgments in the future.

I also recommend this questioning technique to people who are overly critical of themselves. Once they see these thoughts, they see clearly their inner pattern and pain, which is not always the case when criticizing others because the other person is blamed for causing the pain. A manager in our EMBA program reported to me that his critical judge said, "I am the weakest person on this team. I can't hold up my end."

> *Is the statement true?* "It feels like it to me."
>
> *Can you absolutely know that it's true?* "No, I can't. It's my sense of things, my fear. But I still think it."
>
> *How do you react when you think that thought?* "I feel bad about myself. I feel inadequate. Even if I am the weakest person, the thought makes me feel worse."
>
> *Who would you be without that thought?* "I would be someone who is less depressed, less down on myself. Naïve maybe, but happier."
>
> *Can you turn around that thought?* "As I think about it, I have things to offer. I was overwhelmed by people's quant backgrounds. As the negative feeling subsides, I can see that we each bring skills to the group. That original thought is completely untrue. I see it now."

In each of these cases, the inner executive was able to focus inward with a little practice and learn to witness negative or dysfunctional thoughts. With self-inquiry, people can disentangle from the harmful (to themselves) thoughts and no longer accept them as true. As you find this deeper truth—that these thoughts are based on long-past childhood experiences or faulty brain wiring—then you become free of them. You no longer see the thoughts as being "you"—you disidentify with them; this weakens the thoughts, and they will gradually disappear. It takes practice and inward concentration to develop your witness, which will build a stronger inner executive. As you learn to manage your own thought process, you will really be leading yourself. You will be in charge of your inner elephant. That is a complete reversal from leadership based on an unconscious mind that accepts the inner elephant's thoughts, impulses, aversions, and bad habits as who you are and about which you do nothing.

Remember This

Use Radical Self-Inquiry

- Radical self-inquiry is a means of identifying and questioning with close examination the validity of critical or unhelpful thoughts.
- OCD and other unwanted thoughts can be disabled through focus and reinterpretation.
- You can weaken a critical thought toward others or yourself with questions to yourself about the thought's validity. These questions are "Is it true?" "Can you absolutely know the thought is true?" "How do you react when you think that thought?" "Who would you be without that thought?" and "Can you turn around that thought to its opposite?"
- Self-inquiry strengthens the inner executive to have authority over unwanted thoughts from the inner elephant.

Who Am I?

The witness is a powerful aid for seeing and inquiring into the elephant mind. Ramana Maharshi (1879–1950), an Indian sage and spiritual teacher, recommended *self-inquiry* as the highest form of meditation. He urged followers to ponder the question, "Who am I?" The question turns your attention inward to see thoughts that arise. This approach is challenging, but also simple. Focus inward and search for a thought, then inquire into either (1) the intended recipient of the thought or (2) the source of the thought.

When thoughts arise, inquire, "To whom has this thought arisen?" Your answer will be, "To me." Then ask, "Who am I?" to help you find your true "I."[8] This simple act of asking to whom the thought arises or to whom it is intended has deep implications. Once you see that it is intended for "me," then you suddenly realize that you are the receiver of the thought and not the sender—the opposite of what people typically assume. You will see the clear distinction between the sender (inner elephant) and receiver (inner executive) and that "you" have to be the observer-receiver, the higher consciousness.

As your mind is learning to focus enough to see a thought and ask to whom it was sent, you might ask yourself such related questions as

"What is my idea of myself?" "Do I exist?" If yes, then "Who exists?" "Who do I mean by 'I' when I say or think 'I'?" Or when other thoughts or desires appear, ask, "Who feels this pleasure?" "Who feels this fear?" "Who feels this desire?" Self-inquiry can address any thoughts, feelings, or impulses that arise during your inward focus. For example, you might ask the question, "Is that me?" about each automatic thought, feeling, desire, or sensation that arises from within the body. "Is that really me?" You may find yourself saying, "Not this" or "That is not me," along with "Who am I?" You can also inquire into your state of mind, such as by asking, "What is my mood right now?" which may explain the nature of arising thoughts (for example, a bad mood causing negative thoughts). Or "Am I seeing this person with compassion?" to inquire into your underlying attitude toward another.

The second inquiry is into the source of your "I" thought, the source of your assumption about who you are. From where does your thought arise? When you probe beneath your thoughts for the source of your thoughts or the source of your "I" assumption, you are attempting to see the outlines of the inner elephant. The answers take you to the inner elephant's "I." As you see the inner elephant directly, it may begin to disappear and lose its power. To understand the inner elephant, you might also ask such questions as "Who is asking this question?" "Who is providing this answer?" to turn your mind inward. For undesired thoughts, you might ask, "Who sent that thought?" as well as "Who is receiving that thought?" to get back to the underlying "I" assumption.

As you follow the second line of inquiry into the source of the thought, the point is that you may also become aware of another "I," the "I" that sees the thoughts. This takes you back to Maharshi's first line of inquiry. This "I" is the seer, or what this book has been calling the witness or inner executive. Over time, your identification will shift away from the lower, ego-based "I" and toward the seer or witness. You may begin to think of yourself not as the stream of automatic thoughts, desires, and impulses but as the observing witness. The seer or witness watches the noisy thoughts from a place of stillness and peace. You probably assumed that all the thoughts, desires, and sensations going on inside were really you, but maybe they are not. With time, you will figure out the answers.

Generally speaking, I find it easier to answer the question of who received the thought than to identify who sent the thought. You can take the questions in the sequence you prefer. If you gain understanding of the receiver, then you might turn to inquiring into the sender of thoughts, which I think takes more focus and practice. As you find who you are with respect to receiving the thoughts, your inner elephant's thought-generator may quiet down. For example, if I am trapped behind a city bus while driving home from work, a thought may appear in my mind, such as, "That bus is smelly and stops frequently." Or if I receive a flaming e-mail from a theatrical producer, I may feel a rush of emotion and think, "I would like to smash this guy. Why did we ever sign a contract with him?" Immediately following either of those thoughts, I could ask myself, "Who received that thought?" It was me, so I am the observer of the thought. Later, as my concentration becomes more acute, I may ask, "From where did that thought arise?" or "From whence did it come?" and probe inwardly toward its source.

Don't expect ready answers to these questions. The point is to hold your focus inward and probe more deeply into thoughts that appear. As you learn who you are and from where thoughts originate, you will be strengthening your inner executive to take charge of a weaker inner elephant.

It may take a long time to ultimately answer the questions for the two "Who am I?" lines of inquiry. I think the approach suggested by Ramana Maharshi works best for people who are relatively advanced in mental discipline and can focus narrowly and deeply into their inner world. The path of answering "Who am I?" to tame your inner elephant is considered a relatively direct but very steep path to learn who you are, and it is not suited to many people. However, just asking the questions in the moment will shift you into the inner-executive part of your brain so that you are aware of your inner elephant's thoughts, desires, or resistance and will not be seduced by them.

• Try This •

Ask, "Who Am I?"

Asking "Who am I?" is a way to decouple from unwanted automatic thoughts.

- Upon seeing the thought, ask, "To whom has this thought arisen?"
- After answering, "To me," then ask, "Who am I?"
- Probe deeply into the source of the thought by asking, "From where did the thought arise?"

This approach requires one-pointed concentration to probe the thought's destination and its source.

Developing your witness to undertake inward focus and engaging in radical self-inquiry are tools you can use to eliminate the limiting and harmful mental habits that block you from becoming the best leader possible. At the least, just recognizing your thoughts as thoughts will lead to clearer perception and better self-management.

13

Reprogram Yourself

*I must be willing to give up what I am in order to become what
I will be.*
—Albert Einstein

*There's only one corner of the universe you can be certain
of improving, and that's your own self.*
—Aldous Huxley

HERE IS AN INTERESTING STORY about Eastern Orthodox spirituality.
Some hundred pages of notes were written by a thirty-three-year-old man,
a spiritual seeker with a withered left arm, a mendicant wandering from
place to place in Russia during the mid-1800s owning only a knapsack
in which he carried some dry bread. The man's name is not known.
The notes tell the story of how he visited monasteries and churches
seeking teachers to guide his spiritual growth. One day he heard St.
Paul's admonition "Pray without ceasing," which fixed itself in his mind.
What could this mean? Where could he find someone to explain how to
pray without ceasing? He visited many churches with famous preachers,
and none could tell him the answer. Finally, his journey led to a person
of advanced spiritual understanding.

The master taught him the discipline known as the Jesus Prayer—an
uninterrupted mantra-like invocation: "Lord Jesus Christ have mercy

on me." The pilgrim was told to repeat that prayer exactly three thousand times the first two days, then six thousand times each day for the next week, then twelve thousand times, and then without limit. The master gave him rosary beads on which to count. The mendicant moved his lips in his repetitions. The first days were tiring and unsettling—his mind was severely tested. He stayed in a hut and pushed other thoughts aside. After a few days, his heart opened to the mantra. He repeated it constantly. As weeks passed, he felt absolute peace. He began traveling, and could walk forty miles a day and feel as though he was not walking at all. When he was hungry, the invocation prompted him to forget the wish for food. When ill, he did not notice the pain. His lips and tongue seemed to pronounce the words by themselves, without urging. After a time, his mind took over the task, letting his lips rest. He felt light, as if he were walking on air. His world was transformed. "I felt there was no happier person on earth than I. . . . The whole outside world also seemed to me full of charm and delight. Everything drew me to love . . . people, trees, plants, and animals. I saw them all as my kinfolk."[1]

What accounted for this inner transformation? Various religions suggest mental repetition of some form of divine name. But the power of repetition is not limited to the divine. Repeating a thought intentionally and continually *keeps away all other thoughts,* particularly the random, automatic, and unwanted negative images, criticisms, desires, dislikes, and impulses that detract from the best of you. Just as a little boy can plug his ears and speak loudly so that he doesn't hear what his sister is saying, the inner executive can steadily repeat a mantra to block the voice of the inner elephant. The one thought keeps away the many thoughts. The pilgrim was enjoying a life free of influence from his inner elephant. Intentionally repeating one thought constantly anchored him in his higher consciousness.

The inner elephant is highly resistant to giving up its dominion over your mind. Its established program runs your life. A person's self-image is relatively permanent and resistant to change. Self-image is the concept of oneself, based on a system of ideas that are by and large consistent with one other. Self-consistency theory suggests that we think and act consistently with our self-concept or self-image. Indeed, people want to grow and change, but they seem to behave to maintain a consistent image. They seek information and relationships that reinforce their self-image. Ideas outside the self-image are typically rejected, and those that seem consistent are accepted. You might think of your self-image as the center of the idea cluster that represents your enduring beliefs about yourself. Ideas about the self are generated from past successes and failures, and feedback from childhood experiences, including the conclusions drawn about yourself based on how you were treated as a child. Self-image is basically what you think about yourself deep down at an unconscious level where the beliefs and assumptions are held. This is the deepest root of the inner elephant.

I saw self-image at work when I collaborated with an artist in Santa Fe. Many of the people she taught to draw—especially the businessmen in her classes—believed they had no artistic creativity. She did a session for one of my executive programs, and when she asked for a show of hands about creativity, some 80 percent admitted to no creativity at all. The managers were shaking in their boots about trying to draw. This was supposed to be a program about leadership. Most had been told as children that they were not artistic. Others had reached that conclusion on their own. The "I am not creative" aspect of their self-image stuck. The artist then guided them through a series of exercises during which they temporarily forgot that they had no artistic ability. Everyone was pleased and surprised at the realistic human face that appeared on their sketchpad. They had creative potential after all, contrary to self-image!

Self-image is hard to change. Even plastic surgery sometimes fails to help people change their bodily self-image. In one case, after having had a scar removed from her face, a woman could hardly tell the difference, even when shown before and after photos. Her self-image was so negative that when she could finally see the difference, she still could not feel it. Teenage girls suffering from anorexia look in the mirror and see an overweight person, regardless of how skinny they become. Among managers, I often observe differences in those who see themselves as good at judging, controlling, telling, and directing, as opposed to those who see themselves as facilitators of others by helping, developing, supporting, and removing obstacles for others. These self-image differences create wide differences in leadership style.

When a person's self-image is adequate and realistic, it is a gift that keeps on giving through adulthood. If the self-image is distorted, negative, and perhaps self-defeating, it may lead to a life of trials and struggles. Negative self-images arise when people identify with their failures, when they receive and believe negative feedback about themselves, or when they draw negative conclusions about themselves, especially as children, and hence their core beliefs are distorted. I can remember one person telling me, "but it's true, it's really true, that I am worthless." A negative self-concept is surprisingly hard to shake, even when a person can see how she disables herself.

Think of the mind as a limited thought field. That field can hold only one thought at a time. There is a tsunami of thoughts waiting to crowd into that limited space. When your mind is racing, many thoughts get their instant in your head. On a normal day, perhaps 98 percent of your thoughts are automatic responses to your opportunities, problems, pace of living, and other stimuli that prompt an ongoing mental flow of ideas, solutions, cravings, impulses, aversions, criticalness, opinions, and feelings of joy and depression, surprise and concern. These thoughts flood through the gateway to your mind, and they are all unintentional, accepted by you without much of a fight.

Repeat a Mantra

The story of the mendicant illustrates the potential power of repeating a mantra. A mantra can be used to block the flow of unintentional thoughts that flood your mind. A mantra is similar to autosuggestion described in Chapter Five, but with a different historical origin. Autosuggestion started in the West in medicine and psychology. The mantra originated in religious traditions in the East and Middle East. To this day, remembrance and repetition of a divine name is practiced in the Greek Orthodox and Russian Orthodox churches among other Christian affiliations, as well as Eastern religions such as Hinduism and Buddhism.[2] In these religions, remembrance and repetition of the name of a higher power is a potent form of mental discipline. When practiced intensively, it can lead to some form of liberation from the trials and limitations of the ego.

I am using the term *mantra* to mean autosuggestion on steroids. The mantra is an *intentional* thought, pushed forward by the intelligent will of the inner executive. The first value of a mantra is to keep away unwanted thoughts. The second is to use it to make a new suggestion to yourself to reprogram your basic assumptions and self-image. Autosuggestion can be used to facilitate change in your behavior in the short term. It has a positive impact with repetitions of twenty, thirty, fifty times a day, perhaps during specific periods such as early morning or late evening. A mantra, however, repeated continuously, can be used to fundamentally alter the core beliefs or dispositions underlying your personality. The mantra, repeated as often as possible, becomes a reprogramming instruction for your inner elephant, and should be repeated many, many times, even hundreds and thousands of times a day.

Repeating a mantra takes effort and focus and thereby strengthens your executive self by pushing back the tide of unneeded thoughts and feelings that fill up your mind. I like the word *mindshare*—as the share of intentional thought increases, the share of mindless and negative chatter decreases. If your inner executive asserts its own continuous positive thought, there is no longer room for the negative flotsam surging into your mind. And if the mantra has a higher spiritual connotation, such as a divine name that is dear to you, the experience may be even more uplifting.

Why not apply this powerful concept of mantra to a deeper issue, such as self-image? A well-designed mantra can work at a deep level, as it did for the Russian mendicant. As he continued to repeat the mantra, his automatic (and probably negative) thoughts fell away. Those thoughts were no longer accepted or reinforced.

To gain the benefits of a mantra, I typically suggest working up to a repetition of a thousand times a day or more. When I was practicing mantras, I once used a hand counter during a road trip. I found that a short mantra could be repeated about a thousand times in an hour. A longer mantra might take an hour and a half to two hours. Of course, it is hard to stay focused for that length of time. Besides, who has an hour to spare? Actually, you have more time than you think. Your mind is already repeating the tired old reactions, feelings, and scripts that have been with you for years as a predictable response to the world. The negative thoughts about you and others, the criticisms, the fears, anxiety, racing mind, and ups and downs take up much of your day.

If unhelpful thoughts and feelings were replaced by the steady drumbeat of an intentional mantra of positive intent, would you be better off? Yes, almost certainly. There are many moments during a typical day when your mind is passive—perfect moments for repeating the mantra. You can repeat a mantra when exercising, driving, listening to a boring presentation, watching TV—any time you are not fully concentrating on a task. You may need to set reminders for yourself, perhaps in your BlackBerry or cell phone, until your mind is conditioned to repeat the mantra during opportune periods. Otherwise the mind follows its old routines. I found that using a hand counter served as a physical mechanism to keep my mind focused on the mantra. This is important during the early stages when you are cutting a new groove in your thought system. Saying the mantra out loud will also give you more momentum in the early stages. After several days of practice, the mantra will almost keep itself going in the back of your mind. The mantra is perhaps the best way to train your mind in an age of busyness, because it requires no special setting or separate quiet time.

But can it really work? Clyde had low self-confidence compared to what I expected of a graduate from a top business school. Clyde said his older brother was a superstar at everything, including sports and business, and that he was weak by comparison. Clyde set very high goals for himself, and when he did not achieve them he would mentally beat himself up. Somewhere in his early life, things spiraled down to an anxious and melancholy attitude. I noticed that Clyde kept his head down while sitting or walking. He obsessed on negative aspects of his work situation, promotion, family, everything. I suggested therapy, but he said no, because it was not consistent with his cultural heritage. As we talked, it became clear that his devastatingly low confidence was a big problem, reinforced by his inner elephant's ability to see the worst in everything and to articulate it with severely negative self-talk.

Self-confidence is the foundation for practically all effective leadership behavior. I initially suggested that he intentionally keep his head up, with an angle that was slightly upward. His response, "What if I trip and fall down?" indicated to me that he was not welcoming the idea. He admitted to his cynicism toward any suggestions for change. We discussed it some more and then I moved on to a mantra. I explained the idea of replacing those obsessively negative thoughts about himself with a single, intentional positive thought that he would repeat over and over when he could remember to do so. I asked him to help create a mantra that felt good to him. We brainstormed several ideas and ended up with "I am becoming more confident." That was it. That was the core issue. He would repeat it every night before going to sleep, every morning upon awakening, and as often during the day as possible.

Three weeks later, Clyde sent me a note before we met again. He reported that he had been working hard and had achieved positive results. "I am happy to say that there has been a sharp decline in the number of negative notions popping up in my head." Acting like a scientist, he had kept a log; his negative thoughts had dropped by half. Even better, he was experiencing an occasional automatic positive, optimistic thought, which he enjoyed. To my surprise, the mantra helped him keep his head up while sitting, standing, and walking. In his words,

> I have noticed that keeping my head up while sitting, I automatically become more alert and attentive. At other times when I keep my head up, a wave of confidence washes over me. It's hard to explain why this happens, but it's true. Also, by keeping my head up while walking, I tend to see more people around me and I notice my colleagues' faces. I wish them "hello" more often than I otherwise did. Before I only saw people's feet, and not their faces. This may sound hokey, but it reinforces my self-confidence and I don't know why. I intend to keep my head up from now on.

I was interested in the other results of Clyde's mantra. Despite his initial skepticism, he had repeated the mantra more frequently than instructed.

> I derived some wonderful results. The beneficial effects of self-affirmation are simply astounding! This saying has helped me mentally, emotionally, spiritually, and physiologically. I notice that

whenever I chant this saying to myself, my whole body relaxes
and a blissful, almost silly, smile unconsciously comes to my face.
I also feel as though a tremendous weight has been removed from
my chest. I can breathe more deeply and freely. My spirit becomes,
and I become, more receptive to myself and others. My housemates
have noticed the change. One came up to me and said, "Clyde, you
have such a positive attitude. You are a rock star!" I felt immensely
pleased. I had no idea that it took only a little determined effort to
transform my outlook from gloomy to optimistic.

Once a person turns on her own light of understanding, as Clyde
did, she may backslide occasionally, but cannot go all the way back
to old thinking. "Now that I have realized the power of this positive
self-affirmation, I will carry on this fruitful practice every day and will
enjoy the fruits."

The word *mantra* means "to free from the mind." It is a tool used by
the higher mind to free oneself from the vagaries of the lower mind (inner
elephant). This is captured by a story I heard in India. A man came to the
door of a house and offered a housewife the following bargain: he would
do all of her work, and if he ever completed the work so that he was
idle, he would be given possession of her children and be free to leave
with them. The housewife could not imagine running out of work, so she
agreed. The man was most industrious, washing clothes, mopping floors,
preparing food, and cultivating the garden, and after a few weeks the
woman began to fear that she could not keep him busy. Indeed, she was
becoming weary of finding tasks for this superefficient worker. Finally,
she thought of a new task—building a twenty-foot-high pole in back of
her house. Henceforth, whenever she did not have an immediate task for
the man to complete, she ordered him to climb up and down the pole
rather than be idle. Then when a new task came up, she assigned him to
it. When he completed the work, she again assigned him to climb up and
down the pole.

The pole is a metaphor for a mantra. It keeps the mind busy between
important tasks. Most religions have their own form of a mantra. The
Jesus Prayer is from the Christian tradition. So is "Hail Mary full of
Grace," which Catholics recite. I have Hindu friends who repeat "Om
Sai Ram" or "I am that" in the back of their minds throughout the day.
Bahá'ís sometimes repeat "Allah-u-Abah." From the Buddhists I learned,
"May the world have peace and harmony." Some mantras are considered
powerful because they trigger a thought-sound vibration within the mind
and body, which is in tune with the vibration of the universe. The
best-known of these thought-sound vibrations is "Om."[3]

When assisting someone in defining a mantra that will help correct his or her self-image, I use the same guidelines as presented in Chapter Five for autosuggestion. It is important to stay in the present tense and to speak gently, respectfully, and positively. Be fully present and aware of the mantra repeating in your mind during the early stages. When your mind jumps away, just bring it back to the mantra. It helps to feel it, believe it, and mean it. And, as for autosuggestion, I urge people to start with "I am," followed by a verb with an "ing," such as "I am becoming," or "I am feeling." The "I am" seems to have special power, and the "ing" moves them toward their desired future state.

• • •

A mantra can serve as an antidote to a nasty internal judge. Jack was an accomplished manager who joined the EMBA program to obtain a credential for promotion to an anticipated C-level opening. People in high-level positions sometimes feel like frauds. The confident exterior hides massive insecurity and a severe internal judge saying they are worthless, which they believe others will soon discover. Jack believed his success to be due to factors outside his control, and credited his "failures" to himself. As Jack talked, I thought a mantra might help offset his harsh inner voice and perhaps reprogram his self-image. Therapy was out of the question. A mantra could be repeated during his busy days. We considered "I am becoming more confident," which I thought got to the core issue. Jack preferred something to directly counter the inner critic. This was a tough one. However, any intentional thought that replaced the inner critic would be an improvement. Jack liked "I am deserving of my position" and said he would repeat it as often as possible during the day, especially whenever he heard that voice. He could modify the mantra as he figured out what had traction for him.

When I talked to Jack later in the semester, he said the mantra had a valuable effect. It helped him become even more aware of the self-critical thoughts. He saw them more clearly. He learned to shift from those thoughts to the mantra. After a few weeks, the negative thoughts became a trigger to start the mantra. "What a perfect outcome," I thought to myself. "The self-critical thoughts have become the stick that stirs the fire, destroying itself in the process." The mantra was a mechanism to detach from the critical, "I'm a fraud" thoughts that had plagued him. He varied the mantra, but the result was the same: the critical voice was losing steam and losing its power over him. He was training his mind with a mantra to leave those disabling thoughts behind.

I practiced different mantras in different ways for about a year, and found them useful as a way to insert intentional thoughts into my mind to push back on the unintentional junk passing through. I still use a mantra occasionally. Continuously repeating any mantra is a good way to train and focus the mind to replace its constant mindless chatter. The content of the mantra also seems important. For example, a Sanskrit mantra whose meaning I did not know seemed to have less effect than a mantra in English that my inner elephant could understand and absorb. Longer mantras take more intention than a short, easily repeatable phrase. An example of a longer mantra is "From ignorance, lead me to truth; from darkness, lead me to light; from death, lead me to immortality; om, peace, peace, peace." A longer mantra is probably better used during a period of focused meditation. A short, easily repeatable mantra seems the best way to keep the mind climbing up and down the pole during idle periods of the day.

One mantra that had power for me was "I am staying awake." I started to notice that for some brief periods during the day I felt that I was "awake," in the present moment, and fully in my inner executive. But the pace of the day would pull me back into unconscious reactions and behaviors. My inner elephant was productive, but I wanted to extend the periods when I was awake in the sense of being able to observe and influence my mind and emotions rather than be carried along by them. The "I am staying awake" mantra felt right. I was repeating it more than a thousand times a day, and I could sense that my inner executive was successfully taking mindshare away from my inner elephant. I was making progress.

Then my daughter and grandchild moved in with us unexpectedly for several weeks. There was a predictable friction generated by people unused to living together figuring out which household system and family system would prevail. There were numerous points at which frustration might trigger upset within me. But I kept repeating that mantra and . . . something unusual happened. I could sense the upset within me as it began its rush toward filling my mind, as if I had accidentally triggered an avalanche while skiing. But when I kept saying, "I am staying awake," the avalanche did not sweep me away. It was as if I skied up to a higher peak, and the rush of emotion could not quite reach me. If it had, I would have been engulfed with a feeling of anger or frustration and probably would have expressed it, causing a fight and hard feelings. Instead, I repeated the mantra, and the emotional upsurge subsided. I was free. I was able to stay above the avalanche. Instead of being upset, I could see an opposite point of view without getting caught up for or against it. I could help resolve differences rather than add to differences. Indeed, when I repeat that mantra, I feel as though I can stay "awake" for as long as I can continue to repeat it. But there are still periods when I don't repeat the mantra, either because I am absorbed in work or my automatic stream of thoughts takes over.

Remember, *intentions come into being through the power of words.* This is the essence of a mantra. It brings into being a mental intention that gives specific guidance to your inner elephant. Saying a mantra puts a small burst of energy behind the intention. Intention is brought to life by the mantra.

Remember This

Repeat a Mantra

- A mantra is an intentional thought pushed forward by your intelligent will (inner executive).
- Your intentions come into being through the power of words.
- A mantra keeps away unwanted thoughts and provides instruction to the inner elephant.
- Repeat a mantra at every opportunity during the day.
- A mantra can change basic assumptions underlying your self-image.
- Once you have had some practice, a negative thought will serve as a trigger to start repetition of a positive mantra.

A variation is to sing or chant the mantra. One manager told me that he experimented with chanting a short religious mantra. The chanting seemed to add power to his intention. I like that idea. It would be like singing your favorite song over and over in your mind with uplifting intention. I tried chanting (singing) a mantra, and it did seem to help my mind hold on to the mantra for a longer time. It was more fun than simple forced repetition. But for me, simple, quiet repetition seems more natural. However you do it, the payoff comes with a quieter and more focused mind. The manager insisted that chanting lessened his negativity and that after a few days he found life easier and more enjoyable.

If the idea of a mantra or chant appeals to you, I encourage you to try it. Devise a phrase that resonates with your heart and stick with it for several days. The important thing over the long term is to reprogram your mind by training it with the mantra to take over the share of mind normally spent in negative chatter that reinforces some negative aspect of the self-image you no longer want. The outcome can be likened to that of fire. The light and heat of the fire will gradually destroy unwanted thoughts that would rush through your mind automatically. The mantra can calm and quiet the inner elephant, healing its frantic nature, enabling it to focus and follow through on its assignments without resistance or distractions.[4]

Prayer May Help, but Not the Way You Think

A prayer can be similar to a mantra. A prayer is a deliberate, intentional, and willful mental action. Intentional mental action engages the higher inner executive to create thoughts to replace the ad hoc thoughts sent into the mind by the inner elephant. A prayer can be a short phrase similar to the Jesus Prayer, the repetition of a longer memorized prayer, or spontaneously talking to a higher power. Many people think of successful prayer as getting what they want by asking a higher power to give it. I don't know whether that works. But I do believe that one value of prayer is that it harnesses intention, just as a mantra, visualization, or autosuggestion does. Saying a prayer creates an intention in your mind, which is very different from the junk thoughts normally flowing through.

Which of the following thoughts would you like to keep alive in your mind?

1. "I am so worthless, so awful. I can't do anything right. No one likes me. I'll never achieve anything. No one really loves me. Whatever I do, there are mistakes and wasted time. Everyone else is better than me. I hope my boss doesn't figure out that I don't know what I'm doing."

2. "Bestow upon me a heart which, like unto glass, may be illuminated with the light of Thy love, and confer upon me thoughts which may change this world into a rose garden through the outpourings of heavenly grace."[5]

Or consider which of the following types of thoughts would be more likely to uplift or enhance your life.

1. "Those people offend me. Why don't they act correctly? He's an idiot. She's so tactless. She doesn't know how to dress well, she's too loud, and could stand to lose a few pounds. He's so thoughtless, so narcissistic. He just sucks up to everyone. That's why he's done so well. He's not as smart as I am. She gets by on her sex appeal—and sleeping her way to success."

2. "Help me to be generous in prosperity and thankful in adversity. Let me be worthy of the trust of my neighbor, and look upon him with a bright and friendly face. Help me be a treasure to the poor, a help to the needy, fair in judgment, and loving in my speech. Let me possess a pure, kindly and radiant heart. Let integrity and uprightness distinguish all my acts."[6]

What do you want to keep alive in your mind? Without some intentional thoughts of the second kind to fill up the mind, the first kind of words and thoughts will lurk there. Which do you prefer? I think intentional positive thoughts beat negative thoughts every time, but you need to exert effort and intention to keep them at the forefront. If you have a religious orientation, prayer is an excellent way to take charge of your thoughts.

There are various kinds of prayer, which reflect different aspects of a person's relationship with a higher power. Perhaps the commonest prayer is the *petition,* asking for something for oneself. This might be considered a form of "begging" to satisfy one's own physical or ego needs, such as for a job, winning the lottery, a cancer cure, a promotion, food, or a new car. A related prayer is called *intercession,* which asks for an intervention on behalf of other people, perhaps to cure an illness or help them find their way in the world. Another common type of prayer is *confession,* which involves admitting and apologizing for a wrongdoing and requesting forgiveness, and perhaps asking assistance to behave correctly. A prayer of *adoration* gives praise and honor to the vastness and greatness of a higher power. A prayer of *thanksgiving* is an offering of gratitude for the created world and for specific bounty in one's life.

All these prayers are the same in one respect: you are putting your intention into words and making it explicit. You are expending enough energy to bring to life in your mind what you want to have happen. I view asking for material things to meet physical and ego needs as the prayer of the inner elephant. The petition prayer, for example, tends to tell the higher power what to do by requesting specific outcomes or trying to dictate the future. This type of prayer puts the inner elephant in the center of things. The inner elephant wants the higher power to respond to its will.

Other prayers are based in humility and are used to send love or to improve oneself. These prayers arise from the inner executive because they seek assistance toward humility, a higher goal, or something bigger than collecting more things for oneself. The best advice I have heard about prayer is simply to pray for inner peace and contentment, because that reflects the happiness that everyone seems to want and is a good thought to keep alive in your mind. Let your higher power figure out how to provide it.

I have had coaching sessions with a number of people who have strong religious beliefs. Most of them are comfortable with the ideas in this book, including mantras. However, one MBA student, Felix, was distinctly uncomfortable leaving God out of the equation. On his own, he had developed his witness and was able to see his negative thoughts toward other people. Although he did not use a mantra, he would consciously rebut a negative thought with a response such as "No, that's not true. John is a friend of mine and a good person." His concentration was good enough to spot individual thoughts, so we left it at that for handling the criticisms of his inner judge.

Felix wanted my help with his monkey mind. His mind jumped around a lot, landing mostly on judgmental thoughts and worries about the future. He wanted his mind to stay more in the present. Felix was clearly a sparkplug and energizer, and he wanted to feel more executive presence rather than moderate anxiety. We talked about various mantras for staying in the moment, such as, "I am staying present in this moment." He simply converted the mantra into a prayer: "Lord, help me be present in this moment." When I talked to him later, he reported that this prayer seemed to have the same effect for him as a mantra has for other people. He said his mind was more in the moment rather than thinking ahead and worrying about the future. His moderate anxiety seemed to be calming down.

Repeating a prayer may have other benefits. The negative side of the inner elephant seems to be less visible in the lives of people who pray as part of a spiritual practice.[7] A review of research in psychology concluded that religious belief promotes self-control. For example, as early as the 1920s, students who spent more time in Sunday school were found to do better at laboratory tests measuring their self-discipline. "Brain scan studies have shown that when people pray or meditate, there is a lot of activity in two parts of the brain that are important for self-regulation and control of attention and emotion."[8]

I have learned a lot from religious traditions and practices. I like the ideas of mantra and prayer. I especially like the idea of a short prayer, perhaps repeated like a mantra, such as "Let me speak only kind words," "Help me stay in this moment," "Help me stay in the flow with this work," or "Please help me learn the lesson of true humility." These prayers are a useful way to train the mind, take charge of the mind, and pull it away from the inner elephant's meandering thoughts and impulses. The best advice I ever heard for prayer also works for a mantra: pray as though you have fallen into a deep well and are trying to be heard by someone above ground. In other words, pray as though you mean it.

Remember This

Prayer May Help

- A prayer is a deliberate, intentional, and willful mental action.
- A prayer can harness intention just as a mantra or visualization does.
- A prayer keeps alive in your mind what you want to have happen.
- A mantra can be reworded into a short prayer if you prefer that form.
- People who pray seem to have better self-regulation.

Find something that works for you. Even if you are not a religious person, prayer is still helpful because it speaks your intention to your inner elephant if not to a higher power. The outcome can be good either way. And the prayer will keep away automatic thoughts. Just getting rid of some of the negative, harsh, self-defeating chatter will produce an improvement in your mood and your leadership style.

14

Mend Your Mind
with Meditation

*You must learn to be still in the midst of activity, and to be
vibrantly alive in repose.*
—Indira Gandhi

*Let us remember that within us there is a palace
of immense magnificence.*
—Teresa of Avila

THE MOMENT THAT CHANGED David Lynch, best known as the director
of such surrealist feature films as *Lost Highway*, *Blue Velvet*, and
Mulholland Drive, was when his ex-wife called to tell him about her
experience with Transcendental Meditation (TM). "There was something
in her voice. A change. A quality of happiness. And I thought, That's
what I want."[1] So Lynch found a TM instructor who gave him a mantra,
which he repeated silently to himself for twenty minutes. Lynch fell into
something blissful during that first meditation and has meditated twice
a day for twenty minutes ever since. The meditation awakened him,
as if a psychological weight had been lifted from his shoulders. After
about two weeks, his ex-wife came to him and asked, "What's going
on?" He paused for a moment and said, "What do you mean?" And she

responded, "This anger, where did it go?" Lynch hadn't realized that his ever-present anger had lifted.[2]

Meditation did not target a specific bad habit to make Lynch a better leader and movie director; rather, meditation awakened a deep sense of happiness. After meditating, Lynch simply goes about the business of his day with increased joy and creativity, heightened pleasure in living, and disappearing negativity.

His experience was so life changing that Lynch recently started a foundation to promote meditation in middle and high schools. Lynch believes that people need to concentrate on one thing at a time and not have a million different things distracting them. A person's capacity for concentration and creativity grow when he or she starts meditating and diving within. With meditation, wherever you focus your attention becomes "livelier." Work gets better, and people get happier.[3] Lynch likens meditation to removing a rubber suit, which is constraining, uncomfortable, and smelly. Meditation grants freedom from mental constraints and negativity.

Why Meditate?

My experience with meditation has been positive, although not as dramatic as Lynch's. I was initially taught a sitting posture and how to focus on my breath by a Buddhist group in Santa Fe. Experimenting with this practice at home in the mornings, I would occasionally feel a burst of well-being at some point during the day. The sense of well-being was delightful but unpredictable. My best experience followed a Vipassana meditation retreat in Texas in which the group meditated about ten hours a day for ten days. There I was taught to develop a finely tuned focus into the body, using the mind's attention to search for any thoughts, feelings, or physical sensations. Our instruction for back home was to meditate two hours each day, one hour in the morning and one in the late afternoon, using our well-tuned internal focus to search inwardly.

Two hours a day was going to be impossible, but I decided to try it, and managed to perform the assigned meditation for three months before the pressures of the world started chipping away at my meditation time. Those were among the most efficient three months of my life. I seemed to be in the "flow" most the time with respect to work and other activities. By 2:00 P.M. or so, I had finished my normal day's work and would be looking for other things to do. Tasks I normally avoided, such as clearing piles in my office, digging through files, or doing library work, I waded into without hesitation. I felt no distractions. There was no sense of favoring some tasks and avoiding others. Whatever was in front of me I did, as if all work were the same. It was like opening e-mails in the order received rather than based on what I wanted to read or avoid.

There was also a difference in the way I related to people. I didn't feel any new love or compassion for others, but no one bothered me. People's idiosyncrasies and annoyances no longer had meaning for me. I saw each person as just being who he or she was, and I just accepted that I had to work within those limitations—no problem, no stress. Nothing got to me. I was always in a good mood. Life at home was tranquil, partly because nothing bothered me and partly because I had energy and flow for tasks at home as well as more time and presence to devote to family. My desire for snacks declined. As pleasing as that period was, I started meditating less and less as the demands of the world intruded and old habits returned, though with somewhat less strength than previously.

What accounts for the changes based on meditation? Meditation does not focus on correcting a specific problem. With meditation, dysfunctional thoughts or behaviors, like Lynch's anger or my felt resistance to some work, just fall away on their own. In my case, and probably for Lynch as well, it felt as though meditation completely relaxed my inner elephant, such that it was no longer running the show. Its constant negative judgments about tasks and people, its attractions and aversions, its impulses and cravings seemed to disappear, as if the elephant were asleep. Distractions, reactions, and stray impulses were not infecting the flow of my day. My inner executive seemed completely in charge. Whatever I willed, I did. Another explanation is that my inner executive became super strong through meditation and thus had complete dominance over the peculiarities and dysfunctions of my inner elephant. An explanation given for the success of TM by Lynch, for example, is that the mind taps into some sort of universal consciousness or energy. If we normally have a golf-ball-size consciousness of ourselves and the world, then we are stuck in a golf-ball-size set of elephant responses. So if meditation takes us into a larger consciousness, our capacity for asserting our will and enjoying creativity and flow can multiply many times. It felt like that to me.

Many people are not attracted to meditation, and you should trust your instincts. I do not teach meditation in my classes or programs because some people are uncomfortable with that use of class time, although I have held a few sessions outside class for people who request it. Meditation methods and techniques vary widely to suit different personalities and temperaments. If you are interested in meditation, it is important to select an approach that feels right to you. Meditation is a culmination of sorts, drawing on the ability to concentrate, an inward focus, your witness, use of a mantra, and visualization. Use whichever parts are correct for you.

•••

Assuming meditation fits your temperament, what might be its benefit for you? It comes back to the point made in earlier chapters that everyone has an internal judge tossing up critical thoughts about self and others, an internal attorney providing persuasive self-justifications for thoughtless behavior, and an internal magician pushing illusory thinking that avoids reality, particularly about oneself. Thanks to the way your mind works, you probably jump to conclusions, are influenced by impulses and avoidances, misjudge the future value of things, and look for happiness in the wrong places. Meditation is something of an overall solution that can overcome dysfunctional habits of leadership or individual performance. Meditation can improve your intention and your ability to manage yourself. It can quiet egocentric desires and impulses, help you focus attention and energy, and facilitate a positive attitude in your relationships. It has the potential to increase the strength of your inner executive and help you transcend the limits of your inner elephant, whatever your limits are.

Medtronic's former CEO, Bill George, has practiced meditation twice a day for twenty minutes for over thirty years. He says, "Out of anything, it has had the greatest impact on my career."[4] When traveling, he meditates on the airplane during taxiing and takeoff until the flight attendant offers him a drink. Roger Berkowitz, CEO of Legal Sea Foods in Boston, wrote in *Inc.* magazine, "The first thing I do in the morning is retreat to my den and meditate. I meditate twice a day for 20 minutes, closing my eyes, clearing my mind, and repeating my mantra until I'm in a semiconscious state. Sometimes, I'm wrestling with an issue before meditation, and afterwards the answer is suddenly clear."[5] Former Aetna International chairman Michael Stephen started meditating in 1974. He claims meditation helped transform him from an impatient, demanding know-it-all into a more effective leader.[6] Former Time-Warner chieftain Gerald Levin's advice to executives in the thick of a busy professional life is to "find a calm, meditative state every day."[7]

Networking guru Keith Ferrazzi, author of *Never Eat Alone* and sought-after speaker, revealed his secret to networking. It's not about technical skills or working a room. The key to connecting is "not being an asshole." The most effective path he found to achieve that goal is meditation. Ferrazzi spends ten days every year at a silent meditation retreat.[8] Other well-known meditation devotees include junk bond king turned philanthropist Mike Milken, NBA coach Phil Jackson, and

CEO Marc Benioff of Salesforce.com. Google employees have organized twice-weekly meditation hours.[9] A documentary film called *The Dhamma Brothers* showed an intensive ten-day meditation for prisoners in a maximum-security prison in Alabama. The prisoners had harsh personalities in a harsh environment. No one thought these hard-case prisoners could tolerate ten days of meditation. They tolerated it just fine, and disciplinary infractions dropped by 20 percent. The director of treatment at the Alabama Department of Corrections said inmates were "better able to control their anger and better able to conduct themselves."[10]

Over the last decade or so, much research has been conducted to test the impact of meditation, particularly Buddhist meditation practices. In the laboratory, the brain function of monks who have meditated regularly for years was found to be profoundly different from that of the average human brain, with highly developed areas for positive emotion—more gray matter in the prefrontal cortexes, the location of the brain's executive function. This change in physiology enabled monks to respond with calm and equanimity in a crisis. In other words, they respond thoughtfully and with mental clarity (their inner executive) in a crisis situation rather than having a strong emotional reaction. In a related research project, four dozen employees from a biotech company who had no meditation experience meditated once a week for three hours. The researchers discovered that after even this short time meditating, subjects felt much better and recorded positive changes in their brains and bodies.[11] A study of medical and premedical students compared to a control group was undertaken to determine whether meditation helped students cope with enormous stress. The findings reported sharp declines in anxiety and psychological distress such as depression, and sharp increases in empathy and feelings of spirituality.[12] There has been less research on children, but some schools are experimenting with limited meditation quiet times. The idea is to help children slow down, calm down, and think before acting. Fifth graders at Park Day School in California showed increased control of attention and less negative internal chatter. One girl described with some relief the decline in what she called "the gossip inside my head saying I'm stupid, I'm fat or I'm going to fail math."[13]

Remember This

Why Meditate?

- Regular meditation can produce unexpected reductions in dysfunctional thinking and behavior.

- Meditation appears to develop a connection to one's higher consciousness.
- Research supports the beneficial impact of meditation on stress and anxiety.

An Easy Way to Start

If the idea of meditation holds some appeal for you, it is worth investigating. You will find many wonderful books in the library or bookstore on how to meditate. Perhaps the simplest approach is described in *The Relaxation Response,* by Herbert Benson, which contains medical evidence supporting meditation. Another book, *Meditation: The Complete Guide,* by Patricia Monaghan and Eleanor Viereck, provides a thoughtful survey of many techniques. There are a ton of audiotapes of instruction, recorded music, and guided meditations for you to consider. Better yet, attend a meditation workshop or retreat and receive personal instruction from a teacher.

A simple way to begin meditating is with the following steps.

1. Beforehand, pick an anchor word, short phrase, saying, or short prayer that reflects a positive aspiration for your belief system. A word such as "love" or "compassion" is fine, or use a phrase that has meaning for you, such as "May the world have peace and harmony." You can also count backward from three hundred. You can focus on your breath. The point is to have an object on which your mind will focus.

2. Sit quietly in a comfortable position. If you're in a straight chair, your back should be erect with the lower part curved a bit forward rather than rigidly straight, so that the weight of your head and shoulders will rest naturally on your backbone. Think of your backbone as a stack of coins with a curve rather than as a straight rod. Keep your feet flat on the floor, and let your hands rest in your lap.

3. Close your eyes.

4. Relax your body before starting the meditation. Use some technique that relaxes you, perhaps progressive muscle relaxation (tensing each muscle group for three seconds and then relaxing it). Work through your feet, calves, thighs, buttocks, abdomen, hands, forearms, upper arms, shoulders, back, neck, and head. Then relax and let go of all tightness and stress from within.

5. Breathe slowly and naturally. Repeat your anchor word or phrase slowly and with awareness. It may help to synchronize the word repetition or counting with your breathing. Whenever your mind wanders, gently bring it back to your object of concentration.

6. Assume a passive attitude. This means that if a negative thought or emotion arises, do not push it away. Allow whatever happens to happen. Just continue repeating your anchor phrase. The only effort is to concentrate on your object. Let all else pass by. Don't judge yourself in terms of how well you are doing or how deeply you are meditating. Don't try to make something happen, other than repeating your phrase.

7. Continue for ten minutes to start, working up to twenty to thirty minutes as your concentration improves.

8. Practicing twice daily at the same time every day produces the best result. The body and mind will learn more quickly on a fixed schedule.

As your mind learns to quiet down during meditation, you may repeat the anchor phrase more slowly, leaving gaps of quiet between phrases. The space between thoughts is your peace and bliss. As your meditation practice develops, you may want to experiment with different approaches, including different kinds of objects on which to focus, such as visual images, a part of your body such as the spot between your eyebrows, questions, or your breath.

Meditation takes some focus and effort to get started. For example, Marvin, a thirty-two-year-old operations manager, reported to me the following:

> Quiet time for me is rare. One afternoon I got home from work early while my wife was out with the kids. I sat in the back room for twenty minutes trying to meditate and think about nothing. I tried to focus on a short mantra. Initially my mind would scatter among many ongoing projects and pressures. Somewhere in the middle of the session, my elephant calmed down and I was content to think about nothing but the mantra for perhaps five minutes. Then after about ten minutes, I started to get anxious about the many things I needed to complete during the evening. My elephant was taking control over my weak executive. However, during the evening I noticed calmness in my mood and a more positive mindset. I did not feel as irritable as I often do after a day at the office. I had much more patience with my children and a softer attitude toward my wife. I felt a bit happier and more content.

Two Essentials

All meditation practices share two essentials: the mind has to maintain a passive attitude toward whatever is happening, and the mind has to have an object of focus. In my meditations, I found maintaining the passive attitude to be more difficult than developing concentration and focus. A passive attitude means nonattachment to whatever comes into your mind. Something in my mind persistently tried to make things happen and wanted to control the meditation process. To hold a passive attitude means to be an alert observer who concentrates on the present moment rather than tries to control things. Don't try to block unwanted thoughts or push them away. Try not to judge yourself or feel frustrated about your progress. Don't buy into a thought such as, "I should be doing better at this by now." Simply focus on your verbal anchor or breathing. Let go of judgments about how your meditation should proceed, whether you think you are doing well or poorly, or whether your meditation is deep or shallow. Do not set goals. Do not try to achieve goals. Do not try to force anything to happen. These actions take you out of the present moment and back into your inner elephant. Make an effort to concentrate, but nothing more. Just relax and observe whatever thoughts or impulses arise, returning to your object of focus when your mind jumps away. With practice, you will be able to increase the amount of time you are free of the unrelenting mental chatter.

The other essential is a mental object or anchor—a sound, word, mantra, breath, prayer, visualization, even a body part or blank space—used within the mind as a point of focus. The repetition or continuous use of this object trains your mind to focus intentionally on the object and thereby disengage from the random chatter and impulses of the inner elephant. Choose whatever object works for you, but there must be an object of focus. As soon as you are aware of a distracting thought, disengage from the intruding thought and return your attention to your object.

There may be times, such as late afternoon on a busy workday, when the force of random chatter is so great that you cannot maintain focus on your word, phrase, or breathing. The agitated inner elephant will be tossing up too many thoughts to ignore. There are three ways to give a boost to your concentration during such challenging times:

1. If you are repeating a word or phrase in your mind, move your lips and whisper it. Engaging your mouth and lips will help pull your attention away from the onrushing thoughts back to your object of concentration. Go back to repeating it silently in your mind after the involuntary thoughts quiet down.

2. If you are watching your breathing, temporarily take control of your breath until your inner elephant quiets down. Taking control of your breathing simply means you might start with three deep breaths and then return to your normal breathing rate, adding perhaps one second to each in-breath and out-breath. That one second asserts your intention and will help maintain your focus on the breath. When your mind calms down, return to watching your natural breathing.

3. Another aid is to synchronize the word or phrase with your breathing. If using a two-word mantra, you might say one word on the in-breath and the second word on the out-breath. Or you might count to ten synchronously with your breathing. You can say "one" silently (or out loud if needed) during your first in-breath and again with your first out-breath. Then say "two" silently during your second in-breath and again with your out-breath. After counting for ten breaths, start over with the number one. Do not set goals for how far you can count, because that is inner-elephant thinking rather than staying in the present moment. Maintain your passive attitude by being content with counting to ten.

For example, here is one manager's experience with gaining control during a mindfulness meditation:

> On a Sunday morning when my family was out of town, I decided to meditate for thirty minutes with no distractions. It was difficult to remain focused and keep my monkey mind quiet. I noticed the buzz of the cicadas outside, the roar of my neighbor's car, and my cell phone message beeper. The harder I tried to stop the thoughts from coming into my head, the faster they came. I knew I had to just let go and not try so hard to block my thoughts. I said "breathe in" and "breathe out" as I breathed to help reduce distracting thoughts. Counting to eight while inhaling and backwards from eight while exhaling was even more effective. After several minutes of breathing and letting go, I achieved a blank mind for brief intervals, during which I experienced a remarkable sense of peace, intense pleasure, and periods of overwhelming joy and excitement. Was this nirvana? I felt my "presence" increase, and my field of vision seemed wider. When I was distracted with a specific thought, I could feel my field of vision narrow and my presence-in-the-moment shrink.

This is a nice example of positive outcomes from an intentional effort to meditate and calm an otherwise jumping mind.

Remember This

Remember Two Essentials

- Meditation takes mental effort and focus to get started. Practice meditation at the same time and place each day.
- Essential 1 is a passive attitude.
- Essential 2 is to have a mental anchor or object on which to concentrate.
- If you are unable to hold your focus,
    - Repeat the anchor word out loud.
    - Take control of your breathing by extending each natural breath by one second.
    - Synchronize your mental anchor word and your breathing.

Mindfulness Meditation

Mindfulness meditation is a Buddhist technique taught as watching the breath rather than repeating a word or phrase. Paying attention to your breath means focusing on the nostrils, the sensation of air moving in and out of your body, or the movement in your belly. Focusing on the tip of the nostrils and "watching" (or feeling) the touch of the breath on the nostrils works for most people. It is quite simple. Just focus on the breath for ten to twenty minutes, or however long you want to meditate. Focusing on your breath focuses your mind on the present moment. Breathing is happening right now. Of course your elephant mind will jump away to other thoughts. When these thoughts arise, observe them without attachment.

You may experience some dilemma between concentration and relaxed awareness. Initially, most effort goes into concentration. As you progress, the idea is to concentrate on your breathing, but with not too much effort. Relaxed concentration is the key. Mindfulness meditation is about focusing just enough to be aware of your breathing while also being aware of other thoughts and impressions that come into your mind as well as sensations in your body. Try to be aware of your breath *and* notice whatever else is happening inside. Nonattachment means you just observe whatever thoughts and feelings arise and let them come and go without buying in to them, controlling them, or fighting them.

Valerie, an EMBA student, was tired and apprehensive about the first exam of the term.

> I could not quiet my mind and get into studying. So for thirty minutes I let myself relax and do nothing but sit and watch my breath. I had many thoughts, but did not dwell on them, letting them fade away. It worked better than I expected. After thirty minutes, I felt refreshed, calm, and less apprehensive about the amount of work to do in preparation for the exam. I managed to stay focused much better with less anxiety.

You cannot develop nonattachment by force. Like Valerie, try to remain undisturbed, unaffected, and uninvolved with the thoughts and images in your mind. Gently bring your mind back to present-moment breathing whenever a thought takes it away. This is nonattachment toward your inner elephant. This letting go will let your mind settle like a glass of muddy water. If you are patient and don't stir the water, the mud will settle to the bottom of the glass, leaving clear water above. Over time, lessened attachment will quiet your inner elephant and strengthen your inner executive.

Focusing on the breath brings your mind into present-moment awareness and lowers the noise level of constant inner chatter. When the noise has subsided, the reality of peace and being emerges. This new reality has been hidden by the noise of the inner elephant much as the sun is blocked by clouds. The quiet mind allows the sun to shine. If the mind is especially agitated, take a few deep breaths, and with each exhale imagine the tensions and pressures being released from within you. Then let your body breathe normally. Avoid extreme breathing, including holding the breath to get a physical effect, which can cause unintended damage.

Deirdre moved into a new house and was feeling overwhelmed.

> I decided to meditate. I felt the urge to unpack the boxes around me, and my thoughts were self-critical. I felt guilty and unproductive for sitting still. I just watched the urge and focused on my breath. Near the end of twenty minutes, each moment was like a special treat for all the hard work I had been doing. I actually started to relax. Something inside me thanked me for the downtime. I was more focused and productive the rest of the day. This was a profound experience for me. I am now meditating each morning. I get up earlier, have a relaxed breakfast, and start the day off more calm. It is easier to stay in the executive part of my brain when I begin the day with a relaxed mind.

Mindfulness meditation represents a substantive change compared to how people normally handle distracting or negative thoughts and emotions. The idea here is to let go, allow the urge and thought—even a negative depressive thought, a criticism of self or other, the feeling of anger or frustration—and just watch it. Just be with it. View these difficult thoughts with a kind awareness rather than try to fight, suppress, or resist them. There is no need to solve or fix anything that arises. Just let thoughts pass by like a gentle breeze on a spring day. Jon Kabat-Zinn quoted a colleague who said she thought meditation practice "was all about aiming the attention and then sustaining that focus moment by moment."[14] That captures meditation as I understand it. And as you practice mindfulness meditation, you will find value in making it a way of life rather than a technique. Rather than meditate for twenty minutes and then stop, let yourself expand your focus and peaceful state throughout larger portions of the day.

• TRY THIS •

Practice Mindfulness Meditation

1. Sit quietly in a comfortable position with eyes closed.

2. Focus on the breath to stay in the present moment.

3. Expand awareness to thoughts and feelings.

4. Stay nonattached to anything that arises within.

5. Do not resist or suppress unpleasant thoughts and feelings.

6. Extend the peaceful mental state to other parts of your day.

Try Visual Rather Than Verbal

Chapter Six described the power of mental visualization to influence your inner elephant's behavior. The same is true for meditation, for which many visualizations to heal specific emotions have been designed and published in books on visualization. Here is my favorite visualization to use during a short meditation:

> Imagine there is a lump of black coal in the region of your heart. Use your mind to fan the coal with your breath. Visualize the lump of coal in your chest, inhale, and then direct your exhale towards the lump and fan it into ignition. Continue fanning the coal for several minutes until the ember is visualized as red-hot in the region of your

heart. Once fully glowing, this ember will provide inner warmth and peace.[15]

I and several of my acquaintances have also used a light (Jyoti) meditation as a simple and efficient way to tame the inner elephant. It was originally proposed by Zoroaster to his followers and is also included in suggested meditation practices by Indian spiritual teacher Sathya Sai Baba.[16] Here is a shorthand version:

First, sit in a comfortable posture in which your back is relatively straight. Light a candle, the flame of which you can easily observe. Close your eyes, relax your mind, and become calm by whatever means you prefer. When calm and centered, open your eyes and gaze steadily at the candle flame. This might last a minute or so to impress the flame in your mind in the region between the eyebrows. Maintain your focus on the image as you bring it into your mind and hold it for a few seconds.

Now bring the flame downward to the region of the heart. Hold the light near the heart and allow it to gradually expand outward to fill the chest area. Now, slowly and with concentration, begin to move the flame throughout your body. Bring the flame upward to the area of the throat, jaw, and tongue, bathing them in light for several seconds. Then bring the flame upward to the ears for a few seconds, then to the eyes. You may divide the light into two parts and carry the divided flame to the two ears and two eyes. Join the two flames into one and bring it to the top of your head. Let the light inundate your whole head until it is bright and clear. Now bring the light down through the neck and divide it into two and slowly bring it down through the arms into the hands. Bring the flame back up the arms into the chest and slowly move down through the abdomen and buttocks. Then split the light again and move it through your legs down to your feet, shedding light as it travels. Repeat the process of moving the flame carefully around the body with the intention to purify each part.

After ten or fifteen minutes of bathing the inner body in that resplendent light, spend a few moments sharing it with the world. Reestablish the light in the heart and increase the flame to reach out from your heart toward other human beings. Imagine bathing a single person in the light from head to foot, starting with close family members, then move to other relatives, friends, or acquaintances. Then extend the light to people you may consider difficult or antagonistic. Concentrate on bathing them in light and love. Finally, expand the light to shine throughout your home, business, neighborhood, city, country, and finally bathe the whole world in the light that emanates from the center of your heart. When finished, bring the light back into your heart and slowly extinguish the flame. Remain quiet for a few moments and then undertake your daily activities.

The light meditation is similar to Vipassana, a meditation technique taught by the Buddha and currently taught in Vipassana centers around the world. Typical classes are ten-day silent meditation retreats. Experienced meditators can sign up for longer retreats, such as for thirty days. After developing their concentration to a fine focus, participants turn the mind's attention inward to search through the body for sensations. The inner body's arising sensations are the objects of focus during meditation. The mind's attention is moved slowly around the body, through the arms and legs, chest, back, the head, face, hands, and feet, through muscles and over the surface of the skin to detect any sensations. The mind also watches for automatic thoughts that arise. There is no mantra or visualization. The Vipassana practice is to focus on moving the mind's attention through each part of the physical body.

• TRY THIS •

Try Visual Rather Than Verbal

1. Visualize an ember of coal in your heart area to experience warmth and peace.
2. Use the light meditation to bathe your inner form in light and warmth.
3. Learn to extend the light through all parts of your head and body.
4. Then extend the light to other people and the world.

Of the meditation techniques I have tried over the years, I felt I made the greatest progress when I focused directly on the random thoughts that arose in my mind. You can do the same in your mind by imagining yourself as a cat sitting outside a mouse hole, fully alert, waiting to pounce on any mouse that emerges. That mouse is the next thought, and if you concentrate hard, you will see it coming. If you see it, it will fade away. By focusing on the thoughts, at last I was experiencing some quiet space between thoughts, which is called the *still point*. When I was able to see the thoughts directly, suddenly they scattered and disappeared like minnows in a shallow stream. It felt weird at first for the chatter to subside, but it is during the expanding quiet that real meditation occurs. Mental chatter is like a veil blocking the light. As soon as your mind starts to quiet down and remove the veil, you can start to see the light—the empty space, the still point—rather than the veil of thoughts from your inner elephant.

Contemplative Meditation

Another way to quiet the mind's chatter and free up some quiet space is to ask yourself questions or to contemplate a puzzlement. Asking a question gives the mind something to focus on, and if the question or puzzlement is difficult, your mind may stop chattering while it ponders an answer. The inner elephant's noisy chatter is stopped cold when it has no instant reaction to a big question. A deep question or paradox will engage the mind in reflection and listening for an answer. This is similar to meditating on a Zen koan that the elephant mind cannot answer with its simple logic, causing it to shut up temporarily. Deeper rumination is required. An example of a Zen koan would be "What is the sound of one hand clapping?" or "Who hears?" Another example of a puzzlement requiring an answer on a deeper level is "Everything you think you are, you are not; everything you think you are not, you are." Close your eyes right now and ask yourself one of these questions. Does your mind go quiet while it ponders an answer? Retain your inward focus and wait for the answer. During a longer meditation, you can slowly repeat the question to yourself, leaving time between questions for answers to emerge.

Joel S. Goldsmith (1892–1964), a Christian mystic who lived in the United States, suggested that after you have relaxed and turned inward, an effective meditation is to ponder on the subject, "What is God?" You can ask yourself that question, perhaps repeating it slowly, and see what happens. You might find yourself engaged in a dialogue with yourself as possible answers arise. Goldsmith also recommended meditating on biblical (or other scriptural) phrases, such as "I can of mine own self do nothing," "Ye ask, and receive not, because ye ask amiss," or "I am that I am." You can also ponder the meaning of a single word, such as "soul" or "light." Focusing the mind to contemplate deep issues to which there is not an obvious answer tends to subdue random thinking. And the answers can be pretty significant, going well beyond the elephant mind's typical reaction.

Starting with an inspirational or scriptural statement is called *discursive* or *contemplative* meditation, which is an approach to meditation used with religious subjects by Christians. You focus on and think about the subject phrase using your own reasoning and ideas. You can walk around the concept in your mind, seeing it from many angles, developing your own thoughts and interpretation. Discursive meditation takes more effort and concentration than passively watching thoughts or repeating a mantra. It is focused thinking.

Perhaps read over a verse a few times. Ponder what the text means. Then close your eyes and repeat the verse over and over in your mind. After exhausting the thoughts and ideas that come up within you, your thinking may evolve into a conversation with your higher power, asking its interpretation. Or your mind may go quiet, in which case you can adopt a listening attitude. You can ask the higher power to reveal the truth. You may hear something that is not your own thought, as if from a higher consciousness. The point of discursive meditation is similar to other meditation approaches. Because the ego or inner elephant focuses mainly on itself, contemplation refocuses your mind to contemplate issues bigger than yourself, the meaning of scripture, and a higher power. This form of meditation engages and strengthens your inner executive and will weaken your inner elephant's mental meanderings.

• TRY THIS •

Practice Contemplative Meditation

A challenging question or puzzlement will hold the mind's attention.

1. Select a phrase with meaning from scripture or philosophy writings.
2. Ponder the phrase by turning it over slowly in your mind.
3. Hold your focus and wait for answers to arise from within.

This chapter has touched lightly on the profound topic of meditation. Meditation is a general practice of detaching from your inner elephant rather than addressing specific issues you want to correct. The correction will happen on its own. If you are drawn to the practice, I suggest joining a meditation group, finding a teacher, or at least reading a few books. Choose an approach that looks good to you. Regardless of the approach chosen, the ultimate purpose of meditation is first to focus the mind inward rather than outward, and then to make the mind one-pointed to concentrate on one idea or thought to the exclusion of all random thoughts. This practice leads to a quieter mind with more space between thoughts. With practice, the inner elephant's dysfunctional thoughts, desires, and impulses begin to subside as your inner executive becomes dominant. The outcome is often better focus, a heightened mood, and more energy. Although the techniques and practices in the previous six chapters can help achieve outcomes similar to those of meditation, meditation is probably the strongest approach to giving you power over your inner elephant. You will know that your inner elephant is losing influence when you experience more white space in your mind, more flow in your work, more appreciation in your relationships, more creativity, and more concern for other people. There are many, many approaches to meditation to choose from. Remember, the best approach to meditation is the one that appeals to you most.

PART SIX

Can You Lead from a People Frame of Reference?

15

Change Your Frame
to See People

We are what we believe we are.
—Benjamin N. Cardozo

Every man takes the limits of his own field of vision
for the limits of the world.
—Schopenhauer

WHEN I WAS A KID GROWING UP in Nebraska, my Uncle Wes was a puzzle to me. He was married to my dad's sister, and was the holder of a college degree in agriculture, a sign that he'd had more education than most of the family. My puzzlement had to do with his personal style. Weston spent time with his boys, whereas my dad spent most of his time running his small business. Weston and Winnie (my aunt) took my grandmother out for lunch and an ice cream on Sundays, whereas we seldom visited her. Weston had a warmth, kindness, and gentleness about him that I did not understand. He did not square with the macho images in my mind of a strong man.

Weston Furrer was a farm manager. He supervised rental farmland for absentee owners as an employee of Farmers National. He seemed to do well. He and his family had a nice house in Lincoln. As I grew up and went off to college, I would occasionally hear news about Weston. He was promoted to regional manager. Later on he was promoted again. I felt dissonance. How could someone so gentle be promoted upward in a company? He did not personify the kick-butt Lone Ranger–John Wayne style of leadership I envisioned as ideal. He was not a know-it-all, take-charge guy in my view. John Wayne always had the right answers.

I launched into my career as a business school academic, and lost track of Weston's family. The last thing I heard was that Uncle Wes was being considered for promotion to president of his company. He had also been considered for a top position at a competing firm. This blew my mind—the person I saw as an unassuming Mr. Milquetoast being considered to run a company. I was skeptical that it would happen. Then, in 1983, shortly after I started subscribing to magazines to learn about the world of business, I received a copy of *Fortune* magazine. On the cover was a feature story about the farm crisis (thousands of foreclosures). I flipped to the article, and there was a large photo of my uncle and his management team. He had been promoted to president, and the article told about how well managed the company was and what a great job Farmers National was doing by ramping up to take on thousands of additional farms. *Fortune* magazine had legitimacy in my mind. Clearly there was something excellent about Uncle Wes's leadership that I did not understand.

A year later, I heard about a family get-together that Weston would attend. I decided to go and find out directly from Uncle Wes the qualities that propelled him upward at Farmers National. I arrived prior to a meal, and managed to sit next to him. It was great to see him, and after we chatted a bit, I asked the question. "Uncle Wes, how do you account for your rise at Farmers National? What do you do well that took you to the top of the company?" He thought for a moment. "I would say my strength has to do with people. I spend time making sure people are right for the job. A big part of what I have done is to identify people who are wrong for the job. As soon as I saw that someone was not working out, I would talk to them and help them find a position elsewhere. Many of them later thanked me, because they were not suited to the farm management business." As we talked, it became clear to me that this humble person really cared about people and did everything with their best interest in mind. Yet he was no milquetoast. He was quick to hold people accountable and even fire them for poor performance, but he did so out of compassion and helpfulness rather than frustration and anger. The team he assembled at each level as he moved upward was pretty remarkable. Even today, most senior managers at Farmers National are people Uncle Wes hired.

Talking to Wes resolved my dissonance. My youthful images of leadership were based on a myth of a task-focused, self-oriented, individualistic hero. It made more sense that a successful leader would rely heavily on other people, have the interpersonal skills to engage them in achieving a company's purpose, and have the strength to quickly replace people who don't work out. The biggest shift in thinking for me was to embrace the idea that for a leader to be effective, compassion could be as valuable as toughness. Uncle Wes's style crystallized for me as I read more publications on leadership. I grew up with his humility and kindness, but did not recognize it as leadership. As president, he used a combination of kindness and accountability to run the farm management business.

• • •

Your frame of reference is the angle or lens through which you view the world, a perspective based on your ideas, beliefs, theories, and assumptions. We each see our personal version of reality and act from it. This frame is what guides you as a leader. It sets the boundaries within which you make decisions and take action. Your life experience shapes your frame of reference, but as you become conscious of your frame, you can begin to change and expand it, as happened to me via Uncle Wes.

One example of a frame through which people may view the world is that of liberal versus conservative. If you watch the talking heads on cable news programs, you have seen commentators in either camp interpret "hard data" in opposite ways to suit their conservative or liberal frame. Another example of the power of frames is the story of the six blind men who were given the opportunity to learn about an elephant by touching it. They had no previous knowledge of elephants, so they would have to "see" through their fingers. Each man touched a different part and saw a different "elephant." The elephant's leg felt like a tree trunk; its tail, a piece of rope; its side, a wall; the tusk, a spear; the trunk, a large snake; and the flapping ear, a large fan. The six blind men, excited about their discoveries, returned to their village and told others about the elephant. Each was convinced of his own conclusion and persuaded others. The blind men and their followers argued with one another, defending their respective viewpoints. Followers argued the rope philosophy versus the tree trunk philosophy, the fan doctrine versus the big-snake doctrine, the truth of a wall versus the truth of a spear. The respective groups were each convinced of its own view, and never did learn the larger truth about the elephant based on their collective knowledge.

• • •

Previous chapters of this book have dealt with specific practices to strengthen your inner executive to deal with undesired thoughts and actions of your inner elephant. This chapter explores a more fundamental issue: that of the worldview or cognitive frame within which your thoughts arise. Your frame is anchored in your assumptions and most basic beliefs. Your view of the world guides and limits your interpretations and how you think. Mahatma Gandhi expressed the importance of basic beliefs this way:

> Your beliefs become your thoughts,
> Your thoughts become your words,
> Your words become your actions,
> Your actions become your habits,
> Your habits become your values,
> Your values become your destiny.

We thus see things in a somewhat limited and predictable way through our frame of mind, an attitude or worldview that seems real and solid to our inner elephant. A key frame for leaders is the frame through which they view *people*. Through what frame do *you* see other people? This chapter is about how frames of reference shape your leadership style and behavior, and how you can change or expand your perspective about people. Do you operate primarily from the small, self-oriented frame of your inner elephant or from the larger, other-oriented frame of your inner executive?

What Is Your Frame?

Please read the instructions that follow and write down your responses.[1]

1. Think of a specific situation in which you were working with someone who was in a leadership position over you and who did something *wrong* for you. The leader could be a formal or informal authority figure, including a boss, chair, coach, teacher, project manager, committee head at a volunteer organization, and so on. "Wrong" means that the specific behavior reduced your performance or motivation or that of the team of which you were a part. Write a few words that describe what the leader did that was wrong for you. (If you think of multiple examples, write down all of them.)

2. Think of a specific situation in which you were working with someone who was in a leadership position over you and who did something *right* for you. Again, you may think of any formal or informal authority figure, and "right" means that the specific behavior enhanced your performance or motivation or that of the team. Write a few words

that describe what the leader did that was right for you. (Write multiple examples if you can.)

3. Compare your answers to the answers in Table 15.1, which were provided by a group of managers from an international manufacturing company. Are there answers in the list similar to yours?

4. The next step is for you to study the two lists carefully and identify underlying themes associated with wrong (low-performance) and right (high-performance) leadership. What themes do you see that capture the essence of leader wrong and leader right? Take a moment to study the lists before resuming reading.

Management groups typically come up with several themes based on their lists, related to communication, empowerment, respect, recognition, development and support of others, security, direction and vision, and ethics. These themes provide a good model of leadership attributes that will foster high performance among a team of direct reports.

5. What is the *one thing* that best captures or explains the differences between the leader wrong and leader right lists in Table 15.1? You have to dig beneath the surface. Or think of it this way: If a leader had the characteristics of either "wrong" or "right," what personal attribute or quality would underlie the characteristics on the list?

I have used this exercise with about seventy management groups, and the consistent "one thing" answer is the attribute of *self-centeredness* or *ego-centeredness* underlying the characteristics in the left column versus *other-centeredness* underlying those in the right column. The underlying leadership and performance issue is how leaders view others and themselves.

Most of the behaviors in the left column of Table 15.1 are based in ego-centeredness—a worldview concerned primarily with one's own interests. The inner elephant is dominant. This worldview corresponds to Abraham Maslow's "deficiency of love motivation" that puts oneself first and sees other people in terms of one's own needs and desires. The second column represents a larger picture, a focus on and concern for other people. This frame is comparable to Maslow's "love or growth motivation" that can put others first and is able to serve their needs. The two lists represent fundamental frames or viewpoints about others, wherein other people are seen either as a way to meet our needs or as worthy of respect, development, and service from us.[2]

Table 15.1. Leader Wrong and Leader Right

Leader Wrong	Leader Right
Lack of understanding	Praised publicly
Not taking responsibility	Asked my opinion
Threats, scare tactics	Developed people
Overbearing personality	Recognized individual/team
Micromanager	Excellent training
Impulsive reactions	Trusted my decision
No concern for employees	Gave credit
No recognition for achievements	Empowered me
Sell you down the river	Encouraged independence
Lack of respect	Trustworthy and supportive
Self-serving behavior	Criticism at right time
Inconsistent standards	Developed people effectively
Dishonesty	Objective
Demotivating words	Demonstrated integrity
Controlling	Humility
Did not keep word	Consistent
Closed minded	Empowerment
Undermined decision making	Encouragement
Demeaning	Empathy
Ruled by fear	Sincere coaching
Took the credit	Shared responsibility
No direction	Went out of way to support group
Unapproachable	Supported after mistake
No coaching	Listened
Verbally abusive	Provided opportunities
Problem avoidance	Trusted
No commitment to company	Fact-based decision
Only "my way"	Fought for people
Blamed others for his mistakes	Supportive coach
No guidance	Concern for employees
Credit hog	Gave responsibility
Avoidance	Genuinely interested
Unethical	Fair rewards
Knee-jerk reactions	Open minded/flexible
Failure to communicate expectations	Objective
Lack of communication	Sharing power/information
Refusing to listen	Clear goals
Control freak	Listened to business case
Not take accountability	Delegation
Set poor example	Constructive feedback
Poor communication	Did right for company
Blocked promotions	Gave away credit

Remember This

What Is Your Frame?

1. Everyone has a distinct frame of reference.
2. The "leader wrong" frame of reference is based on deficiency of love, puts self first, and sees others as means of serving one's own interests.
3. The "leader right" frame is based on love or growth motivation, puts others first, and respects their needs.
4. A leader's frame influences the motivation of others:
   - Self-centered leadership behaviors lead to lower motivation and performance.
   - Other-centered leadership behaviors lead to higher motivation and performance.
5. People see others through a self-centered frame more often than they realize.

Now, here is the key question: What is *your* frame? The two lists in Table 15.1 are not just about your leaders; they are about you, too. If the behaviors in the second column are more effective, you need to ask yourself how often you come across to others with behaviors perceived to be in the first column. Your inner elephant, with the assistance of your internal attorney and magician, has likely been telling you that your style is in column 2. But I assure you that we all display a bigger portion of column 1 in our behavior toward direct reports and colleagues than we realize.

From Leading Objects to Leading Humans

Please look at the two columns again. The two frames represented by the columns in Table 15.1 see either "objects" or "humanness" with respect to other people. These frames represent the I-It and I-Thou attitudes described by Martin Buber.[3] I-It is a relationship of subject to object characterized by separateness and detachment. People are seen as things that are less real, more distant, and somewhat inferior to how you see yourself. I-Thou is a relationship of subject to subject, characterized by seeing a person's whole being. Other people are seen as just as real and human as you see yourself.

You may not even realize that you view other people as objects to meet your needs. If the nature of your childhood was deficient in love, your natural inner elephant probably sees through an objects frame, requiring intentional effort on your part to see through a humanness frame. If the column 2 humanness frame is more dominant in you, you may find yourself sliding into column 1 objects-frame thinking if you are under stress or pressure, are in a bad mood, or are feeling fearful about your position or job, and hence are trying harder to control things to meet your needs. The objects frame can also dominate if the organizational culture expects and socializes people to see employees or customers as objects.

For example, Sean, an HR manager for a software firm, told me that he saw people through an objects frame during a downsizing. He distanced himself, and said he could hardly look at people who were to be laid off. "I just wanted those people out of my sight." He was unable to reach out and provide emotional support. Kate, a supervisor in a manufacturing plant, said that she "turned into a monster during a product changeover." Kate was responsible for the change project, and as it slipped behind schedule, she saw people as her enemy and would attack them to get things moving faster. Looking back, she saw that the "monster" approach did not work and created resentment and more resistance. Kate wished she could have maintained a more supportive approach to help people through that difficult time. World Bank president Paul Wolfowitz was said to have failed in that job because he demonized bank officers as the enemy rather than see them as partners. He tried to impose his ideas unilaterally, and saw people who disagreed with him as either corrupt or incompetent. Rather than form alliances based on respect, Wolfowitz alienated senior managers, leading to his removal as president, even after he promised to change his management style.[4] The important point is that you, like Sean and Kate and Wolfowitz, see others through an objects frame probably more than you realize.

• • •

Do you doubt that you see others through an objects frame? Here's an easy test. Have you flown on Southwest Airlines? Imagine boarding in the "A" group and finding a comfortable aisle seat. As passengers come down the aisle toward you, do you see them as a potential threat to the middle seat that you would like to keep vacant? Perhaps you read a newspaper to avoid eye contact, or place your briefcase or book in the middle seat to signal that it is taken. Maybe you get out your handkerchief and start coughing as if sick, so no one will sit beside you. Your mind is seeing people as objects who threaten to thwart you in your desire for an empty middle seat. If you were to adopt the humanness frame, you would see people coming down the aisle as tired human beings whom you welcome to rest in the seat beside you.

How do you view other drivers when you drive your car? Do you ever objectify them, honk at them, or criticize them in your mind simply because they don't drive in a way that meets your need? If a driver goes slowly when you are in a hurry, do you see the driver with compassion? More likely you are filled with critical thoughts. I remember being in a hurry to an important meeting when the car in front of me in the left-turn lane broke down. The other lanes were full, so I could not go around the car. My reaction was to honk and think the driver should get that junk heap out of the way. My objects frame was in full bloom. As I calmed down, I was able to see with a more humanistic viewpoint that helping the driver would be the right thing to do for me, the other driver, and the traffic flow. My meeting could wait a few minutes.

The objectification of others that afflicts many managers shows up as a lack of trust and respect and as overmanaging people. The pressures in business combined with the desire for personal success and profit reinforce the view of people as objects to be manipulated for our gain. The objects frame can take over your thinking any time at home or work. In the book *Leadership and Self-Deception,* the authors describe a manager's reaction when his wife wants him to get up in the middle of the night to attend to a crying baby so she can sleep.[5] The husband's objects frame instantly flared up to objectify his wife and judge her as lazy, inconsiderate, insensitive and unappreciative, a faker, and a lousy mom and wife, simply because he did not want to get up. His concern was strictly for himself, as he unconsciously inflated his own value and virtue as a hard-working and important person and a good husband, while casting blame on his wife as an object of derision. The objects frame cannot see the humanness in another person or see another person's needs and concerns as equal to one's own.

Once you see the frame through which you view other people, you can begin to get a handle on it. Nell Minow, cofounder of the Corporate Library, shared her experience:

> One thing that helped move my thinking forward was that I noticed in my first job that there was something very definitional in who was included in somebody's "we" and who was included in somebody's "them." I found generally that the more expansive the assumptions that were within somebody's idea of who is "we"—the larger the group that you included in that "we"—the better off everybody was. I started to really do my best to make sure that my notion of "we" was very expansive and to promote that idea among other people.[6]

Indra Nooyi, head of PepsiCo, said she learned from her father to always assume positive intent. Whatever a person says or does, assume positive intent—a people frame—which means seeing a person as a sincere human being. "When you assume negative intent, you're angry. If you take away that anger and assume positive intent, you will be amazed. . . . You don't get defensive. You don't scream. You are trying to understand and listen."[7] Jacquelyn Kosecoff, CEO of Prescription Solutions, said something similar about meeting with others: "Assume-positive intent. It's one of the ways to sort of keep communication on the high road. Perhaps somebody was misunderstood, or they misheard something. . . . It's very likely to be simply a misunderstanding. And it tends to, I think, breed a lot more trust and respect among us."[8]

Assuming positive intent means seeing through a humanness frame, which is not always easy. When a direct report makes a mistake that really annoys you or hurts your feelings, you may take an unbalanced, overly negative view of that person as a poor team player or a troublemaker causing conflict, as having a bad attitude, lack of motivation, or lack of engagement or commitment. These conclusions are distortions brought on by the inner elephant's fear, hurt, bad mood, and need to protect itself. These negative-frame thoughts are not good data on which to act, because there is no empathy or understanding of the other's view or situation.

When my wife and I were helping produce one of her plays in distant cities, there were often sharp disagreements with other producers or with local theater people. We adopted the rule that we would not make a decision while upset or angry. I offer you the same advice. Don't make decisions when you are in a bad frame of mind, because that is when it feels urgent to speak or take action, usually the wrong action. Don't push the Send button when you are in a bad frame. You will write a different e-mail when your upset passes. Words and actions from a balanced perspective that includes seeing the other person's point of view will be more realistic and have greater positive impact on outcomes.

Remember This

From Leading Objects to Leading Humans

- Two primary frames toward people are the objects frame and the humanness frame.
- The objects frame sees others as "they" and as distant and separate from "we."

- A stressful situation may trigger a strong objects frame toward another.

- You may witness your objects frame during everyday occurrences, such as when driving or when upset.

- When you observe that you are in an objects frame, do not act on it.

How to Change Your Frame

Nirvan told me his story at an academic conference. I was taken by his warmth (for an academic) and his superb teaching scores, so I inquired about them. Nirvan had given up a high-paying executive position at a bank to get a PhD.

He did well teaching as a graduate student, but asked the teaching center to evaluate his performance in class. The evaluation was positive, especially for his excellent organization and presentation of content. But, the evaluator told him, "You didn't ever smile." That statement woke up something in Nirvan. He had never thought about smiling. Later on he looked back at old photos of himself, and, indeed, he was never smiling. He was sullen. As a bank executive, he had had perhaps four hundred people reporting to him. He had been considered "nice," but hadn't really paid attention to people. He had not been disliked, but his interactions had not been satisfying. He had been very serious. "I had intensity, but not passion. I couldn't give a warm response. As a manager, I was all head and no heart." He went on, "One older manager broke down and cried in my office when I gave him a moderate performance evaluation. He said, 'You never encouraged me. You never told me.' I thought I had. The disconnect was in me."

Thanks to the "smile" comment, Nirvan set out to change himself. First, he watched others who had a softer demeanor, and he identified people who could serve as role models. He hung around people who laughed and smiled, who were warm, and who cared about the *person,* not just an idea. He aspired to be lighter, more radiant. Nirvan had a background in Eastern religion, and tried various exercises and practices. His favorite reading was a condensed *Bhagavad Gita,* and he started repeating favorite verses to himself during the day. One of the *Gita* verses said that all people have the same soul. When he dealt with people toward whom he previously would have felt little tolerance for their low intellect, he would look into their heart to see them as the same as himself. He also tried meditation, in which he would focus on sound. He would notice sounds previously unheard—cars on the highway, a garbage truck, a bird's song, the wind, his computer, someone talking. He used his new focus and presence to pay close attention to everyone with whom he spoke. Conversations with his mother were always boring, but now when visiting her he would stay focused for thirty minutes and listen to whatever she wanted to talk about. As he became more present and less judgmental, he noticed positive changes in his relationships, and his new behaviors were easier to repeat.

I asked if other factors helped his dramatic change in frame. One was that he had a friend who understood what he was doing and to whom he could talk about the issues when needed. Also, as a PhD student, he could find time to be introspective, which was harder to do in his executive position. He also said, "I previously told people about what I thought, and waited for them to respond. It was self-centered. I started watching how much I talked in a conversation. I became more of a listener, asking questions." Then he finished with, "Perhaps the most important thing was that I forced myself to smile, and now it comes naturally." I can vouch for that. Whenever I meet Nirvan, I feel warmth from the light of that smile.

• • •

Like Nirvan, many managers see the world through an objects frame much of the time. Many people, myself included, are like a fish unaware of the water because their objects frame of mind is so much a part of their everyday thinking. Our extant worldview is the only thing we know.

How can we change? The first step is to "see" or be the witness to your lack of human concern. A medical resident auditing my class told me he became aware of his lousy bedside manner. He traced his coldness to negative judgments he made toward many patients. Once he saw his negative opinions, he began blocking those negative thoughts, prepping himself with positive thoughts as he met each patient. He used intentional positive thoughts, similar to autosuggestion, to shift the frame of reference through which he saw patients. He was happy with the change.

Tom Coughlin, one of the last of the old school NFL head coaches, came across as an unsmiling martinet, with a tight-lipped, freezing stare. A micromanager of the first order, he was voted the NFL's least-liked coach in a *Sports Illustrated* poll of players.[9] After a disappointing year, Coughlin's bosses at the Giants wanted him to lighten up. Coughlin heard the message. "I may be a dinosaur, but I can change," he said. "I can be more patient."[10] This was the start of his self-initiated personality makeover. He started listening to comments and feedback. He appointed a leadership council of players to meet with him regularly and help players police themselves. Rather than snap and snarl at reporters, he sat down with them individually to get to know them better. He would occasionally make a joke. He canceled practice one day and took the players bowling. The New York Giants as a team came together.[11] The year of Coughlin's personality change was the year the Giants won the Super Bowl.

When do you see people with criticalness or with humanness, with negative judgment or with understanding? It is easy for a manager's mind to be focused on goals, tasks, rewards, costs, profits, operations, marketing, and the next step in a career, and therefore fail to see the humanness in people around him or her. You can use your witness to observe your thoughts toward others, or you can think back over previous work situations and the view you held toward other people. Becoming aware of your own frame of mind is like becoming aware of colored glasses. You can remove the glasses when needed, or at least accommodate your perception to allow for the tint.

How do you awaken a frame of love and compassion? One easy exercise is a mantra. Tom Coughlin made up his own mantras to help him change his frame toward players—for example, "Be smart about it" and "Put a smile on your face."[12] Each time you have a critical thought toward another person, you can replace it with a mantra of kindness and interest in the person's well-being, such as "May you have peace and harmony," or offset it with a counterthought, such as "I am loving people more" or "I am accepting people more." Keep the mantra going until you feel your frame of mind toward the person begin to shift.

Probably the quickest way to shift your frame is to serve others. It is hard to objectify someone during an act of service. Here is an example from the corporate world. The integration of the Borg-Warner Chemicals acquisition into GE Plastics was not going well. After years of intense competition among the companies' managers, mutual trust was low. The cultures were opposite in many ways, and managers were hesitant about working with the "enemy." Joel Hutt and the team charged with the annual corporate meeting had an idea: instead of an annual golf outing, why not perform a service project that would have enduring value? This might knock down the mental barriers between the two camps. Five projects, such as completely refurbishing a rundown YMCA and rebuilding a community center, were selected. Each project would engage about five hundred people for one long day. Members of smaller work teams (windows, carpet, painting, grounds, and so on) were carefully selected to include people from both cultures and various hierarchical levels.

The result was stunning. The camaraderie across cultures was beyond what organizers could have hoped for. After everyone had spent a day pounding nails together in service of a nonprofit, the perception of each other as rivals or enemies or as the "competition" disappeared. The participants saw each other as human beings, friends, and teammates.[13] People cannot hold on to a subject-object perspective toward people when performing service activities elbow-to-elbow with them. Serving a higher purpose and being in close contact engage the higher subject-subject frame through which to view others. The bank KeyCorp gets the same result every year among its employees with its "Neighbors Make the Difference" day that does good works for twelve hundred public and private agencies.[14] When the bosses and underlings get dirt and paint on themselves together, and the underlings are in charge of the service projects, perceived differences between people melt away pretty quickly.

You can also develop the humanness frame by understanding that love is a state that you can choose to be in, not something caused by other people. You may think of love as a special feeling saved for a special relationship with your spouse or children. Or perhaps love is for your favorite team, your new car, golf, or some other activity. Your inner elephant thinks of love as something that happens when favorite people or things awaken good feelings in you. This "love" is typically your inner elephant's identification with or desire for something. The inner executive is bigger. Rather than "do what you love," the inner executive can learn to "love what you do." Rather than "be with the one you love," the inner executive can intentionally "love the one you are with." Your inner executive can override your inner elephant's negative view toward others. Once you are conscious of the negative frame through which you view another person, you can start to change the frame. Awareness is the first 50 percent of the change.

The MBA students and managers I teach and coach have tried many ideas covered in this book to change the mental frame they are in, such as employing a mantra or visualization, or have simply used their rational understanding to see more deeply into people. One exercise I assign is called See with Your Heart, which asks participants to intentionally change their frame toward another person.[15] It harnesses the inner executive's intention to change how one sees other people. Lisa, a highly rational finance major, was one of many students dumbfounded when she saw the sheer volume of her critical thoughts and her objectification of others:

> I have a low threshold for annoying beings. I glare at crying babies
> on airplanes. I frown at the guy who talks too loud in restaurants.

I throw up my hands in disgust at the driver who cuts in front of me. So when I tried to garner caring sentiments for a person who annoys me, it was difficult. I knew immediately a great candidate for this exercise, someone who has annoyed me for a whole year. I first thought about why she acts the way she does. Almost immediately my executive helped me think about the fact that I do not know the big picture. I only see snippets of her life. My elephant is quick to judge on too little information. My next step was visualizing her and repeating, "May you be at peace with yourself and all that is in your life." As I repeated I found my critical judgment softening and I was feeling more empathetic, as if my executive was telling me, "We all want to be at peace." I found myself acting more warmly toward her, and our interactions have become much more positive since.

Another MBA student reported a similar experience.

There are a few people at school who really annoy me based on what I believe to be their shortcomings. It is easy to think about what they should be doing differently. I found that focusing on them and repeating the phrase, "May you have peace and harmony," allowed me to see these two individuals as imperfect human beings just like me. It is easy to fall into the finger-pointing trap and to take inventory of other people's shortcomings. Wishing others goodwill, even those I don't care for, changed my perspective. As I talked to one of the annoyers, I suddenly felt ashamed for being so selfish. I couldn't believe that I had been so blind. This guy was not trying to purposely aggravate me, but was just craving some attention. Now I have an entirely different outlook toward both individuals.

As you became conscious of your objects frame, a successful approach is to slow down and use your rational mind to understand why the person behaved as he or she did. Lisa transformed her viewpoint by using her inner executive to look into individuals and imagine the life circumstances that caused what her inner elephant thought was annoying behavior. She could envision the person's reactions based on childhood conditioning, and understand that the individual was not displaying the behavior to annoy her. Lisa's ability to use rational understanding paid off with a shift in her frame of reference from negative to mildly positive, a big step.

When I was associate dean of the business school, I had to work closely on a project with an associate dean from another school who annoyed the heck out of me. My objects frame of reference took over, and I saw him as an ego-centered jerk. I wanted to avoid him. My solution was similar to Lisa's. I was able to see him more rationally when

I imagined the underlying causes of his personality and actions. I also did visualizations in which I held him in my mind while calling up positive feelings of compassion toward him. I think the visualization helped a lot. Before a meeting with that associate dean, I would prepare myself by understanding his unfortunate background and feeling compassion for him, and visualizing myself accepting his behavior without annoyance. This mental rehearsal solved the issue over time. By the fourth weekly meeting after starting the visualization practice, I could actually feel sympathy toward him during the meeting. This felt much better than the inner annoyance that triggered my feelings of criticalness and dislike. I let his behavior go right past me; hence I could work more rationally with him to get the job done. I didn't realize it at the time, but what I did was similar to a *forgiveness meditation*.

• TRY THIS •

Practice Forgiveness Meditation

1. Sit comfortably, close your eyes, take three deep breaths, and relax.
2. Bring to mind the person and situation in which you felt upset or annoyed.
3. Visualize the situation as it occurred, and feel your negative reaction.
4. Try to let go of your negative feelings. Release them. Let them drift out of you.
5. Visualize yourself not being annoyed in that situation and in future contacts with the annoying person and behavior.
6. Repeat as you visualize the person, "I forgive you."
7. Awaken feelings of compassion and understanding toward the person.

Other exercises I use to help people shift frames ask them to awaken feelings of appreciation. The following activities are effective.

APPRECIATION EXERCISES

1. At the end of the day, ask yourself about each interaction that day, "How was this person my teacher? What do I appreciate about this person?" Can you see the positive learning you received from even the annoying people?

2. Spend seven minutes each morning for one week writing down everything you appreciate. Write down all the things you are grateful for. It is okay to repeat items on the list each day. What kind of feeling does this exercise awaken in you? Feelings of appreciation will pull you out of the objects frame of mind.

3. Make a list of all the people you genuinely appreciate, whether they are professional associates, friends, relatives, service providers, or even the grocery store checkout clerk. Then pick one and contact him or her to express your appreciation.

REMEMBER THIS

Change Your Frame

You can change your mental frame toward other people. The following practices will help.

- Use your witness to observe your frame toward others. Becoming aware of your frame is 50 percent of the way toward changing it.
- Learn to "love what you do" and "love the one you're with."
- Repeat a mantra, such as "May you have peace and harmony," to replace critical thoughts.
- Serve others to awaken your or your team's humanness frame.
- See with your heart, which means to understand and accept why the person behaves that way.
- Try a forgiveness meditation.
- Use an appreciation exercise.

You don't have to give up performance standards to see other people as human beings.

Strong leaders can be soft in their concern for the welfare of others. When asked about his most important leadership lesson, Clarence Otis Jr., CEO of Darden Restaurants, said the following: "It's this notion that leaders really think about others first. They think about the people who are on the team, trying to help them get the job done. They think about the people who they are trying to do a job for. Your thoughts are always there first, and you think about what's the appropriate response for whatever the audience is, and you think last about, 'what does this mean for me?'" Otis learned this lesson from his predecessor, Joe Lee, who was CEO on 9/11. Lee called an all-employee meeting to ascertain the location of all Darden people who were traveling. Then Lee said, "We've got a lot of Muslim teammates, managers in our restaurants, employees in our restaurants, who are going to be under a lot of stress during this period. And so, we need to make sure we are attentive to that." The lesson was not lost on Otis: "And that was pretty powerful. Of all the things you could focus on that morning, he thought about the people who were on the road and then our Muslim colleagues."[16]

If you are ready to change your frame from seeing objects to seeing people, many of the practices in previous chapters will help you. For example, calming yourself down, visualization, conducting an end-of-day review, or using a mantra such as "I am becoming more concerned about people" will help facilitate your mental transition to a more human frame of reference. Remember, you don't have to give up performance standards, boundaries, or self-discipline to see people as human beings. My uncle Wes found it less stressful to treat low-performing people with compassion as he helped them find other work. You will see people more fully and be able to develop their potential, whether in your business or elsewhere. You can become a terrific individual performer by focusing on yourself and objectifying others. You will become a terrific *leader* by focusing your primary concern on others.

16

•

Change Your Frame
to Ask Questions

The most erroneous stories are those we think we know
best—and therefore never scrutinize or question.
—Steven J. Gould

You can tell whether a man is clever by his answers. You can
tell whether a man is wise by his questions.
—Naguib Mahfouz

DAVID WOLFSKEHL STARTED A BUSINESS at age twenty-four. He quickly
found that being top leader of his own company presented a real
challenge. Feeling that he had to gain the respect of his small group of
employees, Wolfskehl acted like an alpha male who had all the answers.
He'd stand before his employees at weekly staff meetings expounding on
what needed to be done and how to do it. But after a few years of not
getting results, Wolfskehl decided to take a different approach. Despite
his fear, he went into the staff meeting one morning and did something
simple yet remarkable: he asked a question! With that one act, Wolfskehl
started his company on a transformation that accelerated the growth
of his small business, Action Fast Print. "I was worried that everyone
was going to tell me all the things I was doing wrong," he says now.

"[But] once I started asking how I could help, amazing things started happening."[1]

From Answering Questions to Asking Questions

Like many of us, Wolfskehl had been socially conditioned to think he had to have the right answers to succeed. From grade school through college and in our first jobs, we are rewarded for giving the right answers to questions. As students, we would wave our hand in class to show we had the right answer, we received high grades for giving the right answers on tests, and we were marked down for wrong answers. Preschool children may start out as question marks, but they end up as periods. We grew up in a right-answer world. As we move on to work and a career, again we believe that having right answers is the way to get ahead.

Is it any wonder that many leaders retain the frame of reference that assumes when someone comes to them with a problem, their job is to provide the right answer? They pride themselves on having right answers to solve problems, knowing how to do things right, and never showing doubt. After all, what is their experience for? Leaders may even fear that not having an answer means that followers will lose respect or confidence in them. And there lies the challenge. How can a leader let go of being the doer, the expert, the answer person? Expecting things to be done your way often comes across as micromanagement, which is not an effective way to motivate people.

How can you stop viewing yourself as the expert and instead encourage people to provide their own right answers and right actions? Greg Cushard, founder and head of Rubicon Oil, would interrupt conversations, call people out on mistakes, and make mundane decisions. To resolve his micromanagement, he started walking away from meetings to let others take turns leading in his place.[2] Other managers solve the problem by setting goals and letting direct reports fill in the details—a good idea, because most employees hate and resist micromanagement.

A simple way to shift your frame out of the right-answer mind-set is to *ask questions*. The higher you go in a company, the more important it becomes to ask questions rather than have answers. The journey to leadership knowledge often begins with curiosity and questions, not answers. A study of geniuses, such as Einstein, Mozart, Aristotle, Freud, and da Vinci, found that a common characteristic was the habit of asking basic questions. "Geniuses tend to emphasize questions more than answers. They are typically very bold about their questions and humble about their answers."[3] Questions make people think, whereas answers bring thinking to a full stop. Questions encourage creativity in others, whereas answers squelch creativity. For example, Tim Brown, CEO of IDEO, said that asking the right question is itself a creative process. "[I]t doesn't matter how good the answers you come up with. If you're focusing on the wrong questions, you're not providing the leadership you should. . . . I think that's something that we forget—as leaders, probably the most important role we can play is asking the right questions."[4] Brown is more likely to lead a debate about the right questions than he is to debate about the right solutions.

There is an important reason to shift your frame from answering to asking questions. A man was walking in the woods and saw a chrysalis hanging from a low branch of a tree. His interest piqued, he examined it and saw movement within. Looking more closely, he saw a leg pushing through the skin of the chrysalis. Wanting to help, he took out a knife and cut open the chrysalis, releasing the butterfly within. The butterfly fell to the ground and lay there wiggling. It could not fly. Later he contacted a butterfly expert, who said that the struggle to free itself from the chrysalis is what develops the butterfly's strength to fly. Having cut open the chrysalis, the man had prevented the butterfly from developing its inherent capability.

People working for you are also trying to develop their strengths and capabilities. Can you patiently enable their growth, or do you intervene for the sake of efficiency, cutting open the chrysalis? A key change is to shift your focus from giving your quick answer to taking some time to allow others to develop their own answer. Most people seek answers; they want a remedy. And you may find it expedient to give the quick answer. It feels good to be in the center of things, to be the answer person. But each time you give an answer, you miss a development opportunity. When you ask a question of someone, you put her on alert in a way that making a statement does not; she has to think in order to respond.[5] If a plant foreman says, "We have to increase production to fill this order for an important customer," workers may not listen or try to speed things up because filling the order is the boss's responsibility. If, instead, the foreman asks plant employees, "What can we do to make sure we fill this order on time?" people can't ignore him; they have to start looking for solutions. Questions can be follower centered, in that they encourage critical thinking, expand people's awareness, and stimulate their learning. Asking questions gets people to accept responsibility for solving their own problems.

A question will nearly always engage another person. I recall sitting through a dreary morning of research presentations at an academic conference. These one-way presentations can be a boring way to get to some facts. The fourth speaker started with a question, and waited a moment for people to formulate an answer in their minds. Suddenly everyone seemed interested. They sat up straight, and several people leaned forward. By using periodic questions, the presenter held everyone's interest for what otherwise would have been a monotonous lecture.

Have you tried to coach people by using questions? Leadership coaching is more about being the person with the right questions than being the person with the right answers. And the higher you go, the more important it is to be the person with the right questions. Consider Ram Charan's example of the CEO who relied on his own curiosity to coach a direct report about how a new strategy would work to increase market share in Germany. Rather than give advice, the CEO asked questions that expanded the thinking of the business unit chief after his strategy presentation. "How are you going to make those gains?" he said, probing into the strength of the powerful German competitor. "Which customers will you acquire? What products and competitive advantages will you need to beat the German competitor?" Other questions pertained to organizational capability. "How many salespeople do you have?" "How many does your main competitor have?" "What is the experience of the people working for you in Germany?" The CEO's simple questions inquiring into how things worked exposed a certain naïveté in the business unit's plans. The CEO, as part of his coaching, suggested his view on picking niches and winning on speed of execution. The unit chief saw the weaknesses and came up with new ideas to strengthen and tighten the strategy.[6]

Asking any question is often better than asking no question. My wife is a master at asking questions. She developed this skill as a professor in which she would guide an entire class session through questions rather than lecture. When I am confused about something, I have asked her to start asking me questions, any questions. Interestingly, some of the questions don't directly apply to my problem, but they force me to think of a response, and new insights emerge upon which my inner executive can act. We have both tried using this approach with our children, who are now adults, and found it always to be more effective than giving advice.

Ask Outcome-Focused Questions

As you develop a frame of curiosity and question asking, you will find that some questions are better than others. For example, asking *problem-focused* questions focus people's thinking on immediate problems, barriers, and difficulties. Asking *outcome-focused* or *results-oriented* questions will direct people's thinking toward the future and stimulate their creative thinking about how to get to the desired future. When I teach the outcome frame to managers, I ask them to think of a work problem and then have a partner ask questions about it. That way they can feel the different impacts of problem-focused versus outcome-focused questions. You can do the exercise in your own mind.

Please think of a specific unresolved work problem you have. Then answer the two sets of questions that follow. It might be a good idea to write down your thoughts to help you arrive at clear answers. Please pay attention to how you feel as you answer the questions.[7]

Answer the following questions while thinking about your problem:

1. Why do you have this problem?

2. Who or what caused this problem?

3. Why hasn't the problem been solved?

4. How likely is it that you will solve this problem?

How do you feel after answering these questions? When you are ready, answer the following questions while thinking about the same problem:

1. What do you really want to have happen? (What is your desired outcome?)

2. How will you know you have achieved this outcome? (Be specific about how things will look, sound, and feel.)

3. What ideas do you have to achieve this outcome?

4. What will you do to get started?

How do you feel after answering these questions? Do you experience anything different between the two sets? Managers tell me they feel more positive emotion and creativity when answering the second set of questions. The mental shift in thinking toward future solutions or outcomes is a positive frame of reference offering hope, awakening creative ideas, and renewing energy and confidence. The first set of questions may bring up feelings of discouragement when thinking about roadblocks and obstacles. The heightened creativity of the second set of questions encourages taking immediate steps toward a solution. What a relief!

The power of this approach is that it shifts the realm of discussion from the past to the future—the realm of possibility rather than the realm of history. Only about 5 percent of statements in normal discourse are in the realm of possibility wherein you create the future.[8] The trick is to get out of past- and problem-focused discussions to awaken people's creativity for reaching a goal. Creating ideas for a better future is fun, and new possibilities drive action. All it takes is a simple question like "What do you want to have happen?"

In my role as associate dean, my inner elephant initially liked to tell other people how to solve their problems. A student might come in complaining about the way a professor assigned a final grade. Rather than drill into the problem and offer solutions, I learned to ask, "What do you want to have happen?" The student might respond with, "I would like the professor to regrade my final exam." Then I would follow up with, "What would be the first step you can take to make that happen?" The student might respond, "Maybe I could call the professor and make an appointment to talk about this." Then I would say, "Good idea. Please do that and let me know what happens." Problem solved. The student figured out his own answer. I was developing their independence rather than make them dependent on me.

Ask a Broad Range of Questions

Gary Marenzi is president of international television at Paramount Pictures and manages about a hundred employees. He regularly has people coming to him upset about a problem and asking for answers. Marenzi instead tells them to relax and starts asking questions: "I tell them that it's not just the numbers that are important—does it make money or doesn't it make money? What's more, how is it going to affect people? Is this how we want to spend our time as managers or as teammates? Is it going to make us happy?" Marenzi broadens people's thinking and shapes the culture of his division by asking questions.[9]

Effective questions can serve a number of purposes, such as expanding the person's perspective to incorporate a bigger picture, shifting the person's thinking toward outcomes, helping the person reflect more deeply, or helping ground the person in reality. The following are examples of some different types of questions:

QUESTIONS THAT SHIFT THE MIND TOWARD FUTURE RESULTS
OR OUTCOMES

What do you want instead of this problem?

What do you really want to accomplish?

What is your ultimate purpose with this?

Can you articulate the long-term direction for your organization?

QUESTIONS THAT SHIFT PEOPLE'S THINKING TOWARD
DEEPER MEANING

What can be learned from this experience?

What is the lesson here?

What has this experience meant to you?

Why have you succeeded when others have failed?

QUESTIONS THAT PROMOTE A BROADER PERSPECTIVE

How do you want things to be different in your area?

What would people in other areas (for example, marketing, top management) think about this?

What will be the impact on people?

How will you help others understand this complex issue?

QUESTIONS THAT GROUND PEOPLE IN REALITY

What is your evidence for (or against) this?

What is your thinking behind this idea?

QUESTIONS THAT PROMPT ACTION

What is the most useful thing to do right now?

How can I help?

QUESTIONS THAT PROMPT DEEPER INQUIRY

Are you focused on the right factors?

What assumptions are you making?

Is your judgment based on intuition or facts?

How can you use this as an opportunity?

Which tasks drain your energy, and which tasks add to your energy?

QUESTIONS THAT SHIFT THINKING TO AN APPRECIATION FRAME

What personal characteristics do you admire in yourself and others?

What factors give life to this organization?

When you feel best about your work, what is happening?

QUESTIONS THAT PROBE INTO UNSTATED ASSUMPTIONS

Why are you doing this?

Why are you doing that?

The last two questions were used by Peter Drucker. He called them "dumb" questions because they forced managers to think about their unconscious assumptions underlying their habitual and routine work. Now in my world, people often believe in theoretical ideas that may not work in practice. To help ground people in reality, I most often ask the question "What is your evidence to support this?" When we start talking about grounded evidence, the speaker starts thinking in more concrete terms.

• • •

If you are ready to change your frame from giving answers to answering questions, many of the practices in previous chapters will help you. For example, conducting an end-of-day review can be a time to examine the situations in which you asked questions and to make plans for when to ask questions tomorrow. Autosuggestions such as "I am developing people by asking questions" or "I am asking more questions" repeated several times morning and evening will facilitate your mental transition to a question-asking frame of reference. You can also repeat the suggestion just before meetings in which you want to ask questions. Remember, you don't have to give up standards, boundaries, or self-discipline to shift from telling to asking. You just need to see people more fully and want to help develop them to their potential.

Remember This

Learn to Ask Questions
- We have all been conditioned to give answers.
- Asking questions is a way to coach and develop other people.
- Asking questions becomes more important as you move higher up in the organization.
- Asking any question is often better than asking no question.
- Outcome-focused questions stimulate creativity and personal responsibility in others.
- Effective questions may be used to expand people's perspective, ground their thinking, probe unstated assumptions, stimulate deeper inquiry, or shift people to an appreciative frame.
- End-of-day review and autosuggestion will help your transition to question asking.

In All Things, Consult

A similar approach that serves to develop others is to consult in all things. Consulting with others is one of the easiest ways to engage them while expanding your mind's awareness to break free of the distortions, fears, and small-mindedness of your inner elephant. The simple act of consulting with other people can produce a profound change toward a more accurate perspective. Consider these two examples:

> I am in a very competitive fantasy football league, and I contemplated a specific trade. I had the perfect answer. Before making the trade, I talked with three friends who are big football fans. I learned two things. One, people love when you ask for their advice. Second, consultation makes the decision so much easier. I spent days thinking about that trade, and after talking with others it was obviously a bad decision. I was headed for a colossal mistake. Instead, I have a winning record in my fantasy league.

> I am an entrepreneur and have developed a great idea for a new business. My plan was well thought out and attainable. Before launching I sought out a local entrepreneur in the same industry. Wow. By the end of the meeting I learned more successful products to carry and a much more effective way to monetize the service aspect of the business. My elephant can be so ignorant. My answers are always the best, right? It is so easy to get lost in what I believe to be accurate. All trains of thought go down the same track. Other people's experiences add so much.

Under the pressure of time and busyness, a person can readily succumb to the temptation of believing his own answer, wanting his view or idea to prevail, and wanting to receive the credit, which reinforces a small viewpoint, narrow insight, and poor decisions. The solution is to break free of the inner elephant's mind-set by engaging the larger mind of other people. You learn more and at the same time are engaging the thinking of direct reports and others.

Bob Lengel, of the University of Texas at San Antonio, and I wrote a couple of papers based on Bob's research that explored how managers made decisions when things were unclear and complicated, such as when something is amiss but the exact problem was not clear and the answer was not obvious. It was amazing how quickly effective managers chose to come out of their offices to consult with others. Their conversations clarified their ambiguity. Indeed, the simple act of talking through an issue, even if no new information was obtained, helped managers clear away the fog in their minds. This is the inner executive at work, doing the smart thing to escape from the limited and distorted thinking of the inner elephant.

Jim Collins, author of *Good to Great,* developed a personal board of directors during his twenties. He drew a conference table and seven chairs on a piece of paper and wrote the names of people he admired. When wrestling with a tough question, he would sometimes imagine what each person would tell him, as a way to pull himself out of his mental box. If really stuck on an issue, he would talk to some of them directly.[10] Some executives use their spouse as a sounding board, engaging in a lengthy discussion over dinner before making an important hire or launching a new strategy. The spouse can often be trusted to provide unvarnished feedback. And just talking it through will clarify fuzzy areas and blind spots in one's own mind.

Jody, head of retail operations for a southeastern brokerage firm, had a personal board of directors. He included a few luminaries, the time of whom he was willing to pay for, as well as local friends and associates. He would call me periodically to go to lunch to talk about a problem, so I think I was on his board. A few days after one of our conversations, Jody called to thank me profusely for my suggestions about establishing a vision for his business. That was interesting, because I hadn't made any suggestions. I had simply asked questions, and the ideas had clarified in his own mind. That is the value of consultation.

Let's face it: the higher you go in an organization, the less clear things become. Talking to others is a great clarifier, even when we think we know the answer. Leonard was assigned responsibility to create a new compensation system for sales agents. He initially worked on it alone—no consultation.

> I spent many hours developing and building the cost-benefit analysis to support the project. However, to try consultation, I posted my ideas to three key executives. Two of the three agreed with my analysis. The third took a unique stance. My first reaction was anger, but I suppressed my inner elephant. This was not easy. I wanted to tell this guy why he was so wrong and why I was so right. As I held back and listened, my opinion started to change. As I let go of my need to be right, I realized that the plan could be substantially improved by his ideas. The end result was a much better plan, and I had an ally when presenting to the board of directors.

Getting back to Bob Lengel's research, when effective managers were confronted with an ambiguous, controversial, or risky issue, they waded right into conversations rather than going it alone or trusting their own right answer. They were quick to consult—getting all relevant information into the open, testing and clarifying their thinking, and then resolving the issue. Rather than staying stuck in their elephant thinking or championing their own beliefs, the highest-rated executives preferred a collective understanding, a larger truth. Executives rated less effective were much less likely to consult, even on urgent issues. The reason for their lower performance was their inability or unwillingness to base action on thinking larger than their own. The process of consultation is to freely express your own thoughts and welcome the thoughts of others.

Successful executives know that debate is essential to expand their thinking. General David Petraeus was warned about the cloistered existence of military officers who don't stop and look around as often as they should. From officer debates, he learned that seriously bright people thought very differently about important issues. Experiencing that not everyone saw the world the same way was good preparation for his leadership in Iraq and Afghanistan.[11] Selina Lo had a reputation as an aggressive, fire-breathing marketing VP who was determined to get her way. When she became CEO of Ruckus Wireless, the yelling and fist pounding to get her way no longer worked. She was responsible for all departments and employees, and would be fighting against her own organization. Impatience was her greatest foe, and changing her habit required a huge effort of will. She adopted a group decision-making process that forced her to listen to others. Now, whenever a disagreement arises, she convenes a meeting of disputants and other people affected by the decision to resolve the issue.[12]

Some of the best advice for consultation comes from spiritual traditions. My favorite form of consultation is from the Bahá'í faith. I have used it with groups, with superb results. The goal of Bahá'í consultation is to discover the larger truth before making a decision, solving a problem, or pursuing a course of action. Bahá'í consultation is not about personal counseling. You should go to a psychologist for that. Consultation is used to move from your inner elephant's small belief or conjecture toward a larger certitude. "The shining spark of truth cometh forth only after the clash of differing opinions." The key principles for consulting on a diverse range of issues is pretty straightforward:[13]

BAHÁ'Í CONSULTATION

○ *Establishment of the facts.* Base the conversation in facts rather than conjecture, opinion, and belief. Investigate relevant information sources. The facts should be viewed objectively rather than distorted to suit one's own opinion.

○ *Broad participation.* Consult with people who have relevant information or perspectives on the problem. Ideally, these people would be brought together in a group to hear one another's voices. When this is not possible, one-on-one consultation is fine.

o *Detachment.* The idea here is that "your" idea or thought
does not belong to you. It belongs to the larger group or organization you serve. People detach from their own viewpoint
or position, and may even speak against it. People express
their views frankly, calmly, and without rancor. They listen
to others without taking offense or belittling other viewpoints. "They must . . . not insist upon their own opinion,
for stubbornness and persistence in one's views will lead ultimately to discord and wrangling and the truth will remain
hidden."[14] The inner executive can do this; the inner elephant
cannot.

o *Agreement.* If an individual is making the decision, the full discussion provides a bigger picture and a clearer truth with which to
decide the correct action. If a group makes the decision, consultation leads to unanimity or to at least a majority vote following a full
discussion.

Consultation really works. It is an easy way to get outside your own
illusions to face reality. One of my EMBA students told me about his
decision to remove a generating unit from service because of a noisy steam
valve. He knew the right decision, but decided to bring all forty-three
employee stakeholders together anyway to hear their thoughts. "They
were pleased to be part of the decision and made many good points I had
not considered. I changed my decision because they would rather deal
with the noise and leave the unit in service. I learned that regardless of my
knowledge or good intentions, soliciting the thoughts of others always
provides a more robust solution."

Another example of consultation was developed by Luis, the manager
of a plant in San Antonio that repaired and reconditioned jet engines for
government aircraft. Luis had a tendency to insert himself into problems
and make the decisions himself. With a little coaching, he was ready for
consultation. Returning from a business trip, he learned about a serious
problem in the plant. Rather than run around to talk to people and then
make a decision, he tried consultation. He asked all stakeholders to meet
together on the shop floor (the conference room was too small). They
sat in a circle, and he asked each person in turn to fully state his or
her perception of the problem. After everyone spoke, he went around
the circle a second time asking each person to comment on his or her
interpretation of the problem and suggest ideas for going forward. By
now, everyone had a big picture of the issues and agreed on the best
approach. People quickly divided into teams to implement their part of
the solution. Luis did not make the decision by himself. A decision was

reached more quickly this way, with full buy-in from everyone. Now that's consultation.

• • •

If you consult in all things, you are more likely to take correct action in all things. This is not a natural behavior for many managers, but the results can be dramatic. Here is how to get started:

1. An easy way to expand awareness of your inner elephant's small mind is simply to consult with one other person. That's all. *Before making your next decision or taking an action, talk to one person.* Just talking to one other person will pull you out of your mental box.

2. Or try this exercise: consult with at least one person for the first five decisions you make tomorrow. These may be personal decisions, such as what to eat for breakfast or the best route to drive. They may be decisions related to the daily flow of activities in your business, such as hiring, spending, or deciding work priorities. You will be pleased at the increased perspective and clarity you gain.

3. Expand the consultation habit by consulting in all things for a few days. Ask at least one person before making a decision, no matter how small. Ask your spouse about what to wear or what to fix for dinner or the best time to head home from work. Ask someone at work about where to go for lunch or the best time to leave for lunch. Work up to bigger decisions, such as replacing a generator or authorizing an expenditure or designing a new policy manual. People will love that you asked and will see the light of your brilliance in asking them, and your mind will be expanding with new ideas while you learn to engage and develop others. You won't go wrong when in all things, you consult.

Remember This

In All Things, Consult

- Consultation, like asking questions, engages others while expanding your mind-set.
- Talking to just one person before you make a decision can change your perspective.
- Effective managers are quick to consult with others.
- Consultation clarifies ambiguities that exist at higher organization levels.

- Consultation takes advantage of seriously bright people seeing things differently.
- Consultation achieves a more accurate truth than does insistence on one's own opinion.
- Practice consulting about decisions large and small for a few days. You will like the result.

17

·

Living and Leading
from Your Inner
Executive

If, with the rope of mindfulness,
You bind firm the elephant of the mind,
You will let go of every fear
And find virtue close at hand.
—Shantideva

Opportunity is missed by most people because it is dressed
in overalls and looks like work.
—Thomas Edison

LUKE SKYWALKER IS BORED AND RESTLESS on a farm on a remote planet.
A little robot appears with a plea from a princess for her rescue. Luke
responds to this call to adventure. His journey takes him to Ben Kenobi,
a wise mentor who understands supernatural powers (the "Force") and
who teaches Luke to trust his higher self when dueling with a light saber.
Luke undergoes many trials, saves the princess, becomes a Jedi warrior,
wins the struggle with the evil Darth Vader, and fulfills his destiny by
destroying the Death Star. Luke discovered his warrior identity and

attained his true powers, which he realized were within him all along. Luke, an ordinary boy, was raised to the status of mythic hero.[1]

Star Wars, like Lord of the Rings and The Wizard of Oz, are fantasies that give voice to our deep longings and hopes for ourselves. These fantasies are not external reality, but they do relate to our dreams of how we would like reality to be. A hero is someone who has been through the crucible of personal change and devoted his or her life to something bigger than the self. In mythology, heroism typically involves breaking free from the status quo to perform a heroic and courageous deed, such as slaying a dragon, which is usually a symbol for destroying one's own ego. In reality, of course, when faced with a difficult challenge, the internal judge is likely to be sending you such thoughts as "Oh no! I couldn't do that!" or "This is stupid." The inner dragon (voice) must be destroyed before you can discover your heroic self. There are many obstacles to finding your life's mission, your happiness. Fantasies like Star Wars indicate the need to go through some kind of death and rebirth in a journey toward self-awareness and wholeness to achieve that happiness.

For most of us, most of the time, the automatic thoughts and behaviors of the inner elephant work just fine. We could not get through the day without our inner elephant, which does most of the work. Most of us are reasonably well adjusted, and there is no need to change the majority of our behaviors. There may be a few gaps, such as when we are not doing what we know we should be doing, but there is no need to slay the inner elephant; it just needs to be fixed a bit.

The practices in this book help you understand your inner elephant well enough to know which opportunities fit your greater potential, and strengthen your inner executive to reduce undesired behaviors. Helping you eliminate bad habits and undesired behaviors from your leadership style, which may reduce your personal effectiveness, is the goal of this book, and there are many exercises and practices to help you achieve that end.

The material in this final chapter is directed toward more ardent seekers of personal growth who are not content with changing the peripheral aspects of their inner elephant. A few people express the desire to work toward elimination of as much of their ego or "false self" as possible. Like Luke Skywalker, they want to live fully from their inner executive—the higher consciousness. They may want to apply the practices in this book to how they live their life rather than just to how they lead others. The purpose of this chapter is to offer a perspective and support for readers whose goal is to achieve some kind of enduring peace and contented happiness in their life. This chapter is for those of you who want to eliminate a big chunk of your inner elephant, to slay your inner dragon, as when drawn to living all aspects of your life from the higher realm of your inner executive. This chapter is for those of you who aspire to say good-bye to the smaller and self-oriented world of your inner elephant.

Higher Consciousness Revisited

How do you become the hero who is hidden within you? What this book has been calling the inner elephant represents the lower level of consciousness that is concerned with physical survival, personal gain, ego satisfaction, and emotional pleasure. The inner elephant is driven by self-interest to fulfill the needs of the body and ego. The inner elephant operates something like a bio-computer sending automatic signals into your head. As described in Chapters Two through Four, the inner elephant is preoccupied with garnering security, prestige, money, power, sex, status, and pleasant sensations. It can be overly reactive to pressures, intrusions, and triggers from without. It can be inflexible and highly judgmental; it wants control, tends to focus on ends rather than means, gets trapped in avoidance and impulsive behaviors, and does not accurately judge itself or the future. The inner elephant's constant struggle to accumulate for itself dominates your mind without really changing you or making you happy and, when the elephant's needs are thwarted, may trigger resentment, worry, anger, jealousy, or fear. The needs of the physical body and ego system dominate the thinking of the inner elephant. An untrained mind is filled continuously with desires and criticisms that arise from the inner elephant's needs and wants.

Higher consciousness is difficult to explain because it is an experiential phenomenon—you have to experience it to know it; you can't know it when immersed in the inner elephant's thoughts and desires. You might think of it as a higher level of awareness, which can observe the inner hubbub of your thoughts, fears, emotions, desires, and anxieties. Entering higher consciousness is a bit like awakening a dormant part of your mind. The ability to see your inner elephant's emotions and impulses gives you some distance from them; hence you identify less with them and are less under their control. Without higher consciousness, the inner elephant's automatic thoughts—memories, fantasies, frustrations, impulses—arise and fill your mind in haphazard fashion. Operating out of your lower consciousness means that you identify with and are attached to the flow of negative thoughts, fears, emotions, and anxieties in your head. The disparate images appearing in your mind also may create warfare within; for example, you may want to work on a project but feel resistance, or you may feel an unwanted craving or anger impulse that you wish to resist but cannot.

As your inner executive grows stronger, you may become aware of changes similar to those described in the list that follows.[2] You may already possess some of these qualities, and others will arise as you work on practices that are right for you. As you distance yourself from the inner elephant, you are developing the inner executive. As you experience your higher consciousness, you will likely find greater flow and peace of mind. Rather than having thoughts, feelings, and decisions dictated by your conditioned attitudes and responses, you are able to take or leave those impulses. Your thinking becomes clearer, and you become capable of focusing intently and penetrating deeply into whatever topic you address. Engaging your inner executive can provide a continuing sense of well-being and perhaps even periods of bliss or joy.

EMERGING QUALITIES OF THE INNER EXECUTIVE

Your inner state

Peace, contentment, and well-being replace anxiety and unease.

A calm and deliberate approach replaces upset and agitation.

The mind is focused and present in the moment rather than distracted.

You patiently accept things in their time rather than want everything now.

Lightness and humor replace a grim and serious demeanor.

Your dominant thought process

You focus on long-term consequences rather than immediate wants.

Thoughtful responses replace urgent cravings and instant reactions.

You serve others or something larger rather than focus on self first.

You interpret things objectively rather than as personal likes and dislikes.

You enjoy fulfilling your own potential rather than seek only material pleasure.

You see problems as puzzles rather than as people's shortcomings.

An open mind replaces skepticism, defensiveness, and strong viewpoints.

You welcome opposite viewpoints rather than triumph from a fixed position.

You detach from rather than hold on to belief in automatic desires, fears, and negative thoughts.

How you view others

You see people as human beings rather than as objects to meet your own needs.

Others are equal to you rather than below you.

Appreciation replaces envy and disrespect.

Generosity and empathic understanding replace criticalness and obsession with self.

Trust and faith replace distrust and suspicion.

Your decisions and actions

You focus on present and future possibilities rather than on past problems.

Self-discipline replaces impulses and overreactions.

Reason, evidence, and what works replace personal beliefs and ideology.

Developing others becomes more important than controlling others.

Immersion and flow replace feelings of resistance and distraction.

Focus on means replaces focus on ends.

Your relationships

You ask questions rather than provide answers.

You prefer listening to telling.

You enjoy building agreement with others rather than competing.

You appreciate head *and* heart rather than belittle anything touchy-feely.

You connect emotionally rather than remain distant from others.

You prefer interdependence to individualism and going it alone.

Compassion and generosity replace self-centeredness.

You take responsibility rather than blame others.

Living from your inner executive brings a sense of mental comfort, security, and calm that the inner elephant's quest for wealth, winning, and prestige cannot. The higher consciousness can see beyond the small focus on your own needs to care about the needs of another person, group, or organization. The higher consciousness is like maturity, the lower consciousness like immaturity. Everyone starts out with a childlike self-centeredness, and most people make some progress toward maturity throughout life. Living from the inner executive can be thought of as living at a high level of maturity. The inner executive also performs the brain's executive functions of conceptualizing, thinking abstractly, planning, developing, envisioning, and appreciating opposite points of view. In contrast, the inner elephant's devotion is to championing its own view, urges, and needs.

Relationships are problematic for the inner elephant, which is concerned mostly with the self. When we are under the sway of the inner elephant, relationships are driven by the need to control others, tell others what to do, get the elephant's own needs met, and blame others when things go wrong; the inner elephant tends to be individualistic and emotionally distant. Relationships based on higher mind are more effortlessly successful. The higher mind's first concern is to develop others, listen, and take personal responsibility, and it welcomes emotional connection and interdependence.

The best way to use the list of the emerging qualities of the inner executive is simply to study and reflect on it. Let the ideas soak in, and think about where you stand. As you absorb the general patterns, you will gain a better sense of where you would like to grow. The list may illuminate some specific areas to develop at work and in your everyday life. It may also help you identify where the inner elephant is strongest in your daily thinking and behavior. This insight can serve as a guideline to develop a practice, mantra, or visualization to help develop selected aspects of your inner executive.

When Her Mind Went Quiet

To help you understand the potential life outcomes of developing the inner executive as a way of living, I want to share a story about a brain scientist who experienced a brain malfunction. At seven o'clock one morning, Jill Taylor awoke sluggishly with a sharp, piercing pain directly behind her left eye. She felt bizarre and confused. She was conscious, but found it hard to think. Her head had stopped providing the usual answers; ideas seemed to flee from her awareness. Despite the physical discomfort, Taylor felt a growing sense of peace. The constant chatter of her mind went silent, leaving only tranquility. The void of language and cognition was filled with a sense of grace, followed by a sense of "all-knowingness or 'being at *one*' with the universe." Jill Taylor, brain scientist, had experienced a severe stroke that disabled the left hemisphere of her brain. The familiar voices of her brain chatter were delightfully silent as she experienced an abrupt major shift in consciousness.[3]

Taylor did recover, but her experience was so profound that part of her life's mission is to share it with others. Her stroke shut down part of her brain circuitry such that it was no longer reminding her of likes and dislikes or making negative judgments. It was as if her inner elephant had been destroyed. Taylor had grown up with lots of emotional baggage and anger, now all gone. She had spent a lifetime committed to *doing* at a fast pace, and now in an instant she was filled with a *being* consciousness. She didn't understand it, but she *liked* it. Taylor saw herself no longer as a physical body but as the atoms and energy she shared with others. She was in touch with what she called her "authentic" self and was almost reluctant to undertake rehabilitation to become "normal" again. With the brain chatter extinguished, her mind experienced a feeling of deep inner peace, the feeling of genuine happiness that everyone seems to want.

Taylor vividly experienced her two distinct selves, or what she called her two minds, which she said were analogous to the two hemispheres of the brain. Having lived a life in her head, now she was living from her heart. Rather than being trapped in what she called her small ego mind or small self, she experienced a bigger mind—her authentic self—that was calm and caring toward others. With the analytical, thinking part of her brain nonfunctional and her brain chatter silenced, she experienced the bliss that others only dream of. The mindshare devoted to degrading, insulting, or criticizing herself or others was now yielding a steady flow of empathy and consideration. Her mind was right here, right now, enjoying the richness of the present moment. There were no more judgments of good and bad or right and wrong. Observations of others were made without negative sentiment. Her new mental state was one of friendliness, and she smiled a lot. Her new state was one of feeling eternally optimistic and open to new possibilities, so she liked to think outside the box.

With treatment and therapy, Taylor regained the use of her brain's left hemisphere to help her function in daily life, but she has not lost the connection with her larger, authentic self. For example, her automatic anger response can once again be triggered, but now she does not act on it; she just watches it disappear within ninety seconds as she returns to her peaceful awareness. Taylor feels in control of her renewed critical thoughts and impulses. "By paying attention to the choices my automatic circuitry is making, I own my power and make more choices consciously," she wrote, relishing her power to stop thinking thoughts that are destructive or unhelpful. "There has been nothing more empowering than the realization that I don't have to think thoughts that bring me pain." When she received a speeding ticket, the voice in her head started to obsess over her mistake. She can now turn off her this unpleasant voice by realigning herself with the present moment.

Taylor spends much of her time teaching others how to develop this higher consciousness similar to what I have been calling the inner executive. She coaches her college students to develop a nonjudgmental witness that can listen to (or watch) their brain's thoughts. Students often complain that it takes too much mental effort to observe what their brain is telling them. This mastery takes practice and patience, and when they gain the new awareness, they are free to step beyond the mental drama of their impulsive thoughts and desires. They can be conscious of their cognitive loops without being seduced into believing or acting on those thoughts.

Here are some ideas from Taylor, who in a flash experienced a mental change that sages, mystics, and saints spend years trying to develop— liberation from their ego and inner elephant.

o She talks directly to her brain cells, respectfully asking them to stop bringing up specific thought patterns.

o She gives her mental chatterbox two half-hour periods each day to whine rampantly about anything it wants.

o She is a believer in paying attention to her automatic self-talk and stopping any internal verbal abuse. Thanks to her heightened awareness, her authentic self has real power over her thoughts.

o She has noted that her negative thought patterns are more likely to emerge when she is either physically tired or emotionally vulnerable.

o To retain her inner peace, she consistently tends the garden of her mind moment by moment during the day. She believes that being able to *observe* one's circuitry as well as engage with it is a boon to mental health.

o If a strong emotion is triggered, she simply resigns to it, accepts the emotion, and lets it run its course for ninety seconds. "Just like children, emotions heal when they are heard and validated. Over time, the intensity and frequency of these circuits usually abate."

o She unconditionally loves her thought-generating brain cells, both positive and negative, with an open heart and grateful mind.

○ She is able to shift her focus away from the churning loops of her chattering mind by using a mantra. To shift back into her higher consciousness, she may breathe deeply and repeat "In this moment I reclaim my joy," "In this moment I am perfect, whole, and beautiful," or "I am an innocent and peaceful child of the universe."

Although her left hemisphere is back online, Taylor retained the capacity to use her higher circuitry on a regular basis. No longer is she devoted solely to physical doing and mentally criticizing. Maintaining a balance between being and doing is her life now. For Taylor, it is a simple choice: "Why would anyone choose anything other than happiness?"

Answers to Individual Questions

I am asked a lot of questions by MBA students and managers about the content covered in this book. Here are answers to a few questions that have arisen.

How do I get started?

The first step is usually to recognize a desire to change some part of the way you think or behave. Once you clarify what you wish to change, it becomes a matter of finding a new approach through reading books or talking to people. I typically suggest finding a single practice, such as one contained in this book, that feels comfortable, and to experiment with it. Start small. Start with what you are drawn to. It is okay to experiment with one or more attractive practices and see what happens.

A few people are drawn to more general self-improvement. Personal growth is part of their life. This is the path of the seeker. In this case, your first step is usually to read a variety of self-help and spiritual books to identify a path that feels right. It may include participation in retreats of various kinds. This pursuit may include a number of spiritual or improvement practices. You might join with other people to assist with your practice, such as in a meditation or discussion group. This book will be just one of many things you explore.

The biggest barrier to getting started is your inner elephant. It wants to continue its old routines, so creating new mental circuitry takes effort. You will often forget about the new practices, perhaps for days at a time. Things that help would be to set up a system to remind you, to have a partner to check in with, and to stick to a schedule for the same time each day. You may have to use some practices from this book to help you do some of the practices from this book. Once your elephant gets some training, things will be easier. Your mind will be trained to accept a practice routine.

Which practice or exercise is best for me?

The best exercise for you is the one that is most appealing to you. If you try it without success, then go to the next one that attracts you. You may have to try various practices to learn what works for you. My personal favorite exercises to teach in class are "in all things, consult," "review the day," and "let people empty their cup."

If there is a silver bullet among the exercises in this book, I think it is intentionally repeating a phrase in your mind, as in autosuggestion or a mantra. I have been pleasantly surprised at this technique's wide applicability to various people and the array of issues that a frequent, intentional repetition of a carefully chosen phrase will ameliorate. Autosuggestion seems relatively easy for many people, and it has been a powerful way to lead their inner elephant toward new intentional behaviors. People who repeat the standard autosuggestion of "Every day, in every way, I am getting better and better," as well as other phrases, report many benefits, some unanticipated. For example, as their mind gets into the rhythm of a mantra to generate a clear intention, the inner elephant usually responds. Moreover, in some cases their mantra will start to automatically replace negative and critical thoughts. It is almost as if the specific words are not that important. Any phrase, repeated intentionally, starts to replace the negative and dysfunctional involuntary thoughts arising in your mind from your automatic circuitry. Hence, of practices I have taught, the mantra has been the most powerful single practice with the widest application. A few people also have told me that when repeating a mantra-like suggestion, they find themselves visualizing the desired behavior at the same time. This strengthens the power of the suggestion to their inner elephant. When any positive suggestion is repeated several times in the morning and evening, as well as during quiet periods during the day, perhaps accompanied by visualization, it can have a transformative effect on your behavior.

I would say that in the literature I have read, meditation is the practice recommended most often for training the mind. However, many people are not drawn to meditation, so it is relevant to fewer people than a mantra. It is hard to find time in a busy day to meditate. But if meditation resonates for you, it will likely help subordinate your inner elephant to your inner executive and thereby eliminate bad habits and dysfunctional behaviors. Find a meditation practice that works for you, and expect to see some results in a few weeks.

My management job keeps me busy from dawn until dusk. How can I practice any of these exercises?

Yes, busyness is the enemy of change. I recall the authors of a book on teaching mindfulness techniques reporting how difficult it was for the authors themselves to do the simple exercises they asked their clients to do.[4] Getting up earlier in the morning or finding time in a busy schedule was very hard. Their excuses for skipping the exercises proliferated. During a busy day in which we confront many and rapid stimuli for which we are responsible, our automatic systems kick in, and there is little time for reflection. High-stress periods cause us to regress to our most basic and automatic responses.

My suggestion is to search for or create small spaces in your schedule. Do you drive or take a train to and from work? Do you ever watch TV? Do you have a meal break? Do you have a few moments early in the morning or late in the evening? If you truly have no time to yourself, you are in a situation that is not conducive to practice. Being caught up completely in external demands will make it hard to focus on internal work. But if you do have occasional pauses or breaks, then many of the practices in this book are accessible to you.

A mantra is probably the best technique for busy people because it can be used during brief mental pauses and can operate in the back of your mind much of the time. You can repeat a mantra or autosuggestion at any time other than when you are talking or immersed in work. Quieting your mind and reflecting for a few moments or creating a visual picture does not take much time, but does require a break. Another idea is to try practices that can become part of your normal workday. You can consult with others, stop interrupting, focus on people, focus on your work, consciously slow down, or calm down during the flow of your day. Another idea is to work with a partner, which would help you focus for a brief time on a specific exercise. In a perfect world, you would allocate a specific time period from ten to thirty minutes each day to develop your inner executive. Any small practice, done periodically, even if only for a moment, will become a new pattern and will grow over time.

How can I go faster to rid myself of bad habits to improve my leadership approach?

My advice is to let go of trying to go fast. Forcing or pushing against the undesirable parts of your mind will strengthen those parts, just as exercising a muscle by applying tension will strengthen that muscle. This was a lesson I was slow to learn. The goal is to strengthen your intention—your intelligent will—and through your doing so, the undesirable parts of your inner elephant will atrophy and fall away. You essentially learn to let go of the unwanted parts. Meditation works, for example, by just observing, relaxing, and letting go of the thoughts or actions arising from your inner elephant. Relaxation is better than applying pressure. As you strengthen your higher mind by focusing on the present and inward toward your inner elephant, the dysfunctional elements weaken. The idea is to see those elements and let them go, or perhaps replace them with an intentional mantra. Your effort is devoted to learning to concentrate the mind and keep it in the present moment, not to forcing away the stuff you don't want. Training the mind is difficult, but easier than you might think, because you do not have to drive away any thoughts and desires. Just seeing them directly and consciously will weaken them. As your inner executive gains strength, you will find changes in mood and outlook. The trick is to practice every day; you will learn to see and let go of the negative aspects of yourself.

Is repeating a mantra similar to cognitive-behavioral therapy?

I think of a mantra as a shortcut to cognitive-behavioral therapy. Cognitive-behavioral therapy is a collection of techniques to help change a person's negative thoughts, images, and interpretations. For example, the therapist may guide a client to gather objective evidence to dispute self-defeating thought patterns. Through this kind of assignment, the client engages the higher consciousness of the inner executive to witness, detach from, and learn to disbelieve his or her conditioned thought patterns. Having a therapist to work with to change thought patterns is of great value.

Repeating a mantra might be considered a cousin of cognitive-behavioral therapy. The intent of replacing negative or self-defeating thought patterns with positive thoughts is the same. One difference is that a mantra is simple enough to do on your own. After selecting a suitable self-enhancing phrase (as described in Chapters Five and Thirteen), you can gradually increase its frequency of use. Whenever a negative or self-defeating thought arises, you can replace it with the intentional positive thought. This is simpler and more straightforward than gathering evidence to dispute the thought, and works especially well for people who have the mental discipline to repeat a predetermined phrase frequently throughout the day. Both the mantra and cognitive-behavioral therapy strengthen the inner executive to have greater influence over the inner elephant.

How does the material you teach differ from the ideas in books on positive thinking, such as The Secret, *in which motivational speakers say you can get what you want by thinking correctly?*

I have researched a large number of books on positive thinking, including the phenomenal best seller *The Secret,* which propose that the best way to get what you want in life is through positive thinking or thinking about what you want. There is certainly a grain of truth in these books that may account for their popularity. What we think *does* determine who we are and what we accomplish in life.

One difference I have tried to incorporate in this book is the emphasis on the *how* of managing yourself. I searched through a number of positive-thinking books looking for specific exercises that would help readers achieve useful new mental states for leadership. I did not find much. The writers or speakers seemed to be saying, "Do as I do, and you too can be rich," "Here is the attitude or mind-set that will make you wealthy," or "Think positive and everything will be better." This advice fails to recognize how difficult it is to change deeply ingrained thought patterns. I had to search beyond these simple prescriptions and go deeper into psychology and religious traditions to find practices, such as the mantra or meditation, that people can do on their own to change their thinking. Some practices, such as visualization, are better known, but the books I read contained little coaching on how to actually use mental tools to change ingrained mental and habit patterns.

There is another major difference between this book and others. The goal of this book is to help you become a better leader or individual performer. It works from the inside out. Other popular books, such as *The Secret,* seem to be appealing to people's desire to go from the outside in, to acquire for themselves what they want from the material world, particularly money and financial success. The practices in this book are designed to strengthen your inner executive so that your inner elephant will behave under its direction. The idea is for the higher mind to have control over the lower mind's impulses. As I interpret other books, they seem to appeal to the inner elephant's desire for material gain, and attempt to use a person's inner executive to fulfill those desires. That approach—putting the inner executive's higher mind in the service of one's small, self-oriented inner elephant—is just the opposite of mine. That would mean using visualization or a mantra, for example, exclusively to acquire more money rather than to improve yourself. For all I know, that might work to some extent, but it is not what this book is about. Leading or living from your higher consciousness will produce much more life satisfaction and success in the long run than trying to use it to meet the lower needs or desires of your inner elephant.

Is it ever okay to objectify other people?

This question has been raised by students in the context of war or intense competition between companies. In extreme cases such as war, objectifying the enemy seems to fit the situation. However, under normal conditions the unconscious objectification of other people is a major cause of problems in the world. People in one social group often see themselves as superior to other social groups in terms of lineage, school, company, political party, religion, country of origin, or race. Racism, for example, prevents a person from seeing members of another racial group in their humanness or as fully equal. Within organizations, mental barriers arise between departments or between HQ and field offices. People in one section often view people in other sections as objects, idiots, and incompetents rather than as human beings with similar issues and concerns. Thus people in different parts of the same company may fight rather than cooperate. The inner elephant quite naturally blames others, and a great deal of a leader's work is to overcome these mind-sets so that departments and groups can work together.

The main thing for you as a leader is not to objectify any of your followers or colleagues. It is easy to slide into a mind-set of frustration and blame toward individuals. When you feel this way, you communicate it in the form of body language and in the different ways you treat people and the opportunities you give them. Direct reports will know when you think or feel another way toward them, objectifying some and not others, which often causes differences in their performance and satisfaction.

How can I know when I am in my inner executive?

The clearest indicator of your inner executive is that you are aware of your own awareness or are conscious of your consciousness. That may sound pretty abstract, but you will know when it happens. If you are focusing on your breath, for example, you are aware of your breath. When you are aware that you are aware of your breath, your mind is completely in the moment, and automatic thoughts from the inner elephant are quiet. There are no distracting thoughts. You can focus your attention on your awareness and extend the amount of time in that place.

You are also in the inner executive when you are using your conscious intention, such as when you are consciously focusing on the present moment. Any time you consciously focus inwardly on a part of your mind or body, you are in the inner executive because the inner elephant focuses outward through the five senses. The inward focus on a mantra, a visualization, or reviewing your day also puts you into the higher consciousness of the inner executive. Any time you are aware of your own thoughts, emotions, cravings, fears, and so on, you are using your inner executive. You are also in the inner executive when you use your higher mental processes to intentionally plan, conceptualize, write, hold back your inner elephant, talk directly to your inner elephant, or do something your inner elephant doesn't want to do. However, when you are carried away by random thoughts or automatic reactions to external stimuli, you are unconscious and in your inner elephant. In the early stages of your practice, you will likely find that you are unconscious most of the day.

What about intuition? Does it arise from the inner executive or the inner elephant?

This question usually arises from someone who is tuned in to his or her inner elephant and inner executive and can't determine from which an intuitive thought arises. In my experience, intuition tends to fall into the hazy middle region between the inner elephant and inner executive.

The inner elephant does have intuition. Based on the elephant's store of life experiences, a new idea or intuitive feeling may arise into your awareness, and typically it is accurate and should be trusted. This is similar to the intuitive decision making described in *Blink*, by Malcolm Gladwell. The long experience of the inner elephant can translate into a useful intuitive response. The distinctive aspect of intuition is its emotional neutrality. It does not contain the negative and judgmental edge associated with many of the inner elephant's critical thoughts and reactions.

The inner executive is highly intuitive. It seems to rely more on intuition than on rational thought. To the extent that an intuitive thought can be traced to some combination of your previous experiences, then I would say it arises from the inner elephant. To the extent that the intuitive thought is completely new and inspired, I would say it arises from the inner executive, which may be accessing something broader than your elephant's previous life experience, such as the collective unconscious.

I am not attracted to any of the practices you have offered. I am interested in becoming a better leader and in pursuing personal growth. What should I do?

Most people can find some practices in this book to which they are attracted and that will provide some value. If nothing in this book appeals to you, it may be because there are two fundamental paths toward personal growth—the head path and the heart path. This book is written primarily from the perspective of the head or mind. Most of the people I work with are pursuing a career in business, and they are primarily thinkers, analyzers, organizers, and controllers—they primarily use thinking processes in their leadership. The same is true for me—left-brain thinking is my dominant mode for dealing with the world. So the approach taken in this book is the mental path that is focused inward on training the mind to become a witness to your inner elephant's thoughts and impulses and to gradually take charge of them. Most people have some left-brain capacity; hence some practices in this book will have value for them.

Having said that, however, I acknowledge that many people are better suited to the heart path. Their dominant mode of dealing with the world is through feelings, creativity, and relationships rather than through systematic thinking and analysis. This approach is typically more extroverted because it focuses outwardly on other people or on some form of higher power rather than inward. On the heart path of development, the inner elephant can be weakened or eliminated—and the inner executive strengthened—through love and devotion, through service to society or service to a higher power. If you have ever performed any act of pure service, you know how good it feels. Service to others is a way to short-circuit the inner elephant to go directly to the sense of well-being and bliss that those on the "mental" path have to train their minds to achieve. Focusing your attention inward to quiet the extant patterns of thought and habit takes a mental discipline that is unattractive to someone naturally suited to the heart path. If you feel an inclination toward the heart path, it would be a good idea to pursue your personal growth through love and devotion rather than through inward concentration and self-awareness.

I am a champion of the heart path for people suited to it, but it is not my thing to teach. A few years ago, I was serving food to homeless men in a small Catholic charity center in St. Louis. Helping those disadvantaged people for a couple of hours felt great. The lasting impression, however, was of the look on the face of the nun in charge of the center. She was absolutely radiant. Her face glowed. By spending her life doing this work, she seemed filled with uncontainable bliss. Speaking to her, there was no ego to be found. She had surrendered her ego to a higher power in the form of service to those unfortunate clients of the center. Realistically, you have to have some thinking and head skills to get along in the world, but that's all. If you feel inclined toward the heart path, the fastest way to diminish your inner elephant is to select a career in which you can serve others. Indeed, many leadership positions provide opportunities to teach and serve others if you will use the position in that way.

Final Thoughts

Writing this book reawakened all of this material in my mind. I found myself practicing the exercises in whatever chapter I was writing. I am beginning to understand the Buddha's teaching that desire is the basis for suffering. Or the saying I heard in India that the richest person in the world is the one with the fewest desires. I would attribute my increased feelings of contentment and peace over the last few years to the practices described in this book. One thing that I appreciate most is the flow arising from lowered resistance to working on important projects, which feels wonderful and peaceful, and leaves me lighter and happier. With the mental blocks removed, my immersion in ongoing projects is a source of daily satisfaction. The absence of inner struggle—of one part of me wanting to do one thing, the other part the opposite—is a feeling of freedom, as though I was just released from jail. Although still an introvert, I find myself more interested in people. My critical and negative judgments toward other people's seemingly dysfunctional behavior have all but disappeared. I see people as doing or saying what is in their mind in that moment rather than as doing something to upset me. I see their behavior as playing out the thoughts and impulses that arise in their heads, just like everyone else, and they really don't know any better. If their behavior is inappropriate to their mission or team, I may have to call them on it, but without personal dislike or anger.

Most of the exercises in this book are simply training the mind to stay in the present moment. I still practice many of them, because if I don't, old habits reappear. I meditate each day for fifteen to thirty minutes when I awaken, again for a few minutes before going to sleep, for the thirty minutes I exercise on my elliptical (with eyes closed to concentrate inwardly), and while driving to and from work (radio off). Meditation to me means time for observing the dynamics of my mind and training my mind with some kind of mental exercise. I may repeat a mantra to correct some issue on which I am working, or simply stay in the present moment by repeating a phrase such as "I am staying aware." I may focus on watching my body as it exercises, concentrate on my breathing, and bring my mind back to that focus when it jumps away. I may focus on watching for any thought that arises, focus down into the center of my body, or just focus on the now. Any of these things improves concentration and keeps my mind in the present, and thereby does not give license to my automatic circuitry to fill my head with its involuntary critical thoughts, impulses, and dislikes. My inner elephant seems to be weaker, and I am able to stay in the flow of work and personal relationships.

What will make this stuff work for you? I would say two things: a little willingness and a little effort. Is it enough to read the prescription, or do you have to be willing to swallow the medicine? You must be willing to try it to receive the benefit. A little willingness means being open to trying something new. Willingness means being open minded and ready, and lowering your resistance to trying a technique or behavior that may seem strange or different. A little effort means you actually practice some new mental habit and start cutting a mental groove or circuit for it. There is simply no way to avoid doing the work. There is no fast track. Just reading this book and acquiring "book knowledge" won't help much because reading is a familiar mental habit. You have to practice something new to create a new mental pattern. Progress requires intentional effort. Reading one book a day for one hundred days about leadership growth will not have as much impact as practicing one exercise every day for one hundred days. You change yourself by strengthening your inner executive and by quieting the inner elephant, not with mental gymnastics or mental cleverness that perpetuates your inner elephant. Practicing something new from this book or other books is the best way to lead yourself toward your leadership inner excellence.

You are in for something of a fight with the established mental circuitry of your inner elephant. It will try to keep your attention. Major changes, lasting changes, require months and years of practice, not days and weeks. You can expect some traction in a few days, but not a change of major proportion. The great thing, however, is that once you start and become a little bit aware of the present moment, and as you begin to engage your inner executive to become a witness to the antics of your inner elephant, there is no going back. The process will continue on its own, albeit slowly if you don't practice regularly. Start small. Make it easy on yourself. Have faith. With regular daily practice, you will gain enough traction to feel some change in the shorter term, and experience more substantive changes in the longer term.

Any or all of the practices in this book will lead to a leadership style more characteristic of Luke Skywalker or Ben Kenobi than of Darth Vader. The call to adventure is an inward rather than outward call. You may want to slay a dragon externally, which would be fun and rewarding, but a greater victory will be to slay your internal dragon. The challenge of inner excellence is to gain mastery over your leadership habits and personal behaviors the way Luke Skywalker did. Do you accept the call? You can lead yourself to become a superb leader of other people. You are bigger than your selfish wants. Let go of your childish ways. Align with your higher angels. Then you will become the hero who lies within you—the ideal leader who lies within you.

Notes

•

CHAPTER ONE: THE PROBLEM OF MANAGING YOURSELF

1. Ram Charan and Geoffrey Colvin, "Why CEOs Fail," *Fortune*, June 21, 1999, 69–78.

2. Jeffrey Pfeffer and Robert I. Sutton, *The Knowing-Doing Gap: How Smart Companies Turn Knowledge into Action* (Boston: Harvard Business School Press, 1999).

3. Romans 7:15–19, King James Version.

4. Mark Gunther, "Soul Trainer," *Fortune*, January 7, 2002, 119–121.

5. "Oprah Winfrey I Fell 'Off the Wagon,'" *People*, December 22, 2008, http://www.people.com/people/archive/article/0,,20252101,00.html.

6. Alex Williams, "New Year, New You? Nice Try," *New York Times*, December 31, 2008, http://www.nytimes.com/2009/01/01/fashion/01change.html; Atul Gawande, "The Man Who Couldn't Stop Eating," *New Yorker*, July 9, 2001, 66–75.

7. Alan Deutschman, *Change or Die* (New York: Regan, 2007).

8. Marilee C. Goldberg, *The Art of the Question: A Guide to Short-Term Question-Centered Therapy* (Hoboken, NJ: Wiley, 1998).

9. Timothy D. Wilson, *Stranger to Ourselves: Discovering the Adaptive Unconscious* (Cambridge, MA: Belknap Press, 2002).

10. Howard Rachlin, *The Science of Self-Control* (Cambridge, MA: Harvard University Press, 2000).

11. Walter Mischel and Ozlem Ayduk, "Willpower in a Cognitive-Affective Processing System: The Dynamics of Delay of Gratification," in *Handbook of Self-Regulation: Research, Theory, and Applications*, ed. Roy F. Baumeister and Kathleen D. Vohs (New York: Guilford Press, 2004), 99–129.

12. Amanda Fortini, "Special Treatment: The Rise of Luxury Rehab," *New Yorker*, December 1, 2008, 40–48.

13. The elephant as a metaphor for the unconscious ego-mind is in the teachings of Sathya Sai Baba and Ramana Maharshi. Jonathan Haidt, *The Happiness Hypothesis: Finding Modern Truth in Ancient Wisdom* (New York: Basic Books, 2006), suggested the boy rider and elephant as a metaphor for the conscious and unconscious minds.

CHAPTER TWO: RECOGNIZE YOUR TWO SELVES

1. Elkhonon Goldberg, *The Executive Brain: Frontal Lobes and the Civilized Mind* (New York: Oxford University Press, 2001).

2. John A. Bargh and Tonya L. Chartrand, "The Unbearable Automaticity of Being," *American Psychologist* 54, no. 7 (1999): 462–479.

3. Ken Keyes Jr., *Handbook to Higher Consciousness* (Coos Bay, OR: Love Line Books, 1988).

4. Timothy D. Wilson, *Strangers to Ourselves: Discovering the Adaptive Unconscious* (Cambridge, MA: Belknap Press, 2002).

5. Pujan Roka, *Bhagavad Gita on Effective Leadership: Timeless Wisdom for Leaders* (New York: iUniverse, 2006); Arvind Sharma, *Classical Hindu Thought: An Introduction* (London: Oxford University Press, 2000); *Bhagavad Gita,* ch. 3, v. 42.

6. Roka, *Bhagavad Gita on Effective Leadership;* Sharma, *Classical Hindu Thought; Bhagavad Gita,* ch. 3, v. 42.

7. *A Course in Miracles* (Mill Valley, CA: Foundation for Inner Peace, 1992).

8. Martin E. P. Seligman, *Learned Optimism: How to Change Your Mind and Your Life* (New York: Vintage Books, 2006).

9. Wilson, *Strangers to Ourselves.*

10. Brandon J. Schmeichel and Roy F. Baumeister, "Self-Regulatory Strength," in *Handbook of Self-Regulation: Research, Theory, and Applications,* ed. Roy F. Baumeister and Kathleen D. Vohs (New York: Guilford Press, 2004), 84–98.

11. Adam Bryant, "Meetings, Version 2.0, at Microsoft," *New York Times,* May 17, 2009, B2.

12. The research by Michael Kane, a psychologist at UNC Greensboro, was reported in Malcolm Ritter, "Mind-Wandering Intrigues Psychologists," *Tennessean,* March 20, 2007, 5A.

13. Eckhard Tolle, *A New Earth: Awakening to Your Life's Purpose* (New York: Dutton, 2005), 31–32.

14. Belle Linda Halpern and Kathy Lubar, *Leadership Presence* (New York: Gotham Books, 2003).

15. Jodi Kantor, "For a New Political Age, a Self-Made Man," *New York Times,* August 28, 2008, A1, A21; David Brooks, "Thinking About Obama," *New York Times,* October 17, 2008, A33; Jodi Kantor, "Barack Obama, Forever Sizing Up," *New York Times,* October 26, 2008, http://www.nytimes.com/2008/10/26/weekinreview/26kantor.html?page wanted=print.

16. Adam Bryant, "In a Near-Death Event, a Corporate Rite of Passage," *New York Times,* August 2, 2009, B2.

17. Jim Fannin, *S.C.O.R.E. for Life: The Secret Formula for Thinking Like a Champion* (New York: HarperCollins, 2005).

18. Jonathan Haidt, *The Happiness Hypothesis: Finding Modern Truth in Ancient Wisdom* (New York: Basic Books, 2006).

19. Jerome Groopman, *How Doctors Think* (Boston: Houghton Mifflin, 2007).

20. Sent-ts'an, "On Trust in the Heart," in *Buddhist Texts Through the Ages,* ed. E. Conze (New York: HarperCollins, 1954), 295.

21. Richard L. Daft, *The Leadership Experience,* 4th ed. (Mason, OH: South-Western, 2008).

22. Ram Charan, *Know-How: The 8 Skills That Separate People Who Perform from Those Who Don't* (New York: Crown, 2007), 83.

23. Adam Bryant, "At Yum Brands, Rewards for Good Work," *New York Times,* July 12, 2009, B2.

CHAPTER THREE: THREE TENDENCIES THAT DISTORT YOUR REALITY

1. Mitchell Zuckoff, "The Perfect Mark," *New Yorker,* May 15, 2006, 36–43.

2. Larry Bossidy and Ram Charan, *Confronting Reality: Doing What Matters to Get Things Right* (New York: Crown Business, 2004), 11.

3. Timothy D. Wilson, *Strangers to Ourselves: Discovering the Adaptive Unconscious* (Cambridge MA: Belknap Press, 2002).

4. These research findings were summarized in Daniel Gilbert, *Stumbling on Happiness* (New York: Knopf, 2006).

5. Gilbert, *Stumbling on Happiness;* Jonathan Haidt, *The Happiness Hypothesis: Finding Modern Truth in Ancient Wisdom* (New York: Basic Books, 2006).

6. Haidt, *Happiness Hypothesis,* 29.

7. Eric Klein and John Izzo, *Awakening Corporate Soul: Four Paths to Unleash the Power of People at Work* (Beverly, MA: Fair Winds Press, 1999); "John Izzo Leadership Speaker," http://www.youtube.com/watch?v= R9C3wJbjsN4.

8. Holly Hom and Jonathan Haidt, "The Bonding and Norming Functions of Gossip" (in preparation, University of Virginia), cited in Haidt, *Happiness Hypothesis,* 54.

9. John Gottman, *Why Marriages Succeed or Fail* (New York: Simon & Schuster, 1995); Marcial Losada and Emily Heaphy, "The Role of Positivity and Connectivity in the Performance of Business Teams," *American Behavioral Scientist* 47, no. 6 (2004): 740–765.

10. M. W. McCall Jr. and M. M. Lombardo, *Off the Track: Why and How Successful Executives Get Derailed,* Technical Report No. 21 (Greensboro, NC: Center for Creative Leadership, 1983).

11. Michael Ray and Rochelle Myers, *Creativity in Business* (New York: Broadway Books, 1986).

12. Riccardo Orizio, *Talk of the Devil: Encounters with Seven Dictators* (New York: Walker, 2004).

13. Helen Phillips, "Mind Fiction: Why Your Brain Tells Tall Tales," *New Scientist,* October 7, 2006, http://www.newscientist.com/article/mg19225720 .100-mind-fiction-why-your-brain-tells-tall-tales.html.

14. G. H. Estabrooks, *Hypnotism* (New York: Dutton, 1943), 78.

15. Gilbert, *Stumbling on Happiness.*

16. Sydney Finkelstein, Jo Whitehead, and Andrew Campbell, "The Illusion of Smart Decision Making: The Past Is Not Prologue," *Journal of Business Strategy* 30, no. 6 (2008): 36–43.

17. Gilbert, *Stumbling on Happiness.*

18. Chris Argyris, *Strategy, Change and Defensive Routines* (Boston: Pitman, 1985).

19. Ibid.

20. Robert Wright, *The Moral Animal* (New York: Pantheon, 1994), 280.

CHAPTER FOUR: EVERY LEADER'S SIX MENTAL MISTAKES

1. Adam Bryant, "In Praise of All That Grunt Work," *New York Times,* May 31, 2009, B2.

2. Adam Bryant, "There's No Need to Bat .900," *New York Times,* April 5, 2009, B2.

3. Adam Bryant, "He Wants Subjects, Verbs and Objects," *New York Times,* April 26, 2009, B2.

4. Paul Tough, "Can the Right Kinds of Play Teach Self-Control?" *New York Times Magazine,* September 27, 2009, 30–35.

5. Adapted from "The Bosses and John, Their Subordinate," case UVA-OB-0217 (Charlottesville: Darden Business Publishing, University of Virginia).

6. Robert Lee Hotz, "The Science Journal: Get out of Your Own Way," *Wall Street Journal*, June 27, 2008, A9.

7. Adam Bryant, "He Was Promotable, After All," *New York Times*, May 3, 2009, B2.

8. Srikumar S. Rao, *Are You Ready to Succeed? Unconventional Strategies for Achieving Personal Mastery in Business and Life* (New York: Hyperion, 2006).

9. Benedict Carey, "A Shocker: Partisan Thought Is Unconscious," *New York Times*, January 24, 2006, F8.

10. Michael B. Metzger, "Managing Our 'Inner Lawyer,'" *Business Horizons* 52, no. 1 (2009): 7–12.

11. Marshall Goldsmith with Mark Reiter, *What Got You Here Won't Get You There* (New York: Hyperion, 2007), 45–46.

12. Maia Szalavitz, "10 Ways We Get the Odds Wrong," *Psychology Today*, January/February 2008, 96–101.

13. Tom Vanderbilt, *Traffic: Why We Drive the Way We Do (and What It Says About Us)* (New York: Knopf, 2008).

14. Chris Argyris, *Strategy, Change and Defensive Routines* (Boston: Pitman, 1985), 11–12.

15. David C. Glass and Jerome E. Singer, *Urban Stress: Experiments on Noise and Social Stressors* (New York: Academic Press, 1972).

16. Ellen J. Langer, *The Psychology of Control* (Thousand Oaks, CA: Sage, 1983), 241–250.

17. Shelley E. Taylor, *Positive Illusions: Creative Self-Deception and the Healthy Mind* (New York: Basic Books, 1989).

18. Adam Bryant, "Planes, Cars, and Cathedrals," *New York Times*, September 6, 2009, B2.

19. This definition was drawn from the "Procrastination Central" Web site of the University of Calgary, http://www.procrastinus.com/.

20. Dominique Browning, "Woman's Estate," *New York Times Book Review*, January 4, 2009, 10.

21. Sumantra Ghoshal and Heike Bruch, "Going Beyond Motivation to the Power of Volition," *MIT Sloan Management Review* 44, no. 3 (Spring 2003): 51–57.

22. Dan Lovallo and Danielle Kahneman, "Delusions of Success: How Optimism Undermines Executives' Decisions," *Harvard Business Review*, July 2003, 56–63, 117.

23. Douglas R. Hofstadter, *Gödel, Escher, Bach: An Eternal Golden Braid*, 20th anniv. ed. (New York: Basic Books, 1999), 152; Jane Collingwood, "Hofstadter's Law and Realistic Planning," *PsychCentral*, http://psychcentral.com/lib/2009/hofstadters-law-and-realistic-planning/.

24. Martin Wolk, "Cost of Iraq War Could Surpass $1 Trillion," MSNBC, updated March, 17, 2006, http://www.msnbc.msn.com/id/11880954/.

25. Thom Shanker, "New Strategy Vindicates Ex-Army Chief Shinseki," *New York Times,* January 12, 2007, A13.

26. Sigmund Freud, *Civilization and Its Discontents*, vol. 1, *Standard Edition of the Complete Psychological Works of Sigmund Freud* (1930; London: Hogarth Press and Institute of Psychoanalysis, 1953), 75–76.

27. Edward L. Deci and Richard M. Ryan, *Intrinsic Motivation and Self-Determination in Human Behavior* (New York: Plenum, 1985).

28. Alfie Kohn, *Punished by Rewards: The Trouble with Gold Stars, Incentive Plans, A's, Praise, and Other Bribes* (Boston: Houghton Mifflin, 1999).

29. Adam Bryant, "Can You Pass a CEO Test?" *New York Times*, March 15, 2009, B2.

30. Jonathan Roof, *Pathways to God* (Prasanthi Nilayam, India: The Convener, Sri Sathya Sai Books and Publications Trust, 2006), 3:96.

31. Kohn, *Punished by Rewards*.

32. Nouk Sanchez and Tomas Vieira, *Take Me to the Truth: Undoing the Ego* (Winchester, England: O Books, 2007), 64–65.

33. This term was coined by Philip Brickman and Donald Campbell, "Hedonic Relativism and Planning the Good Society," in *Adaptation Level Theory: A Symposium,* ed. M. H. Apley (New York: Academic Press, 1971), 287–302.

CHAPTER FIVE: ENGAGE YOUR INTENTION

1. Lynne McTaggart, *The Intention Experiment: Using Your Thoughts to Change Your Life and the World* (New York: Free Press, 2007), 127.

2. "Muhammad Ali's Biography," Blogs.com, http://www.biogs.com/famous/alimuhammad.html.

3. McTaggart, *Intention Experiment,* 128.

4. Gary Mack with David Casstevens, *Mind Gym: An Athlete's Guide to Inner Excellence* (New York: McGraw-Hill, 2001), 112.

5. This exercise was developed by Janet Simmons and Don Irwin of the Developmental Educational Learning Institute in Des Moines, Iowa, 1993.

6. Dan Heath and Chip Heath, "Make Goals Not Resolutions," *Fast Company,* February 2008, 58–59.

7. Mack with Casstevens, *Mind Gym*.

8. A. H. Dorfman and Karl Kuehl, *The Mental Game of Baseball: A Guide to Peak Performance*, 3rd ed. (South Bend, IN: Diamond Communications, 2002), 139.

9. Charles Garfield, "Peak Performers," *Success*, February 1986, cited in Dorfman and Kuehl, *Mental Game of Baseball*, 143–144.

10. Much of this discussion is based on McTaggart, *Intention Experiment*, ch. 9.

11. D. Smith, P. Holmes, D. Collins, and K. Layland, "The Effect of Mental Practice on Muscle Strength and EMG Activity," *Proceedings of the British Psychological Society Annual Conference* 6, no. 2 (1998): 116.

12. Robert Scaglione and William Cummins, *Karate of Okinawa: Building Warrior Spirit* (North Clarendon, VT: Total Publishing, 1993); "Creative Visualization," Wikipedia, http://en.wikipedia.org/wiki/Creative_visualization.

13. McTaggart, *Intention Experiment*.

14. Ibid.

15. Jim Fannin, *S.C.O.R.E. for Life: The Five Keys to Optimal Achievement* (New York: HarperCollins, 2005), 30–35.

16. Dan Hill, *Emotionomics: Leveraging Emotions for Business Success* (London: Kogan Page, 2009).

17. Adam Bryant, "Stumping for Votes, Every Day," *New York Times*, June 27, 2009, B2.

18. Emile Coué, *Self Mastery Through Conscious Autosuggestion* (New York: American Library Service, 1922).

19. These examples are drawn from Timothy D. Wilson, *Strangers to Ourselves: Discovering the Adaptive Unconscious* (Cambridge, MA: Belknap Press, 2002), 32; and Jonathan Haidt, *The Happiness Hypothesis: Finding Modern Truth in Ancient Wisdom* (New York: Basic Books, 2006), 13–14.

20. Grainne M. Fitzsimons and John A. Bargh, "Automatic Self-Regulation," in *Handbook of Self-Regulation: Research, Theory, and Applications*, ed. Roy F. Baumeister and Kathleen D. Vohs (New York: Guilford Press, 2004), 155–170.

21. Lauren Collins, "The Vertical Tourist," *New Yorker*, April 20, 2009, 69–79.

CHAPTER SIX: FOLLOW THROUGH ON YOUR INTENTIONS

1. Timothy D. Wilson, *Strangers to Ourselves: Discovering the Adaptive Unconscious* (Cambridge, MA: Belknap Press, 2002), 176–178.

2. Donald G. Phillips, *Lincoln on Leadership: Executive Strategies for Tough Times* (New York: Business Plus, 1992).

3. Judy Battista, "Secret to Stealers Coach Tomlin's Success: Take Notes," *New York Times,* January 26, 2009, D1, D7.

4. Peter M. Gollwitzer, "Implementation Intentions: Strong Effects of Simple Plans," *American Psychologist* 54, no. 7 (July 1999): 493–503.

5. Cornelius J. Koenig and Martin Kleinmann, "Time Management Problems and Discounted Utility," *Journal of Psychology* 141, no. 3 (May 2007): 321–335.

6. Cornelius J. Koenig and Martin Kleinmann, "Deadline Rush: A Time Management Phenomenon and Its Mathematical Description," *Journal of Psychology* 139, no. 1 (January 2005): 33–45.

7. Dan Ariely and Klaus Wertenbroch, "Procrastination, Deadlines, and Performance: Self-Control by Precommitment," *Psychological Science* 13, no. 3 (May 2002): 219–224.

8. Amos Tversky and Daniel Kahneman, "Judgment Under Uncertainty: Heuristics and Bias," *Science* 185, no. 4157 (September 27, 1974): 1124–1131.

9. Adam Bryant, "For This Guru, No Question Is Too Big," *New York Times,* May 24, 2009, B2; Jim Collins, "Forget Strategy. Build Mechanisms Instead," *Inc.,* October 1997, 45–47.

10. Steve Ballmer's comments on his time management can be viewed at http://online.wsj.com/public/page/lessons-in-leadership.html.

11. Adam Bryant, "He Was Promotable, After All," *New York Times,* May 3, 2009, B2.

12. Terri Cullen, "The $500 Rule: Managing His, Mine and Our Money," *Wall Street Journal,* January 24, 2008, D1.

13. Colette A. Frayne and J. Michael Geringer, "Self-Management Training for Improving Job Performance: A Field Experiment Involving Salespeople," *Journal of Applied Psychology,* 83, no. 3 (2005): 361–372.

14. Pamela Weiler Grayson, "Dieting? Put Your Money Where Your Fat Is," *New York Times,* February 5, 2009, E8.

15. Atul Gawande, "A Life-Saving Checklist," *New York Times,* December 30, 2007, http://www.nytimes.com/2007/12/30/opinion/30gawande.html?_r= 2&oref=slogin.

16. Mike Stobbe, "Checklists Cut Surgery Errors in Half, Study Finds," *Tennessean,* January 15, 2009, 12A; Liz Szabo, "Studies: Surgeons Could Save Lives, $20B by Using Checklist," *USA Today,* January 14, 2009, http://www.usatoday.com/news/health/2009-01-14-surgery-checklist_N.htm.

17. Atul Gawande, "The Checklist," *New Yorker,* December 10, 2007, 86–101.

18. David Allen, *Getting Things Done: The Art of Stress-Free Productivity* (New York: Viking Penguin, 2001).

CHAPTER SEVEN: CALM DOWN TO SPEED UP

1. Laraine Herring, *Writing Begins with the Breath: Embodying Your Authentic Voice* (Boston: Shambhala, 2007), 113.

2. James's essay was described in Maxwell Maltz, *Psycho-Cybernetics: A New Way to Get More Living out of Life* (Upper Saddle River, NJ: Prentice Hall, 1960), 73.

3. Sivi Hustvedt, "Arms at Rest," *New York Times,* February 7, 2008, http://migraine.blogs.nytimes.com/2008/02/07/arms-at-rest/?scp=1&sq=%22arms%20at%20rest%22&st=cse.

4. John Paul Newport, "When 3 Feet Is a Mile," *Wall Street Journal,* August 2–3, 2008, W5.

5. Carol Hymowitz, "Executive Adopts Motto for Job Stress: Work Hard, Be Nice," *Wall Street Journal,* April 16, 2007, B1.

6. Cassell Bryan-Low, "Yoga Bears: It's No Stretch to Say Traders Are Taking Deep Breaths," *Wall Street Journal,* July 24, 2008, A1, A12.

7. Stacey Forster, "Companies Say Yoga Isn't a Stretch—Physical, Emotional Benefits Are Praised as More Firms Look to Cut Health Costs,"*Wall Street Journal,* October 14, 2003, D4.

8. Herring, *Writing Begins with the Breath,* 79–80.

9. The importance of willingness compared to wishing or forcing is mentioned in Beatrice Bruteau, *Radical Optimism: Practical Spirituality in an Uncertain World* (Boulder, CO: Sentient, 2002), 35; and in *A Course in Miracles* (Mill Valley, CA: Foundation for Inner Peace, 1992).

CHAPTER EIGHT: SLOW DOWN TO STOP YOUR REACTIONS

1. Kevin Maney, "Marc Andreessen Puts His Money Where His Mouth Is," *Fortune,* July 20, 2009, 39–48.

2. Michael Bloomberg, "The Best Advice I Ever Got," *Fortune,* May 12, 2008, 73.

3. Adam Bryant, "He Wants Subjects, Verbs and Objects," *New York Times,* April 26, 2009, B2.

4. Adam Bryant, "Imagining a World of No Annual Reviews," *New York Times,* October 18, 2009, B2.

5. Adam Bryant, "Can You Pass a CEO Test?" New York Times, March 13, 2009, BU2.

6. Adam Bryant, "The Benefit of a Boot out the Door," *New York Times,* November 8, 2009, B2.

7. Donald T. Phillips, *Lincoln on Leadership: Executive Strategies for Tough Times* (New York: Business Plus, 1992).

8. Jerome Groopman, *How Doctors Think* (Boston: Houghton Mifflin, 2007), 74.

9. Danny Meyer, "The Saltshaker Theory," *Inc.,* October 2006, 69–70; adapted from Danny Meyer, *Setting the Table: The Transforming Power of Hospitality in Business* (New York: HarperCollins, 2006).

10. Marshall Goldsmith with Mark Reiter, *What Got You Here Won't Get You There* (New York: Hyperion, 2007), 55.

11. The use of mental stimuli has been described in various books on neurolinguistic programming. The application to food cravings is also described in Paul McKenna, *I Can Make You Thin* (New York: Sterling, 2008).

CHAPTER NINE: GET TO KNOW YOUR INNER ELEPHANT

1. Coeli Carr, "Redesigning the Management Psyche," *New York Times,* May 26, 2002, B3, B14.

2. W. Timothy Gallwey, *The Inner Game of Tennis* (New York: Random House, 1997).

3. Colette A. Frayne and J. Michael Geringer, "A Social Cognitive Approach to Examining Joint Venture General Managers," *Group and Organization Management* 19, no. 2 (1994): 240–262.

4. Bill George, Peter Sims, Andrew N. McLean, David Mayer, and Diana Mayer, "Discovering Your Authentic Leadership," *Harvard Business Review,* February 2007, 129–138.

5. This list is taken from Christopher Peterson, *A Primer in Positive Psychology* (New York: Oxford University Press, 2006), 142–146. This text is an excellent source for a deeper explanation of each strength.

6. Ibid., 158–159.

7. Jerry L. Fletcher, *Patterns of High Performance: Discovering the Ways People Work Best* (San Francisco: Barrett-Koehler, 1993).

8. Ibid., 49.

9. These suggestions are from Peterson, *A Primer in Positive Psychology,* 159–162.

10. Eliyahu M. Goldratt, *What Is This Thing Called Theory of Constraints and How Should It Be Implemented?* (Great Barrington, MA: North River Press, 1990).

11. Timothy D. Wilson, *Stranger to Ourselves: Discovering the Adaptive Unconscious* (Cambridge, MA: Belknap Press, 2002).

12. Gary Rivlin, "He Naps, He Sings. And He Isn't Michael Dell," *New York Times,* September 11, 2005, 1, 7.

13. George, Sims, McLean, Mayer, and Mayer, "Discovering Your Authentic Leadership."

14. Adam Bryant, "The Keeper of That Tapping Pen," *New York Times,* March 22, 2009, B2.

15. Adam Bryant, "Knock-Knock: It's the CEO," *New York Times,* April 12, 2009, B2.

16. Stephen P. Kaufman, "Evaluating the CEO," *Harvard Business Review,* October 2008, 53–57.

17. Adam Bryant, "Feedback in Heaping Helpings," *New York Times,* March 29, 2009, B2.

18. Adam Bryant, "There's No Need to Bat .900," *New York Times,* April 5, 2009, B2.

19. Adam Bryant, "Imagining a World of No Annual Reviews," *New York Times,* October 18, 2009, B2.

20. Eric Schmidt, "The Best Advice I Ever Got," *Fortune,* July 6, 2009, 48.

21. Julia Lawlor, "Personality 2.0," *Red Herring,* April 1, 2001, 98–103.

22. Ram Charan, *Know-How: The 8 Skills That Separate People Who Perform from Those Who Don't* (New York: Crown Business), 170–172.

23. Quoted by Michael Eisner, in an interview by Laura Rich, "Talk About Failure," *Industry Standard,* July 30, 2001, 41–47.

24. Patricia Sellers, "Lessons of the Fall," *Fortune,* June 9, 2008, 70–80.

25. Warren G. Bennis and Robert J. Thomas, *Geeks and Geezers: How Era, Values, and Defining Moments Shape Leaders* (Cambridge, MA: Harvard Business School Press, 2002).

26. Chris Argyris, "Teaching Smart People How to Learn," *Harvard Business Review,* May/June 1991, 100.

27. Patricia Sellers, "So You Fail. Now Bounce Back!" *Fortune,* May 1, 1995, 48–66.

28. For research on the benefits of trauma, see Camille B. Wortman, "Posttraumatic Growth: Progress and Problems," *Psychological Inquiry* 15, no. 1 (2004): 81–90. Studies on posttraumatic growth are reported in Richard G. Tedeschi and Lawrence G. Calhoun, "Posttraumatic Growth: Conceptual Foundations and Empirical Evidence," *Psychological Inquiry* 15, no. 1 (2004): 1–18; Susan Nolen-Hoeksema and Christopher G. Davis, "Positive Responses to Loss," in *Handbook of Positive Psychology,* ed. C. R. Snyder

and Shane J. Lopez (New York: Oxford University Press), 598–607; Richard G. Tedeschi, Crystal L. Park, and Lawrence G. Calhoun, eds., *Posttraumatic Growth: Positive Changes in the Aftermath of Crisis* (Mahwah, NJ: Erlbaum, 1998).

29. The quoted image is from Sobonfu E. Some, "Wisewoman: The Other Side of Failure," *Essence,* March 2004, 141, excerpted from Sobonfu E. Some, *Falling out of Grace: Meditations on Loss, Healing, and Wisdom* (El Sobrante, CA: North Bay Books, 2003).

30. Haidt, *Happiness Hypothesis,* 136–141, provides a clear overview of the theories of posttraumatic growth.

31. Thomas Cleary, trans., *Zen Lessons: The Art of Leadership* (Boston: Shambhala, 1989), 43.

32. Kahlil Gibran, *The Prophet* (New York: Knopf, 1987), 58.

33. Quoted in Jonathan Roof, *Pathways to God* (Faber, VA: Leela Press, 1991), 168.

34. Adam Bryant, "Connecting the Dots Isn't Enough," *New York Times,* July 19, 2009, B2.

35. Sellers, "So You Fail."

CHAPTER TEN: EXPAND YOUR AWARENESS

1. Marshall Goldsmith with Mark Reiter, *What Got You Here Won't Get You There* (New York: Hyperion, 2007), 167.

2. Adam Bryant, "There's No Need to Bat .900," *New York Times,* April 5, 2009, B2.

3. Adam Bryant, "The Keeper of That Tapping Pen," *New York Times,* March 22, 2009, B2.

4. Adam Bryant, "Charisma? To Her, It's Overrated," *New York Times,* July 5, 2009, B2.

5. Kent W. Siebert and Marilyn W. Daudelin, *The Role of Reflection in Managerial Learning: Theory, Research, and Practice* (Westport, CT: Quorum, 1999).

6. Rick Smith, "What Jack Welch Taught Me," *New York Times,* December 21, 2008, B8.

7. Adam Bryant, "Can You Pass a CEO Test?" *New York Times,* March 15, 2009, B2.

8. Patricia Raber Hedberg, "Learning Through Reflective Classroom Practice: Applications to Educate the Reflective Manager," *Journal of Management Education* 33, no. 1 (February 2009): 10–36.

9. Quoted in Jonathan Gosling and Henry Mintzberg, "Reflect Yourself," *HR Magazine,* September 2004, 151–156.

CHAPTER ELEVEN: SHARPEN YOUR CONCENTRATION

1. Alice Schroeder, *The Snowball: Warren Buffett and the Business of Life* (New York: Bantam Books, 2008).

2. Maggie Jackson, "May We Have Your Attention, Please?" *BusinessWeek,* June 23, 2008, 55–56.

3. Kabir Edmund Helminski, *Living Presence: A Sufi Way to Mindfulness and the Essential Self* (New York: Penguin Putnam, 1992).

4. David Brooks, "The Frozen Gaze," *New York Times,* June 17, 2008, http://www.nytimes.com/2008/06/17/opinion/17brooks.html?scp=1&sq=%22the%20frozen%20gaze%22&st=cse; Michael Sokolov, "The Tiger Files," *New York Times,* July 14, 2002, http://www.nytimes.com/2002/07/14/magazine/the-tiger-files.html?scp=1&sq=%22the%20tiger%20files%22&st=cse.

5. William James, *Principles of Psychology,* vol. 1 (New York: Henry Holt, 1910), 403–404.

6. Patricia Monaghan and Eleanor G. Viereck, *Meditation: The Complete Guide* (Novato, CA: New World Library, 1999).

7. Adam Bryant, "He Wants Subjects, Verbs and Objects," *New York Times,* April 25, 2009, B2.

8. Colin Powell, "The Best Advice I Ever Got," *Fortune,* July 6, 2009, 48.

9. John Paul Newport, "Golf Journal: Tiger's Search for Golf Stamina," *Wall Street Journal,* March 7–8, 2009, W4.

10. Richard J. Machowicz, *Unleash the Executive Within* (New York: Harlow, 2002), 138.

11. Jon Kabat-Zinn, *Coming to Our Senses: Healing Ourselves and the World Through Mindfulness* (New York: Hyperion, 2005), 73.

CHAPTER TWELVE: DEVELOP YOUR WITNESS

1. Mark Williams, John Teasdale, Zindel Segal, and Jon Kabat-Zinn, *The Mindful Way Through Depression: Freeing Yourself from Chronic Unhappiness* (New York: Guilford Press, 2007).

2. As told in Osho, *Osho Upanishad* (India: Rebel Publishing House, 2001), available at http://www.messagefrommasters.com/Life_of_Masters/Jiddu/Observer_is_the_Observed.htm.

3. Williams, Teasdale, Segal, and Kabat-Zinn, *Mindful Way.*

4. Ibid., 153.

5. David Brooks, "Lost in the Crowd," *New York Times,* December 16, 2008, A37.

6. Sharon Begley, *Train Your Mind, Change Your Brain* (New York: Ballantine Books, 2007), 140–141.

7. J. M. Schwartz, P. W. Stoessel, L. R. Baxter Jr., K. M. Martin, and M. E. Phelps, "Systematic Changes in Cerebral Glucose Metabolic Rate After Successful Behavior Modification Treatment of Obsessive-Compulsive Disorder," *Archives of General Psychiatry* 53, no. 2 (February 1996): 109–113.

8. *Who Am I: The Teachings of Bhagavan Sri Ramana Marashi*, 24th ed. (Tamil Nadu, India: Sri Ramanasramam Tiruvannamalai, 2008).

CHAPTER THIRTEEN: REPROGRAM YOURSELF

1. *The Way of a Pilgrim and The Pilgrim Continues His Way,* trans. R. M. French (San Francisco: HarperOne, 1991), 93.

2. Jonathan Roof, *Pathways to God* (Faber, VA: Leela Press, 1990).

3. Thomas Ashley-Farrand, *Healing Mantras: Using Sound Affirmations for Personal Power, Creativity, and Healing* (New York: Wellspring, 1999).

4. Ibid.

5. Abdu'l-Bahá, *Tablets of Abdul-Bahá Abbas,* vol. 3 (New York: Bahá'í Publishing Committee, 1930), 641.

6. Bahá'u'lláh, *Epistle to the Son of the Wolf* (Wilmette, IL: Bahá'í Publishing Trust, 1988), 93.

7. Debra Williams, "Scientific Research of Prayer: Can the Power of Prayer Be Proven?" *PLIM Report* 8, no. 4 (1999), http://www.plim.org/PrayerDeb.htm.

8. John Tierney, "For Good Self-Control, Try Getting Religious About It," *New York Times,* December 30, 2008, D2.

CHAPTER FOURTEEN: MEND YOUR MIND WITH MEDITATION

1. David Lynch, *Catching the Big Fish: Meditation, Consciousness, and Creativity* (New York: Tarcher, 2006), 4.

2. Ibid., 7.

3. Ibid., 75.

4. Michelle Conlin, "Meditation: New Research Shows That It Changes the Brain in Ways That Alleviate Stress," *BusinessWeek,* August 23, 2004, 136–137.

5. Roger Berkowitz, "The Way I Work," *Inc.,* July 2008, 85–87.

6. Conlon, "Meditation."

7. Maria Bartiromo, "Facetime: Jerry Levin on What He's Learned in His Second Life," *BusinessWeek,* July 14, 2008, 23–24.

8. Oliver Ryan, "Om Work," *Fortune,* July 23, 2007, 193–194.

9. Ibid.

10. Whitney Joiner, "Staring at Death, and Finding Their Bliss," *New York Times,* September 17, 2007, http://www.nytimes.com/2007/09/13/movies/ 13dhar.html?scp=1&sq=%22staring%20at%20death%22&st=cse.

11. Conlon, "Meditation."

12. Shauna L. Shapiro, Gary E. Schwartz, and Ginny Bonner, "Effects of Mindfulness-Based Stress Reduction on Medical and Premedical Students," *Journal of Behavioral Medicine* 21, no. 6 (1998): 581–599.

13. Patricia Leigh Brown, "In the Classroom, a New Focus on Quieting the Mind," *New York Times,* June 16, 2007, A8.

14. Jon Kabat-Zinn, *Coming to Our Senses: Healing Ourselves and the World Through Mindfulness* (New York: Hyperion, 2005), 75.

15. Adapted from Sai Baba, *Meditation,* pamphlet published under the auspices of the Sri Sathya Sai Baba Spiritual Council of Canada (n.d.).

16. Ibid.

CHAPTER FIFTEEN: CHANGE YOUR FRAME TO SEE PEOPLE

1. These questions are modified from an exercise in Melvin R. McKnight, "Organizational Behavior as a Phenomenological, Free-Will Centered Science" (unpublished manuscript, College of Business Administration, Northern Arizona University, 1997).

2. This discussion is based on McKnight, "Organizational Behavior," and Abraham H. Maslow, *Toward a Psychology of Being* (New York: Van Nostrand, 1963).

3. Martin Buber, *I and Thou,* trans. Ronald Gregor Smith (New York: Scribner's, 1958).

4. Steven R. Weisman, "For Wolfowitz, a 2nd Chance Dissolves into Failure," *New York Times,* May 17, 2007, A1, A12.

5. The Arbiter Institute, *Leadership and Self-Deception: Getting out of the Box* (San Francisco: Barrett-Kohler, 2000).

6. Adam Bryant, "Think 'We' for Best Results," *New York Times,* April 19, 2009, B2.

7. Indra Nooyi, "The Best Advice I Ever Got," *Fortune,* May 12, 2008, 74.

8. Adam Bryant, "The Divine, Too, Is in the Details," *New York Times,* June 21, 2009, B2.

9. Sally Jenkins, "Coughlin's Successful Formula," *Washington Post,* December 22, 2005, E1; Ralph Vacchiano, "There's a Softer Side of Tom

Coughlin," *New York Daily News,* January 30, 2008, 56; "Tom Coughlin, Giants Roll with Changes," *New York Daily News,* January 27, 2008, http://www.nydailynews.com/sports/football/giants/2008/01/27/2008-01-27_tom_coughlin_giants_roll_with_changes.html.

10. George Vecsey, "Living and Learning, Changing and Winning," *New York Times,* July 27, 2008, http://www.nytimes.com/2008/07/27/sports/football/27vecsey.html?scp=3&sq=%22living%20and%20learning%22&st=cse; Greg Garber, "Tom Coughlin's Startling Personality Makeover Remains Intact," ESPN.com, January 17, 2008, http://sports.espn.go.com/nfl/playoffs07/columns/story?columnist=garber_greg&id=3200779.

11. Ernie Palladino, "Coughlin's Changes Helped Giants Come Together," *USA Today,* January 18, 2008, http://sports.espn.go.com/nfl/playoffs07/columns/story?columnist=garber_greg&id=3200779.

12. Vecsey, "Living and Learning."

13. David Bollier, "Building Corporate Loyalty While Rebuilding the Community," *Management Review,* October 1996, 17–22.

14. Kent Clarke, "Key Assets," *Sky,* September 1997, 103–107; KeyCorp, "2,600 KeyCorp Employees to Work on 'Neighbors Make the Difference Day' Volunteer Project in Cleveland," press release, September 6, 2006.

15. I want to thank Michael Ray, Stanford Business School, for providing me with his exercise "Do What You Love," on which my exercises are based.

16. Adam Bryant, "Ensemble Acting, in Business," *New York Times,* June 6, 2009, B2.

CHAPTER SIXTEEN: CHANGE YOUR FRAME TO ASK QUESTIONS

1. Leigh Buchanan, "In Praise of Selflessness; Why the Best Leaders Are Servants," *Inc.,* May 2007, 33–35.

2. Cari Tuna, "Micromanagers Miss Bull's-Eye," *Wall Street Journal,* September 3, 2008, B4.

3. Robert B. Dilts, *Strategies of Genius,* vol. 1 (Capitola, CA: Meta Publications, 1994), 282.

4. Adam Bryant, "He Prizes Questions More Than Answers," *New York Times,* October 25, 2009, B2.

5. Dorothy Leeds, *Smart Questions: The Essential Strategy for Successful Managers* (New York: Berkley Books, 1988).

6. Larry Bossidy and Ram Charan, *Execution: The Discipline of Getting Things Done* (New York: Crown Business, 2002).

7. This discussion and questions are based on Vikki Clawson and Robert Bostrom, "Outcome-Directed Thinking: Questions That Turn Things

Around" (unpublished paper, Athens, GA, Bostrom & Associates, 2003), http://www.terry.uga.edu/~bostrom/Outmodel.doc.

8. Kim H. Krisco, *Leadership and the Art of Conversation: Conversation as a Management Tool* (Rocklin, CA: Prima, 1997).

9. Curtis Sittenfeld, "The Most Creative Man in Silicon Valley," *Fast Company*, December 19, 2007, http://www.fastcompany.com/magazine/35/ray.html.

10. "Good to Great Expectations: Jim Collins on Getting to the Next Level," *BusinessWeek,* August 25, 2008, 32–33.

11. David Petraeus, "The Best Advice I Ever Got," *Fortune,* May 12, 2008, 75.

12. Leigh Buchanan, "The Personality Makeover," *Inc.,* March 2009, 60–61.

13. Principles of Bahá'í consultation can be found at the following Web sites: http://www.bci.org/bahaistudies/courses/consult_principles.htm, http://www.netcomuk.co.uk/~vickers/warwick_bookshop/pages/consultation.html, and http://www.google.com/search?sourceid=navclient&ie=UTF-8&rlz=1T4GPTB_enUS294US294&q=%22some+aspects+of+baha%27i+consultation%22.

14. "Consultation," Bahá'ís of Warwick Bookshop, http://www.netcomuk.co.uk/~vickers/warwick_bookshop/pages/consultation.html.

CHAPTER SEVENTEEN: LIVING AND LEADING FROM YOUR INNER EXECUTIVE

1. Andrew Gordon, "*Star Wars:* A Myth for Our Time," http://web.clas.ufl.edu/users/agordon/starwars.htm.

2. This list draws from Jon Kabat-Zinn, *Full Catastrophe Living: Using the Wisdom of Your Body and Mind to Face Stress, Pain, and Illness* (New York: Delta Trade Paperbacks, 1990), 33–45; and David R. Hawkins, *Transcending the Levels of Consciousness: The Stairway to Enlightenment* (West Sedona, AZ: Veritas, 2006), 167–185.

3. This discussion was drawn from Jill Bolte Taylor, *My Stroke of Insight: A Brain Scientist's Personal Journey* (New York: Plume, 2006).

4. Zindel V. Segal, J. Mark G.Williams, and John D. Teasdale, *Mindfulness-Based Cognitive Therapy for Depression: A New Approach to Preventing Relapse* (New York: Guilford Press, 2002), 57.

About the Author

•

Richard L. Daft is the Brownlee O. Currey Jr. Professor of Management in the Owen Graduate School of Management, Vanderbilt University, where he specializes in the study of leadership, organizational performance, and change management. Daft received his MBA and PhD from the University of Chicago, is a Fellow of the Academy of Management, and has served on the editorial boards of *Academy of Management Journal* and *Administrative Science Quarterly*. He also served as associate dean at Owen, was the associate editor in chief of *Organization Science,* and served for three years as associate editor of *Administrative Science Quarterly*.

Daft has authored or coauthored thirteen books, including his worldwide best-selling textbooks, *Organization Theory and Design,* 10th ed. (Cengage/South-Western, 2010) and *Management,* 9th ed. (Cengage/South-Western, 2010). Daft also wrote *The Leadership Experience,* 5th ed. (Cengage/South-Western, 2010). He has authored dozens of scholarly articles, papers, and chapters on the topics of organization design, innovation and change, and information processing. He is listed among the world's most highly cited authors in the fields of economics and business.

Daft also is an active teacher and consultant. He has taught leadership, change management, organization design, organizational behavior, management consulting, and strategic management. He has been involved in leadership development and organizational change consulting for many companies and government organizations, including the National Academy of Science, American Banking Association, Bell Canada, Bristol-Myers Squibb, Bridgestone/Firestone, J. C. Bradford & Co., Aegis Technology, Central Parking System, the U.S. Army, the U.S. Air Force, Tennessee Emergency Pediatric Services, Vanderbilt University Medical Center, Vanderbilt Medical Group, Jacoby & Meyers Law Offices, TVA, Allstate Insurance, State Farm Insurance, Oak Ridge National Laboratory, Pratt & Whitney, Nortel, United Methodist Church, USAA, and First American National Bank.

Exercise Index

•

Index

•

A

Action, and conflict with intention, 5–7

Adversity, benefits of, 159

"Aha" moments, 169

Alcoholics Anonymous, 109

Ali, M., 71–72

Allen, D., 105

Allen, J., 177

Amos, D., 81

Anderson, R., 54, 127, 181

Andreessen, M., 126

Anger, 54, 127, 137

Argyris, C., 48–49, 58, 159

Arnold, M., 147

Asking questions, and changing frame of reference, 262–268

Attention, focus of, 179–180

Attorney, internal. *See* Internal attorney

Attraction behavior, 61–63

Authentic Happiness Web site, 149

Automatic mental processes, 17–19, 22–27, 31–33, 47, 82–89, 200–207

Autosuggestion, 82–89, 128, 131, 198, 268, 284. *See also* Mantra

Aversive mental stimulus, 142, 143

Avoidance behavior, 60–63, 78, 108–115, **120–124**

B

Bahá'í faith, 215, 271–272

Ballmer, S., 28, 100

Bartz, C., 127, 156

Baudouin, C., 82

Bearden, J., 147–148, 149, 152

Behavior, 5–7, 108–115. *See also* Avoidance behavior

Bennett, A., 125

Bennis, W. G., 158

Benson, H., 228

Berkowitz, R., 226

Bhagavad Gita 2:67, 15

Blink (Gladwell), 289

Bloomberg, M., 126–127

Borg-Warner Chemicals, 255–256

Bossidy, L., 38

Brain, and concept of divided self, 16–17

Brain scientist, story of, 280–283

Brecht, B., 90

Brenneman, G., 65–66, 127, 171

Brooks, D., 199

Brown, T., 263

Buber, M., 249

Buddha, 15

Buddhism, 40, 195, 212, 215, 232, 236

Buffet, W., 149, 153, 177–178

Busquet, A., 160

Busyness, and change, 285

C

D

E